ACCLAIM FOR JOSEPH J. ELLIS's

Founding Brothers

"Lively and illuminating . . . leaves the reader with a visceral sense of a formative era in American life. . . . A shrewd, insightful book."
—*The New York Times*

"Masterful. . . . Fascinating. . . . Ellis is an elegant stylist. . . . [He] captures the passion the founders brought to the revolutionary project. . . . [A] very fine book."
—*Chicago Tribune*

"Splendid. . . . Revealing. . . . An extraordinary book. Its insightful conclusions rest on extensive research, and its author's writing is vigorous and lucid."
—*St. Louis Post-Dispatch*

"Ellis has shown here the considerable power of knowledge—his knowledge. . . . [He] unpacks the real issues for his readers, revealing the driving assumptions and riveting fears that animated Americans' first encounter with the organized ideologies and interests we call parties."
—*The Washington Post Book World*

"Lucid. . . . Bustling stories that . . . describ[e] how our early republic 'looked and felt.' . . . *Founding Brothers* takes on timeworn topics and leavens them with telling details. . . . Ellis has such command of the subject matter that it feels fresh, particularly as he segues from psychological to political, even to physical analysis. . . . Ellis's storytelling helps us more fully hear the Brothers' voices."
—*Business Week*

JOSEPH J. ELLIS

Founding Brothers

Joseph J. Ellis is the author of several books of American history, among them *Passionate Sage: The Character and Legacy of John Adams* and *American Sphinx: The Character of Thomas Jefferson,* which won the 1997 National Book Award. He was educated at the College of William and Mary and Yale University and lives in Amherst, Massachusetts, with his wife, Ellen, and three sons.

Founding Brothers

THE REVOLUTIONARY GENERATION

JOSEPH J. ELLIS

Vintage Books

A Division of Random House, Inc.

New York

FIRST VINTAGE BOOKS EDITION, FEBRUARY 2002

Copyright © 2000 by Joseph J. Ellis

All rights reserved under International and Pan-American Copyright Conventions.
Published in the United States by Vintage Books, a division of Random House, Inc.,
New York, and simultaneously in Canada by Random House of Canada Limited,
Toronto. Originally published in hardcover in the United States by Alfred A. Knopf,
a division of Random House, Inc., New York, in 2000.

Vintage and colophon are registered trademarks of Random House, Inc.

The Library of Congress has cataloged the Knopf edition as follows:
Ellis, Joseph J.
Founding brothers : the revolutionary generation / by Joseph J. Ellis.—1st ed.
p.   cm.
ISBN 0-375-40544-5 (alk. paper)
1. Statesmen—United States—Biography—Anecdotes.
2. Presidents—United States—Biography—Anecdotes.
3. United States—History—1783–1815—Anecdotes.
4. United States—Politics and government—1783–1809—Anecdotes.
I. Title.
E302.5.E45 2000
973.4′092′2—dc21   99-059304
CIP

Vintage ISBN: 0-375-70524-4

Book design by Robert C. Olsson

www.vintagebooks.com

Printed in the United States of America
30 29 28 27 26 25 24 23

For Ellen

CONTENTS

Acknowledgments ix

Preface: *The Generation* 3

Chapter One: *The Duel* 20

Chapter Two: *The Dinner* 48

Chapter Three: *The Silence* 81

Chapter Four: *The Farewell* 120

Chapter Five: *The Collaborators* 162

Chapter Six: *The Friendship* 206

Notes 249

Index 279

ACKNOWLEDGMENTS

THE IDEA that gives this book its shape first came to mind while rereading a mischievous little classic by Lytton Strachey entitled *Eminent Victorians*. My problem, at least as I understood it at that early stage, was a matter of scope and scale. I wanted to write a modest-sized account of a massive historical subject, wished to recover a seminal moment in American history without tripping over the dead bodies of my many scholarly predecessors, hoped to render human and accessible that generation of political leaders customarily deified and capitalized as Founding Fathers.

Eminent Victorians made Strachey famous for the sophistication of his prejudices—his title was deeply ironic—but I want to thank him for giving me the courage of mine. His animating idea, a combination of stealth and selectivity, was that less could be more. "It is not by the direct method of scrupulous narration," Strachey wrote,

> that the explorer of the past can hope to depict a singular epoch. If he is wise, he will adopt a subtler strategy. He will attack his subject in unexpected places; he will fall upon the flank and rear; he will shoot a sudden revealing searchlight into obscure recesses, hitherto undivined. He will row out over the great ocean of material, and lower down into it, here and there, a little bucket, which will bring up to the light of day some characteristic specimen, from those far depths, to be examined with a careful curiosity.

With this model in mind, I rowed out over the great ocean of material generated in the founding era of American nationhood, lowered my little bucket as far down as my rope could reach, then made sense out of the characteristic specimens I hoisted up with as much storytelling skill as my imagination allowed.

The characteristic specimens were drawn from that rich depository of published letters and documents generated by scholarly editors over the past half-century. Like everyone else who has tried to make sense out of America's revolutionary generation, I am deeply indebted to the modern editions of their papers. The endnotes reflect my dependence on specific collections, but let me record here a more comprehensive appreciation for the larger project of preservation and publication that, thanks to federal and private funding, permit us to recover the story of America's founding in all its messy grandeur.

As soon as I had drafted a chapter, I sent it out for criticism to fellow scholars with specialized knowledge about the issues raised in that particular story. The following colleagues saved me from countless blunders: Richard Brookhiser, Andrew Burstein, Robert Dalzell, David Brion Davis, Joanne Freeman, Donald Higginbotham, Pauline Maier, Louis Mazur, Philip Morgan, Peter Onuf, and Gordon Wood. As anyone familiar with the historical profession can attest, I had the benefit of criticism from some of the best minds in the business. What I chose to do with it, of course, remains my responsibility.

Three friends and mentors read the entire manuscript and offered substantive or stylistic suggestions on the book as a whole: Eric McKitrick, who knows more about the political culture of the early republic than anyone else; Edmund Morgan, who first taught me to do American history and still does it better than anyone else; Stephen Smith, whose current position as editor of *U.S. News and World Report* somewhat conceals his calling as the sharpest pencil inside or outside the beltway.

The entire manuscript was handwritten in ink, not with a quill but with a medium-point rollerball pen. The art of deciphering my scrawl and transcribing the words onto a disk fell first to Helen Canney, who worked with me on three previous books but was taken away at an early stage of this one. Holly Sharac picked up where she left off without missing a beat.

My agent, Gerald McCauley, handled the contractual intricacies of publication and then became a one-man cheering section on the side-lines. Ashbel Green, my editor at Knopf, lived up to his reputation as the salt of the earth. His able assistant, Asya Muchnick, supervised the editing process with a hard eye and a soft heart.

My older sons, Peter and Scott, drifted to different ends of the earth while these pages filled up. My youngest son, Alexander, doodled in the margins of several pages while practicing his own handwriting. Taken together, my children served as models for the affectionate rivalry that is brotherhood.

My wife endured the vacant stares of a partner whose physical presence belied the mental absence of an author living back there in the eighteenth century. For that, but not for that alone, she deserves the dedication offered at the start.

Joseph J. Ellis
Amherst, Massachusetts

Founding Brothers

The Generation

No EVENT in American history which was so improbable at the time has seemed so inevitable in retrospect as the American Revolution. On the inevitability side, it is true there were voices back then urging prospective patriots to regard American independence as an early version of manifest destiny. Tom Paine, for example, claimed that it was simply a matter of common sense that an island could not rule a continent. And Thomas Jefferson's lyrical rendering of the reasons for the entire revolutionary enterprise emphasized the self-evident character of the principles at stake.

Several other prominent American revolutionaries also talked as if they were actors in a historical drama whose script had already been written by the gods. In his old age, John Adams recalled his youthful intimations of the providential forces at work: "There is nothing . . . more ancient in my memory," he wrote in 1807, "than the observation that arts, sciences, and empire had always travelled westward. And in conversation it was always added, since I was a child, that their next leap would be over the Atlantic into America." Adams instructed his beloved Abigail to start saving all his letters even before the outbreak of the war for independence. Then in June of 1776, he purchased "a Folio Book" to preserve copies of his entire correspondence in order to record, as he put it, "the great Events which are passed, and those greater which are rapidly advancing." Of course we tend to remember only the prophets who turn out to be right, but there does seem to have been a broadly shared sense within the revolutionary generation that they were "present at the creation."[1]

These early premonitions of American destiny have been reinforced and locked into our collective memory by the subsequent triumph of the political ideals the American Revolution first announced, as Jefferson so nicely put it, "to a candid world." Throughout Asia, Africa, and Latin America, former colonies of European powers have won their independence with such predictable regularity that colonial status has become an exotic vestige of bygone days, a mere way station for emerging nations. The republican experiment launched so boldly by the revolutionary generation in America encountered entrenched opposition in the two centuries that followed, but it thoroughly vanquished the monarchical dynasties of the nineteenth century and then the totalitarian despotisms of the twentieth, just as Jefferson predicted it would. Though it seems somewhat extreme to declare, as one contemporary political philosopher has phrased it, that "the end of history" is now at hand, it is true that all alternative forms of political organization appear to be fighting a futile rearguard action against the liberal institutions and ideas first established in the United States in the late eighteenth century. At least it seems safe to say that some form of representative government based on the principle of popular sovereignty and some form of market economy fueled by the energies of individual citizens have become the commonly accepted ingredients for national success throughout the world. These legacies are so familiar to us, we are so accustomed to taking their success for granted, that the era in which they were born cannot help but be remembered as a land of foregone conclusions.[2]

Despite the confident and providential statements of leaders like Paine, Jefferson, and Adams, the conclusions that look so foregone to us had yet to congeal for them. The old adage applies: Men make history, and the leading members of the revolutionary generation realized they were doing so, but they can never know the history they are making. We can look back and make the era of the American Revolution a center point, then scan the terrain upstream and downstream, but they can only know what is downstream. An anecdote that Benjamin Rush, the Philadelphia physician and signer of the Declaration of Independence, liked to tell in his old age makes the point memorably. On July 4, 1776, just after the Continental Congress had finished making its revisions of the Declaration and sent it off to the printer for publication, Rush overheard a conversation between Benjamin Harrison of Virginia and Elbridge Gerry of Massachusetts: "I shall have a great advantage over you, Mr. Gerry," said Harrison, "when we are all hung for what we are now doing. From the size and weight of my body I shall die in a few minutes, but from the lightness of your body you will dance in the air an hour or two before you are dead." Rush recalled that the comment "procured a transient smile, but it was soon succeeded by the solemnity with which the whole business was conducted."[3]

Based on what we now know about the military history of the American Revolution, if the British commanders had prosecuted the war more vigorously in its earliest stages, the Continental Army might very well have been destroyed at the start and the movement for American independence nipped in the bud. The signers of the Declaration would then have been hunted down, tried, and executed for treason, and American history would have flowed forward in a wholly different direction.[4]

In the long run, the evolution of an independent American nation, gradually developing its political and economic strength over the nineteenth century within the protective constraints of the British Empire, was probably inevitable. This was Paine's point. But that was not the way history happened. The creation of a separate American nation occurred suddenly rather than gradually, in revolutionary rather than evolutionary fashion, the decisive events that shaped the political ideas and institutions of the emerging state all taking place with dynamic intensity during the last quarter of the eighteenth century. No one present at the start knew how it would turn out in the end. What in retrospect has the look of a foreordained unfolding of God's will was in reality an improvisational affair in which sheer chance, pure luck— both good and bad—and specific decisions made in the crucible of specific military and political crises determined the outcome. At the dawn of a new century, indeed a new millennium, the United States is now the oldest enduring republic in world history, with a set of political institutions and traditions that have stood the test of time. The basic framework for all these institutions and traditions was built in a sudden spasm of enforced inspiration and makeshift construction during the final decades of the eighteenth century.

If hindsight enhances our appreciation for the solidity and stability of the republican legacy, it also blinds us to the truly stunning improbability of the achievement itself. All the major accomplishments were unprecedented. Though there have been many successful colonial rebellions against imperial domination since the American Revolution, none had occurred before. Taken together, the British army and navy constituted the most powerful military force in the world, destined in the course of the succeeding century to defeat all national competitors for its claim as the first hegemonic power of the modern era. Though the republican paradigm—representative government bottomed on the principle of popular sovereignty—has become the political norm in the twentieth century, no republican government prior to the American Revolution, apart from a few Swiss cantons and Greek city-states, had ever survived for long, and none had ever been tried over a landmass as large as the thirteen colonies. (There was one exception, but it proved the rule: the short-lived Roman Republic of Cicero, which succumbed to the imperial command of Julius Caesar.) And finally the thirteen colonies, spread along the eastern seaboard and stretching inward to the Alleghenies and beyond into unexplored forests occupied by hostile Indian tribes, had no history of enduring cooperation. The very term "American Revolution" propagates a wholly fictional sense of national coherence not present at the moment and only discernible in latent form by historians engaged in after-the-fact appraisals of how it could possibly have turned out so well.

Hindsight, then, is a tricky tool. Too much of it and we obscure the all-pervasive sense of contingency as well as the problematic character of the choices facing the revolutionary generation. On the other hand, without some measure of hindsight, some panoramic perspective on the past from our perch in the present, we lose the chief advantage—perhaps the only advantage—that the discipline of history provides, and we are then thrown without resources into the patternless swirl of events with all the time-bound participants themselves. What we need is a form of hindsight that does not impose itself arbitrarily on the mentality of the revolutionary generation, does not presume that we are witnessing the birth of an inevitable American superpower. We need a historical perspective that frames the issues with one eye on the precarious contingencies felt at the time, while the other eye looks forward to the more expansive consequences perceived dimly, if at all, by those trapped in the moment. We need, in effect, to be nearsighted and farsighted at the same time.

On the farsighted side, the key insight, recognized by a few of the political leaders in the revolutionary generation, is that the geographic isolation of the North American continent and the bountiful natural resources contained within it provided the fledgling nation with massive advantages and almost limitless potential. In 1783, just after the military victory over Great Britain was confirmed in the Treaty of Paris, no less a figure than George Washington gave this continental vision its most eloquent formulation: "The Citizens of America," Washington wrote, "placed in the most enviable condition, as the sole Lords and Proprietors of a vast Tract of Continent, comprehending all the various soils and climates of the World, and abounding with all the necessaries and conveniences of life, are now by the late satisfactory pacification, acknowledged to be possessed of absolute freedom and Independence; They are, from this period, to be considered as Actors on a most conspicuous Theatre, which seems to be peculiarly designed by Providence for the display of human greatness and felicity." If the infant American republic could survive its infancy, if it could manage to endure as a coherent national entity long enough to consolidate its natural advantages, it possessed the potential to become a dominant force in the world.[5]

On the nearsighted side, the key insight, shared by most of the vanguard members of the revolutionary generation, is that the very arguments used to justify secession from the British Empire also undermined the legitimacy of any national government capable of overseeing such a far-flung population, or establishing uniform laws that knotted together the thirteen sovereign states and three or four distinct geographic and economic regions. For the core argument used to discredit the authority of Parliament and the British monarch, the primal source of what were called "Whig principles," was an obsessive suspicion of any centralized political power that operated in faraway places beyond the immediate supervision or surveillance of the citizens it claimed to govern. The national government established during the war under the Articles of Confederation accurately embodied the cardinal conviction of revolutionary-era republicanism; namely, that no central authority empowered to coerce or discipline the citizenry was permissible, since it merely duplicated the monarchical and aristocratic principles that the American Revolution had been fought to escape.[6]

Combine the long-range and short-range perspectives and the result becomes the central paradox of the revolutionary era, which was also the apparently intractable dilemma facing the revolutionary generation. In sum, the long-term prospects for the newly independent American nation were extraordinarily hopeful, almost limitless. But the short-term prospects were bleak in the extreme, because the very size and scale of the national enterprise, what in fact made the future so promising, overwhelmed the governing capacities of the only republican institutions sanctioned by the Revolution. John Adams, who gave the problem more concentrated attention than anyone except James Madison, was periodically tempted to throw up his hands and declare the task impossible. "The lawgivers of antiquity . . . legislated for single cities," Adams observed, but "who can legislate for 20 or 30 states, each of which is greater than Greece or Rome at those times?" And since the only way to reach the long-run glory was through the short-run gauntlet, the safest bet was that the early American republic would dissolve into a cluster of state or regional sovereignties, expiring, like all the republics before it, well short of the promised land.[7]

The chief reason this did not happen, at least from a purely legal and institutional point of view, is that in 1787 a tiny minority of prominent political leaders from several key states conspired to draft and then ratify a document designed to accommodate republican principles to a national scale. Over the subsequent two centuries critics of the Constitutional Convention have called attention to several of its more unseemly features: the convention was extralegal, since its explicit mandate was to revise the Articles of Confederation, not replace them; its sessions were conducted in utter secrecy; the fifty-five delegates were a propertied elite hardly representative of the population as a whole; southern delegates used the proceedings to obtain several assurances that slavery would not be extinguished south of the Potomac; the machinery for ratification did not require the unanimous consent dictated by the Articles themselves. There is truth in each of these accusations.

There is also truth in the opposite claim: that the Constitutional Convention should be called "the miracle at Philadelphia," not in the customary, quasi-religious sense, whereby a gathering of demigods received divine inspiration, but in the more profane and prosaic sense that the Constitution professed to solve what was an apparently insoluble political problem. For it purported to create a consolidated federal government with powers sufficient to coerce obedience to national laws—in effect, to discipline a truly continental union—while remaining true to the republican principles of 1776. At least logically, this was an impossibility, since the core impulse of these republican principles, the original "spirit of '76," was an instinctive aversion to coercive political power of any sort and a thoroughgoing dread of the inevitable corruptions that result when unseen rulers congregate in distant places. The Antifederalist opponents of the Constitution made precisely these points, but they were outmaneuvered, outargued, and ultimately outvoted by a dedicated band of national advocates in nine of the state ratifying conventions.

The American Revolution thus entered a second phase and the constitutional settlement of 1787–1788 became a second "founding moment," alongside the original occasion of 1776. The first founding declared American independence; the second, American nationhood. The incompatibility of these two foundings is reflected in the divisive character of the scholarship on the latter. Critics of the Constitution, then and now, have condemned it as a betrayal of the core principles of the American Revolution, an American version of France's Thermidorian reaction. Strictly speaking, they were and are historically correct. Defenders of the Constitution, then and now, have saluted it as a sensible accommodation of liberty to power and a realistic compromise with the requirements of a national domain. That has turned out, over time, to be correct, though at the time even the advocates were not sure.

Uncertainty, in fact, was the dominant mood at that moment. Historians have emphasized the several compromises the delegates in Philadelphia brokered to produce the constitutional consensus: the interest of large versus small states; federal versus state jurisdiction; the sectional bargain over slavery. The most revealing feature in this compromise motif is that on each issue, both sides could plausibly believe they had gotten the best of the bargain. On the all-important question of sovereignty, the same artfully contrived ambiguity also obtained: Sovereignty did not reside with the federal government or the individual states; it resided with "the people." What that meant was anyone's guess, since there was no such thing at this formative stage as an American "people"; indeed, the primary purpose of the Constitution was to provide the framework to gather together the scattered strands of the population into a more coherent collective worthy of that designation.

This latter point requires a reflective review of recent scholarship on the complicated origins of American nationhood. Based on what we now know about the Anglo-American connection in the pre-Revolution era—that is, before it was severed—the initial identification of the colonial population as "Americans" came from English writers who used the term negatively, as a way of referring to a marginal or peripheral population unworthy of equal status with full-blooded Englishmen back at the metropolitan center of the British Empire. The word was uttered and heard as an insult that designated an inferior or subordinate people. The entire thrust of the colonists' justification for independence was to reject that designation on the grounds that they possessed all the rights of *British* citizens. And the ultimate source of these rights did not lie in any indigenously American origins, but rather in a transcendent realm of natural rights allegedly shared by all men everywhere. At least at the level of language, then, we need to recover the eighteenth-century context of things and not read back into those years the hallowed meanings they would acquire over the next century. The term *American,* like the term *democrat,* began as an epithet, the former referring to an inferior, provincial creature, the latter to one who panders to the crude and mindless whims of the masses. At both the social and verbal levels, in short, an American nation remained a precarious and highly problematic project—at best a work in progress.[8]

This was pretty much how matters stood in 1789, when the newly elected members of the federal government gathered in New York City and proceeded to test the proposition, as Abraham Lincoln so famously put it at Gettysburg, "whether any nation so conceived and so dedicated can long endure." We have already noted some of the assets and liabilities they brought along with them. On the assets side of the historical ledger, the full list would include the following: a bountiful continent an ocean away from European interference; a youthful population of nearly 4 million, about half of it sixteen years of age or younger and therefore certain to grow exponentially over subsequent decades; a broad dispersion of property ownership among the white populace, based on easy access to available land; a clear commitment to republican political institutions rooted in the prowess and practice of the colonial assemblies, then sanctified as the only paradigm during the successful war for independence and institutionalized in the state constitutions; and last, but far from least, a nearly unanimous consensus that the first chief executive would be George Washington, only one man, to be sure, but an incalculable asset.

On the liability side of the ledger, four items topped the list: First, no one had ever established a republican government on the scale of the United States, and the overwhelming judgment of the most respected authorities was that it could not be done; second, the dominant intellectual legacy of the Revolution, enshrined in the Declaration of Independence, stigmatized all concentrated political power and even, its most virulent forms, depicted any energetic expression of governmental authority as an alien force that all responsible citizens ought to repudiate and, if possible, overthrow; third, apart from the support for the Continental Army during the war, which was itself sporadic, uneven, and barely adequate to assure victory, the states and regions comprising the new nation had no common history as a nation and no common experience behaving as a coherent collective (for example, while drafting the Declaration in Philadelphia in June of 1776, Jefferson had written back to friends in Virginia that it was truly disconcerting to find himself deployed at that propitious moment nearly three hundred miles from "my country"); fourth, and finally, according to the first census, commissioned by the Congress in 1790, nearly 700,000 inhabitants of the fledgling American republic were black slaves, the vast majority, over 90 percent, concentrated in the Chesapeake region and points south, their numbers also growing exponentially in a kind of demographic defiance of all the republican rhetoric uttered since the heady days of 1776.[9]

If permitted to define a decade somewhat loosely, then the next decade was the most crucial and consequential in American history. Other leading contestants for that title—the years 1855–1865 and the 1940s come to mind—can make powerful claims, to be sure, but the first decade of our history as a sovereign nation will always have primacy because it was first. It set the precedents, established in palpable fact what the Constitution had only outlined in purposely ambiguous theory, thereby opening up and closing off options for all the history that followed. The Civil War, for example, was a direct consequence of the decision to evade and delay the slavery question during the most vulnerable early years of the republic. Similarly, America's emergence as the dominant world power in the 1940s could never have occurred if the United States had not established stable national institutions at the start that permitted the consolidation of the continent. (From the Native American perspective, of course, this consolidation was a conquest.) The apparently irresistible urge to capitalize and mythologize as "Founding Fathers" the most prominent members of the political leadership during this formative phase has some historical as well as psychological foundation, for in a very real sense we are, politically, if not genetically, still living their legacy. And the same principle also explains the parallel urge to demonize them, since any discussion of their achievement is also an implicit conversation about the distinctive character of American imperialism, both foreign and domestic.

A kind of electromagnetic field, therefore, surrounds this entire subject, manifesting itself as a golden haze or halo for the vast majority of contemporary Americans, or as a contaminated radioactive cloud for a smaller but quite vocal group of critics unhappy with what America has become or how we have gotten here. Within the scholarly community in recent years, the main tendency has been to take the latter side, or to sidestep the controversy by ignoring mainstream politics altogether. Much of the best work has taken the form of a concerted effort to recover the lost voices from the revolutionary generation—the daily life of Martha Ballard as she raised a family and practiced midwifery on the Maine frontier; the experience of Venture Smith, a former slave who sustained his memories of Africa and published a memoir based on them in 1798. This trend is so pronounced that any budding historian who announces that he or she wishes to focus on the political history of the early republic and its most prominent practitioners is generally regarded as having inadvertently confessed a form of intellectual bankruptcy.[10]

Though no longer a budding historian, my own efforts in recent years, including the pages that follow, constitute what I hope is a polite argument against the scholarly grain, based on a set of presumptions that are so disarmingly old-fashioned that they might begin to seem novel in the current climate. In my opinion, the central events and achievements of the revolutionary era and the early republic were political. These events and achievements are historically significant because they shaped the subsequent history of the United States, including our own time. The central players in the drama were not the marginal or peripheral figures, whose lives are more typical, but rather the political leaders at the center of the national story who wielded power. What's more, the shape and character of the political institutions were determined by a relatively small number of leaders who knew each other, who collaborated and collided with one another in patterns that replicated at the level of personality and ideology the principle of checks and balances imbedded structurally in the Constitution.

Mostly male, all white, this collection of public figures was hardly typical of the population as a whole; nor was it, on the other hand, a political elite like anything that existed in England or Europe. All of its members, not just those like Benjamin Franklin and Alexander Hamilton with famously impoverished origins, would have languished in obscurity in England or France. The pressures and exigencies generated by the American Revolution called out and gathered together their talents; no titled and hereditary aristocracy was in place to block their ascent; and no full-blown democratic culture had yet emerged to dull their elitist edge. They were America's first and, in many respects, its only natural aristocracy. Despite recent efforts to locate the title in the twentieth century, they comprised, by any informed and fair-minded standard, the greatest generation of political talent in American history. They created the American republic, then held it together throughout the volatile and vulnerable early years by sustaining their presence until national habits and customs took root. In terms of our earlier distinction, they got us from the short run to the long run.

There are two long-established ways to tell the story, both expressions of the political factions and ideological camps of the revolutionary era itself, and each first articulated in the earliest histories of the period, written while several members of the revolutionary generation were still alive. Mercy Otis Warren's *History of the American Revolution* (1805) defined the "pure republicanism" interpretation, which was also the version embraced by the Republican party and therefore later called "the Jeffersonian interpretation." It depicts the American Revolution as a liberation movement, a clean break not just from English domination but also from the historic corruptions of European monarchy and aristocracy. The ascendance of the Federalists to power in the 1790s thus becomes a hostile takeover of the Revolution by corrupt courtiers and moneymen (Hamilton is the chief culprit), which is eventually defeated and the true spirit of the Revolution recovered by the triumph of the Republicans in the elections of 1800. The core revolutionary principle according to this interpretive tradition is individual liberty. It has radical and, in modern terms, libertarian implications, because it regards any accommodation of personal freedom to governmental discipline as dangerous. In its more extreme forms it is a recipe for anarchy, and its attitude toward any energetic expression of centralized political power can assume paranoid proportions.

The alternative interpretation was first given its fullest articulation by John Marshall in his massive five-volume *The Life of George Washington* (1804–1807). It sees the American Revolution as an incipient national movement with deep, if latent, origins in the colonial era. The constitutional settlement of 1787–1788 thus becomes the natural fulfillment of the Revolution and the leaders of the Federalist party in the 1790s—Adams, Hamilton, and, most significantly, Washington—as the true heirs of the revolutionary legacy. (Jefferson is the chief culprit.) The core revolutionary principle in this view is collectivistic rather than individualistic, for it sees the true spirit of '76 as the virtuous surrender of personal, state, and sectional interests to the larger purposes of American nationhood, first embodied in the Continental Army and later in the newly established federal government. It has conservative but also protosocialistic implications, because it does not regard the individual as the sovereign unit in the political equation and is more comfortable with governmental discipline as a focusing and channeling device for national development. In its more extreme forms it relegates personal rights and liberties to the higher authority of the state, which is "us" and not "them," and it therefore has both communal and despotic implications.[11]

It is truly humbling, perhaps even dispiriting, to realize that the historical debate over the revolutionary era and the early republic merely recapitulates the ideological debate conducted at the time, that historians have essentially been fighting the same battles, over and over again, that the members of the revolutionary generation fought originally among themselves. Though many historians have taken a compromise or split-the-difference position over the ensuing years, the basic choice has remained constant, as historians have declared themselves Jeffersonians or Hamiltonians, committed individualists or dedicated nationalists, liberals or conservatives, then written accounts that favor one camp over the other, or that stigmatize one side by viewing it through the eyes of the other, much as the contestants did back then. While we might be able to forestall intellectual embarrassment by claiming that the underlying values at stake are timeless, and the salient questions classical in character, the awkward truth is that we have been chasing our own tails in an apparently endless cycle of partisan pleading. Perhaps because we are still living their legacy, we have yet to reach a genuinely historical perspective on the revolutionary generation.[12]

But, again, in a way that Paine could tell us was commonsensical and Jefferson could tell us was self-evident, both sides in the debate have legitimate claims on historical truth and both sides speak for the deepest impulses of the American Revolution. With the American Revolution, as with all revolutions, different factions came together in common cause to overthrow the reigning regime, then discovered in the aftermath of their triumph that they had fundamentally different and politically incompatible notions of what they intended. In the dizzying sequence of events that comprises the political history of the 1790s, the full range of their disagreement was exposed and their different agenda for the United States collided head-on. Taking sides in this debate is like choosing between the words and the music of the American Revolution.

What distinguishes the American Revolution from most, if not all, subsequent revolutions worthy of the name is that in the battle for supremacy, for the "true meaning" of the Revolution, neither side completely triumphed. Here I do not just mean that the American Revolution did not "devour its own children" and lead to blood-soaked scenes at the guillotine or the firing-squad wall, though that is true enough. Instead, I mean that the revolutionary generation found a way to contain the explosive energies of the debate in the form of an ongoing argument or dialogue that was eventually institutionalized and rendered safe by the creation of political parties. And the subsequent political history of the United States then became an oscillation between new versions of the old tension, which broke out in violence only on the occasion of the Civil War. In its most familiar form, dominant in the nineteenth century, the tension assumes a constitutional appearance as a conflict between state and federal sovereignty. The source of the disagreement goes much deeper, however, involving conflicting attitudes toward government itself, competing versions of citizenship, differing postures toward the twin goals of freedom and equality.

But the key point is that the debate was not resolved so much as built into the fabric of our national identity. If that means the United States is founded on a contradiction, then so be it. With that one bloody exception, we have been living with it successfully for over two hundred years. Lincoln once said that America was founded on a proposition that was written by Jefferson in 1776. We are really founded on an argument about what that proposition means.

This does not mean that the political history of the early republic can be understood as a polite forensic exercise conducted by a marvelously well-behaved collection of demigods. Nor is the proper image a symphony orchestra; or, given the limited numbers involved at the highest level of national politics, perhaps a chamber music ensemble, each Founding Father playing a particular instrument that blends itself harmoniously into the common score. The whole point is that there was no common score, no assigned instruments, no blended harmonies. The politics of the 1790s was a truly cacophonous affair. Previous historians have labeled it "the Age of Passion" for good reason, for in terms of shrill accusatory rhetoric, flamboyant displays of ideological intransigence, intense personal rivalries, and hyperbolic claims of imminent catastrophe, it has no equal in American history. The political dialogue within the highest echelon of the revolutionary generation was a decade-long shouting match.[13]

How, then, did they do it? Why is it that Alfred North Whitehead was probably right to observe that there were only two instances in Western history when the leadership of an emerging imperial power performed as well, in retrospect, as anyone could reasonably expect? (The first was Rome under Caesar Augustus and the second was the United States in the late eighteenth century.) Why is it that there is a core of truth to the distinctive iconography of the American Revolution, which does not depict dramatic scenes of mass slaughter, but, instead, a gallery of well-dressed personalities in classical poses?[14]

My own answers to these questions are contained in the stories that follow, which attempt to recover the sense of urgency and improvisation, what it looked and felt like, for the eight most prominent political leaders in the early republic. They are, in alphabetical order, Abigail and John Adams, Aaron Burr, Benjamin Franklin, Alexander Hamilton, Thomas Jefferson, James Madison, and George Washington. While each episode is a self-contained narrative designed to illuminate one propitious moment with as much storytelling skill as I can muster, taken together they feature several common themes.

First, the achievement of the revolutionary generation was a collective enterprise that succeeded because of the diversity of personalities and ideologies present in the mix. Their interactions and juxtapositions generated a dynamic form of balance and equilibrium, not because any of them was perfect or infallible, but because their mutual imperfections and fallibilities, as well as their eccentricities and excesses, checked each other in much the way that Madison in *Federalist* *10* claimed that multiple factions would do in a large republic.

Second, they all knew one another personally, meaning that they broke bread together, sat together at countless meetings, corresponded with one another about private as well as public matters. Politics, even at the highest level in the early republic, remained a face-to-face affair in which the contestants, even those who were locked in political battles to the death, were forced to negotiate the emotional affinities and shared intimacies produced by frequent personal interaction. The Adams-Jefferson rivalry and friendship is the outstanding example here, though there are several crucial moments when critical compromises were brokered because personal trust made it possible. Though the American republic became a nation of laws, during the initial phase it also had to be a nation of men.

Third, they managed to take the most threatening and divisive issue off the political agenda. That issue, of course, was slavery, which was clearly incompatible with the principles of the American Revolution, no matter what version one championed. But it was also the political problem with the deepest social and economic roots in the new nation, so that removing it threatened to disrupt the fragile union just as it was congealing. Whether or not it would have been possible to put slavery on the road to extinction without also extinguishing the nation itself remains an open question; it is the main subject of one of the following stories. Whatever conclusion one reaches concerning that hypothetical question, with all the advantage of hindsight and modern racial attitudes as a moral guide, the revolutionary generation decided that the risks outweighed the prospects for success; they quite self-consciously chose to defer the slavery question by placing any discussion of it out-of-bounds at both the national and federal levels.

Fourth, the faces that look down upon us with such classical dignity in those portraits by John Trumbull, Gilbert Stuart, and Charles Willson Peale, the voices that speak to us across the ages in such lyrical cadences, seem so mythically heroic, at least in part, because they knew we would be looking and listening. All the vanguard members of the revolutionary generation developed a keen sense of their historical significance even while they were still making the history on which their reputations would rest. They began posing for posterity, writing letters to us as much as to one another, especially toward the end of their respective careers. If they sometimes look like marble statues, that is how they wanted to look. (John Adams is one of my favorite characters, as you will see, because he was congenitally incapable of holding the pose. His refreshing and often irreverent candor provides the clearest window into the deeper ambitions and clashing vanities that propelled them all.) If they sometimes behave like actors in a historical drama, that is often how they regarded themselves. In a very real sense, we are complicitous in their achievement, since we are the audience for which they were performing; knowing we would be watching helped to keep them on their best behavior.[15]

Chronology, so the saying goes, is the last refuge of the feeble-minded and only resort for historians. My narrative, while willfully episodic in character—no comprehensive coverage of all events is claimed—follows a chronological line, with one significant exception. The first story, about the duel between Aaron Burr and Alexander Hamilton, is out of sequence. In addition to being a fascinating tale designed to catch your attention, it introduces themes that reverberate throughout all the stories that follow by serving as the exception that proves the rule. Here is the only occasion within the revolutionary generation when political differences ended in violence and death rather than in ongoing argument. And Burr, if I have him right, is the odd man out within the elite of the early republic, a colorful and intriguing character, to be sure, but a man whose definition of character does not measure up to the standard.

Enough justifying and generalizing. If the following stories converge to make some larger point, the surest way to reach it is through the stories themselves. It is a hot summer morning in 1804. Aaron Burr and Alexander Hamilton are being rowed in separate boats across the Hudson River for an appointment on the plains of Weehawken. The water is eerily calm and the air thick with a heavy mist . . .

CHAPTER ONE

The Duel

THE MOST succinct version of the story might go like this:

On the morning of July 11, 1804, Aaron Burr and Alexander Hamilton were rowed across the Hudson River in separate boats to a secluded spot near Weehawken, New Jersey. There, in accord with the customs of the *code duello,* they exchanged pistol shots at ten paces. Hamilton was struck on his right side and died the following day. Though unhurt, Burr found that his reputation suffered an equally fatal wound. In this, the most famous duel in American history, both participants were casualties.

While all the information in this version of the story is accurate, its admirable brevity creates some unfortunate historical casualties of its own. After all, if the duel between Burr and Hamilton was the most famous encounter of its kind in American history, we should be able to conjure up a mental image of this dramatic moment, a more richly textured picture of "The Duel." Only a fuller rendering will allow what was called "the interview at Weehawken" to assume its rightful place of primacy among such touted competitors as *Gunfight at the O.K. Corral* or the film classic *High Noon.* In matters of this sort, succinct summaries will simply not do. And so, in an effort to give this episode its requisite density of detail, to recover the scene in its full coloration, here is a more comprehensive version, which attempts to include all the available and indisputable evidence that survives.[1]

AARON BURR left his home on Richmond Hill near the southern end of Manhattan at first light on Wednesday, July 11, 1804. Although he slept that night on his couch and in his clothes, the vice president of the United States was a lifelong disciple of Lord Chesterfield's maxim that a gentleman was free to do anything he pleased as long as he did it with style. So Colonel Burr—the military title a proud emblem of his service in the American Revolution—was elegantly attired in a silklike suit (actually made of a fabric known as bombazine) and carried himself toward the barge on the bank of the Hudson River with the nonchalant air of a natural aristocrat strolling to an appointment with destiny.

His grandfather, the great theologian Jonathan Edwards, had once said that we were all depraved creatures, mere spiders hanging precariously over a never-ending fire. But Burr's entire life had been a sermon on the capacity of the sagacious spider to lift himself out of hellish difficulties and spin webs that trapped others. No one can be sure what was in Burr's mind as a single oarsman rowed him and William Van Ness, his devoted disciple and protégé, toward the New Jersey Palisades on the other side, but the judgment of posterity would be that Burr had finally trapped Hamilton in his diabolical web, and he was now moving in for the kill.[2]

Meanwhile, just north of Richmond Hill, near present-day Wall Street, Hamilton was boarding a small skiff with two oarsmen, his physician, Dr. David Hosack, and his own loyal associate Nathaniel Pendleton. Like Burr, Hamilton was properly attired and also carried himself with a similar air of gentlemanly diffidence. He also carried a military title, thus outranking Burr with his honorary designation as "General Hamilton," based on his last appointment, that of inspector general of the New Army in 1799. At forty-nine, he was a year older than Burr and, like him, was a relatively short man—an inch taller, at five feet seven inches—with similarly small hands and feet, a somewhat delicate bone structure, and a truly distinctive head and face. He was called "the little lion of Federalism" because he was, in truth, little.

But the head was the place where God had seen fit to mark the two men as polar opposites. Burr had the dark and severe coloring of his Edwards ancestry, with black hair receding from the forehead and dark brown, almost black, eyes that suggested a cross between an eagle and a raven. Hamilton had a light peaches and cream complexion with violet-blue eyes and auburn-red hair, all of which came together to suggest an animated beam of light to Burr's somewhat stationary shadow. Whereas Burr's overall demeanor seemed subdued, as if the compressed energies of New England Puritanism were coiled up inside him, waiting for the opportunity to explode, Hamilton conveyed kinetic energy incessantly expressing itself in bursts of conspicuous brilliance.

Their respective genealogies also created temperamental and stylistic contrasts. Unlike Burr's distinguished bloodline, which gave his aristocratic bearing its roots and biological rationale, Hamilton's more dashing and consistently audacious style developed as a willful personal wager against the odds of his impoverished origins. John Adams, who despised Hamilton, once referred to him as "the bastard brat of a Scotch pedlar." While intended as a libelous description, Adams's choice of words was literally correct.

Hamilton had been born on the West Indian island of Nevis, the illegitimate son of a down-on-her-luck beauty of French extraction and a hard-drinking Scottish merchant with a flair for bankruptcy. In part because of his undistinguished origins, Hamilton always seemed compelled to be proving himself; he needed to impress his superiors with his own superiority. Whether he was leading an infantry assault against an entrenched British strong point at Yorktown—first over the parapet in a desperate bayonet charge—or imposing his own visionary fiscal program for the new nation on a reluctant federal government, Hamilton tended to regard worldly problems as personal challenges, and therefore as fixed objects against which he could perform his own isometric exercises, which usually took the form of ostentatious acts of gallantry. Though he had not sought out the impending duel with Burr, there was nothing in Hamilton's lifelong pattern that would permit a self-consciously bland and supremely triumphant refusal of the challenge. He was moving across the nearly calm waters of the Hudson toward Weehawken, then, because he did not believe he could afford to decline Burr's invitation.[3]

We actually know a good deal more about the thoughts in Hamilton's mind at this propitious moment. The previous evening he had drafted a personal statement, which he enclosed with his last will and testament, declaring that he had sincerely hoped to avoid the interview. Moreover, he claimed to feel "no *ill-will* to Col. Burr, distinct from political opposition, which, as I trust, has proceeded from pure and upright motives." What's more, he had decided to expose himself to Burr's fire without retaliating: "I have resolved, if our interview is conducted in the usual manner, and it pleases God to give me the opportunity, to *reserve* and *throw away* my first fire, and I have thoughts even of reserving my second fire—and thus giving a double opportunity to Col. Burr to pause and to reflect." He did not think of this course of action as suicidal, but as another gallant gamble of the sort he was accustomed to winning.[4]

The usual description of the duel's location—the plains of Weehawken—is misleading. Indeed, if one were to retrace the Burr-Hamilton route across the Hudson and land just upstream from the modern-day Lincoln Tunnel, one would come face-to-face with a sheer cliff 150 feet high. Anyone attempting to scale these heights would hardly be capable of fighting a duel upon arrival at the top. The actual site of the duel was a narrow ledge, about ten feet wide and forty feet long, located only twenty feet above the water. It was a popular spot for duels precisely because of its relative isolation and inaccessibility. By prearranged agreement, the Burr party arrived first, just before 7:00 a.m., and began clearing away the incidental brush and rocks on the ledge.[5]

Hamilton's party arrived shortly thereafter, and the two seconds, Van Ness for Burr and Pendleton for Hamilton, conferred to review the agreed-upon rules of the interview. It was called an "interview" because dueling was illegal in many states, including New York. Therefore, in addition to the established etiquette of the *code duello,* veteran duelists had developed an elaborately elusive vocabulary, what we would now call the "language of deniability," so that all participants could subsequently claim ignorance if ever brought to court. None of the oarsmen, for example, was permitted on the ledge to witness the exchange of fire. The physician, David Hosack, was also required to turn his back to the proceedings.[6]

Because Hamilton had been challenged, he had the choice of weapons. He had selected a custom-made pair of highly decorated pistols owned by his wealthy brother-in-law, John Church. Apart from their ornate appearance, the weapons were distinctive for two reasons. First, they had been used in two previous duels involving the participants: once, in 1799, when Church had shot a button off Burr's coat; then, in 1801, when Hamilton's eldest son, Philip, had been fatally wounded defending his father's honor only a few yards from the site at Weehawken. Second, they also contained a concealed device that set a hair-trigger. Without the hair-trigger, the weapon required twenty pounds of pressure to fire. With the hair-trigger, only one pound of pressure was needed. While Hamilton knew about the hair-triggers, Burr almost certainly did not.

After Pendleton and Van Ness loaded the pistols, which were smooth-bore and took a quite large .54-caliber ball, Pendleton whispered to Hamilton, "Should I set the hair-trigger?" Hamilton responded: "Not this time." As they prepared to take their designated places, then, both men were armed with extremely powerful but extremely erratic weapons. If struck in a vital spot by the oversized ball at such close range, the chances of a serious or mortal injury were high. But the inherent inaccuracy of a projectile emerging from a smoothbore barrel, plus the potent jerk required to release the cocked hammer, ignite the powder, and then send the ball toward its target, meant that in this duel, as in most duels of that time, neither party was likely to be hurt badly, if at all.[7]

Burr and Hamilton then met in the middle to receive their final instructions. Hamilton, again because he was the challenged party, had the choice of position. He selected the upstream, or north, side, a poor choice because the morning sun and its reflection off the river would be in his face. The required ten paces between contestants put them at the extreme ends of the ledge. It was agreed that when both principals were ready, Pendleton would say, "Present"; then each man would be free to raise and fire his weapon. If one man fired before the other, the non-firer's second would say, "One, two, three, fire." If he had not fired by the end of the count, he lost his turn. At that point, or if both parties had fired and missed, there would be a conference to decide if another round was required or if both sides agreed that the obligations of honor had been met.[8]

Upon reaching his designated location, just before the final command, Hamilton requested a brief delay. He pulled his eyeglasses out of his breast pocket, adjusted them, then squinted into the glare, raised his pistol, sighted down the barrel at several imaginary targets, then pronounced himself ready. Burr waited with patience and composure through this delay. Not only is there no evidence that he had any foreknowledge of Hamilton's declared intention to reserve or waste his first shot, but Hamilton's behavior at this penultimate moment certainly suggested more harmful intentions. Why he would don his eyeglasses if he did not plan to shoot at Burr remains a mystery.

What happened next is an even greater mystery. In fact, the contradictory versions of the next four to five seconds of the duel might serve as evidence for the postmodern contention that no such thing as objective truth exists, that historic reality is an inherently enigmatic and endlessly negotiable bundle of free-floating perceptions. For our story to proceed along the indisputable lines established at the start, we must skip over the most dramatic moment, then return to it later, after the final pieces of the narrative are in place.

Two shots had rung out and Hamilton had just been hit. The one-ounce ball had struck him on the right side, making a hole two inches in diameter about four inches above his hip. The projectile fractured his rib cage, ricocheted off the rib and up through his liver and diaphragm, then splintered the second lumbar vertebra, where it lodged. Even with all the benefits of modern medical science, the internal damage would have made Hamilton a likely fatality, most certainly a lifetime cripple. Given the limitations of medical science available then, there was no hope. Hamilton himself recognized his own condition almost immediately. When Dr. Hosack rushed forward to examine him, Hamilton calmly declared, "This is a mortal wound, Doctor," then lapsed into unconsciousness.[9]

Meanwhile, Burr seemed surprised and regretful at the outcome of his shot. He started toward the fallen Hamilton, but Van Ness stopped him and ushered him away from the scene and toward his boat, all the while shielding Burr behind an umbrella so that—the deniability motive again—the members of Hamilton's party could claim in some prospective court that they had never seen him. Halfway down the path toward the river, Burr stopped and insisted on going back. "I must go & speak to him," he pleaded. But Van Ness refused to comply and headed Burr into his barge and back across the river to New York.[10]

Hosack half-expected Hamilton to die on the spot. After a few minutes of ministrations, however, it was clear that the unconscious Hamilton was breathing regularly, so they carried him down to the river. On the trip back, Hamilton recovered consciousness for a time and muttered to Hosack, "Pendleton knows I did not mean to fire at Colonel Burr the first time." When one of the oarsmen tried to move Hamilton's pistol, which lay on the seat, Hamilton warned him, "Take care of that pistol; it is undischarged and still cocked; it may go off and do harm," clearly indicating that Hamilton himself did not seem to realize the weapon had been fired. Upon arrival on the New York side, he was carried to the nearby home of James Bayard, a longtime friend and political disciple, where Hosack administered liberal doses of laudanum and waited for the end. Hamilton died at two o'clock on the afternoon of July 12, 1804, surrounded by the Episcopal bishop of New York, Benjamin Moore, as well as by David Hosack, Hamilton's wife, Elizabeth, and their seven surviving children.[11]

The funeral two days later was an extravaganza of mourning. The mahogany coffin was trailed by Hamilton's gray horse, with his boots and spurs reversed astride the empty saddle. Behind it marched his widow and children, the political and legal leaders of the city, the students and faculty of Columbia College, bank presidents, army and navy officers, local clergy and foreign dignitaries, followed by several hundred ordinary citizens. Gouverneur Morris, an old family friend and Federalist colleague, delivered the funeral oration in an overflowing Trinity Church.[12]

The overwhelming popular consensus was that Burr had murdered Hamilton in cold blood. The anti-Burr character of the newspaper stories fed the popular frenzy with concocted claims (for example, Burr had worn a suit, specially prepared for the duel, made of material that could deflect bullets) and melodramatic fabrications (for example, while Hamilton's widow and children shed tears over his dead body, Burr and his followers drank toasts to Hamilton's death in the local tavern, Burr only expressing regret that he had not shot him in the heart). A wax replication of the duel depicted Hamilton being shot by Burr and several hidden accomplices from ambush. The sign beneath the wax version read:

> *O Burr, O Burr, what has thou done?*
> *Thou has shooted dead great Hamilton.*
> *You hid behind a bunch of thistle,*
> *And shooted him dead with a great hoss pistol.*

With indictments pending against him for both dueling and murder, with newspaper editors comparing him to Benedict Arnold as the new exemplar of treachery, with ministers making his behavior the centerpiece for sermons against dueling as a barbaric throwback to medieval notions of justice, Burr fled the city in disgrace, not stopping until he reached Georgia.[13]

So there you have it: Hamilton safely buried and assuming legendary proportions as a martyr; Burr slipping out of town, eventually headed toward bizarre adventures in the American West, but already consigned to political oblivion. This seems the most appropriate closing scene in our attempted recovery of "The Duel" as a famous and eminently visual story.

THE MISSING ingredient in the story, of course, is the four- or five-second interval when the shots were actually fired. Postponing the recovery of this most crucial moment was not only unavoidable—there is no agreed-upon version to recover—but also matches the historical timing of the debate that generated the only evidence on which any narrative must be based. Which is to say that, in the wake of the actual duel, there was another duel of words between witnesses to the event, chiefly Pendleton and Van Ness, and then the inevitable collection of pro-Hamilton and pro-Burr advocates who filled up the newspapers and pamphlets of the day with corroborating testimony for their own conflicting versions.

But before the after-action accounts of the duel degenerated into a duel of its own, the only two eyewitnesses, Pendleton and Van Ness, published a "Joint Statement." Its chief purpose was to claim that both principals had conducted themselves in accord with the *code duello,* so that even though the practice of dueling was illegal, Burr and Hamilton had behaved according to the higher law of honor appropriate for proper gentlemen. Along the way to that principled point, however, Pendleton and Van Ness agreed on several significant particulars worthy of notice because of the light they shed on the looming disagreement over what, in fact, had happened.

First, Pendleton and Van Ness agreed that both principals fired their weapons. There were two shots, not one. This was an important fact to establish, because several published accounts of the duel by friends of Hamilton, undoubtedly influenced by various versions of his preduel pledge not to fire at Burr, had preemptively concluded that Hamilton had withheld his fire; that is, had not fired at all. Since the sound of the gunfire was audible to Hosack and the oarsmen, even though they did not see the exchange, no misrepresentation or falsification of this elemental point was feasible anyway, unless the two shots occurred simultaneously. And Pendleton and Van Ness agreed that they did not.

This led to the second and most intriguing agreement—namely, that an interval lasting "a few seconds" occurred between shots. Just how many seconds they could not agree on. They did concur, however, that a discernible gap of time separated the two shots. One of the two principals had fired first; the other had paused for a discreet and noticeable interval, and then he had fired. The two shots had not gone off simultaneously.[14]

It is not easy to square what was to become the Hamiltonian version of the duel with this agreed-upon point. The crucial ingredient in the Hamiltonian account was that Burr fired first. If one began with the assumption, as Pendleton's and Hamilton's disciples insisted one should, that Hamilton arrived at Weehawken with a firm resolve not to fire at Burr, then it followed logically that Hamilton could not have fired first. Instead, Burr fired while Hamilton's pistol was still raised in the air. The impact of Burr's round then allegedly produced an involuntary jerk on Hamilton's trigger finger, which sent a round sailing harmlessly above Burr and into the trees. Van Ness claimed to have revisited the ledge the following day and found the severed branch of a cedar tree about twelve feet high and four feet to the side of where Burr had stood. This rendition of the story was also compatible with Hamilton's remark in the boat afterward, when he seemed to think his pistol was still loaded. He obviously had not realized that Burr's shot had caused an accidental firing of his own weapon. On the other hand, if one accepted the Hamiltonian version of the exchange, how could one explain the interval between the shots? In the Hamiltonian account, the exchange would have been nearly simultaneous.

Although the Burr version of what occurred presents some problems of its own, it is more compatible with the agreed-upon timing of the shots. According to Van Ness, Hamilton took aim at Burr and fired first, but missed. Burr then delayed his shot for "four or five seconds," waiting for the smoke to clear from around Hamilton and also waiting for Pendleton to begin the count—"One, two, three, fire." But Pendleton's attention had been fixed on his own chief and he apparently had lacked the wherewithal to say anything in this drawn-out moment of the drama. Burr then took it upon himself to fire rather than lose his shot. Hamilton fell instantly. Van Ness was adamant about the sequence of events: "It is agree'd I believe, by all who were within hearing, but particularly attested by Doctr. Hossack [*sic*], that several seconds intervened between the two discharges; and it is also agree'd that Gen. H. fell *instantly* on Mr. B's firing, which contradicts the idea that Mr. B. fired first." Van Ness went on to provide additional detail about Burr's behavior during the dramatic interval.

On the point of the first firing . . . I was never more confident of any matter subject to the examination of my senses. If any doubt had ever existed it would have been removed by the following circumstances: 1st When Genl. H fired I observed a jar or slight motion in Mr. B's body, from which I supposed he was struck; but seeing him immediately afterwards standing firm at his station—I concluded the wound could not be serious. Under the impression still, however, that he was wounded, as soon as I had the opportunity I enquired where he was struck?—and after explaining to him the reason of my impression, he informed me that his foot had got upon a stone or piece of wood which gave him pain and had sprained his Ancle.

In other words, Burr's instinctive reaction to Hamilton's shot was a discernible flinch and an impulsive physical jerk that Burr, seeking afterward to emphasize his composure, blamed on a stone or piece of wood at his feet.[15]

While the palpable detail of this version has the ring of truth, and while the contours of the Burr story align themselves more comfortably with the timing of the shots, two pieces of evidence do not fit. First, how does one explain Hamilton's obviously sincere conviction, delivered to Hosack and Pendleton in the boat afterward, that he had never fired his pistol? And second, if Hamilton did fire at Burr, how does one account for the severed branch so high above and off to the side of Burr's position?

There is a plausible and quite persuasive answer to the second question, which will then lead us to a plausible but more speculative answer to the first. The key insight, possessing the potential to unlock the mystery produced by the contradictory versions of what happened during the duel, is that both sides constructed their explanations around self-serving and misguided assumptions. The Hamilton side needed to claim that their fallen chief was a martyr who had arrived at Weehawken fully intending to expose himself to Burr's fire without shooting back. The Burr side needed to claim that their hero had behaved honorably, in accord with the principles of the *code duello,* and, after exposing his own life to Hamilton's pistol, had responded in kind but with better aim. The Hamiltonian story required a distortion in the sequence of the exchange in order to preserve Hamilton's posthumous reputation. The Burr story required a distortion of Hamilton's honorable intentions in order to justify Burr's fatal response. Both versions misrepresent what, in all likelihood, really happened.

Hamilton did fire his weapon intentionally, and he fired first. But he aimed to miss Burr, sending his ball into the tree above and behind Burr's location. In so doing, he did not withhold his shot, but he did waste it, thereby honoring his preduel pledge. Meanwhile, Burr, who did not know about the pledge, did know that a projectile from Hamilton's gun had whizzed past him and crashed into the tree to his rear. According to the principles of the *code duello,* Burr was perfectly justified in taking deadly aim at Hamilton and firing to kill.[16]

But did he? This is not a question we can resolve beyond a reasonable doubt. In that sense the secret is locked forever in the vast recesses of Burr's famously enigmatic mind at that most pregnant moment. But consider the following pieces of circumstantial evidence: By killing Hamilton, Burr had nothing to gain and everything to lose, as he almost certainly knew at the time and as subsequent events confirmed quite conclusively; Burr's initial reaction to Hamilton's collapse, as described by both Pendleton and Van Ness, was apparent surprise and regret, followed soon thereafter by an urge to speak with the wounded

Hamilton; moreover, in the latter stages of the preduel negotiations, when Hamilton's side proposed that David Hosack serve as physician for both parties, Burr had concurred that one doctor was sufficient, then added, "even that unnecessary"; finally, when duelists wished to graze or wound their antagonist superficially, the most popular targets were the hips and legs; Burr's ball missed being a mere flesh wound on the hip by only two or three inches, the damage to vital organs resulting from the ricochet off Hamilton's rib.[17]

In the end, we can never know for sure. And it is perfectly possible that Burr's smoldering hatred for Hamilton had reached such intensity that, once he had his tormentor standing helplessly in his sights, no rational calculation of his own best interests was operative at all. What is virtually certain, and most compatible with all the available evidence, is that Hamilton fired first and purposely missed. The only plausible explanation for his remark in the boat about the pistol still being loaded is that he was semiconscious, in shock, and did not know what he was saying. Or, less likely, that Pendleton and Hosack made it up to support their version of the story. What is possible, but beyond the reach of the available evidence, is that Burr really missed his target, too, that his own fatal shot, in fact, was accidental. Indeed, one of the most disarming features of the Burr version—a feature that enhances its overall credibility—is that it made Burr's shot a more deliberate and premeditated act. (Why emphasize the interval if one's intention was to diminish Burr's culpability?) In those few but fateful seconds, the thoughts racing through Burr's head would provide the ultimate answer to all questions about his character. But they are, like most of Burr's deepest thoughts, lost forever.

OUR INTENSE focus on what happened on that ledge beneath the plains of Weehawken makes eminent historical sense, for the elemental reason that the Hamilton version of the story has dominated the history books, and it is most probably wrong. But by straining to recover the factual ingredients in the story, we have inadvertently ignored the most obvious question—namely, what were these two prominent American statesmen doing on the ledge in the first place? Granted, they were there because Burr challenged Hamilton, and Hamilton concluded he could not refuse the challenge without staining his honor. But what had Hamilton done to so enrage Burr? And what was at stake for both men that was worth risking so much?

The short answer is that, just as there was a duel of words after the actual duel—won by Hamilton's advocates—there was also a duel of words beforehand, which Burr won with equivalent decisiveness. The somewhat longer answer is that the exchange of words that preceded the exchange of shots was itself merely a culmination of long-standing personal animosity and political disagreement that emerged naturally, in retrospect almost inevitably, out of the supercharged political culture of the early republic.

In the verbal exchanges before the duel, there can be no question that Burr fired first. On June 18, 1804, he called Hamilton's attention to a letter published almost two months earlier in the *Albany Register* in which the author, Dr. Charles Cooper, recalled a harangue Hamilton had delivered against Burr the preceding February. Burr was then running for governor of New York and Hamilton had attacked his qualifications. Exactly what Hamilton said was not reported in Cooper's letter, but it concluded with the following statement: "I could detail to you a still more despicable opinion which General HAMILTON has expressed of Mr. BURR." The offensive word was *despicable*. Burr wanted Hamilton to explain or disavow the word: "You might perceive, Sir, the necessity of a prompt and unqualified acknowledgment or denial of the use of any expressions which could warrant the assertions of Dr. Cooper."[18]

Knowing as we do that Burr's request triggered a chain reaction that eventually produced the fatal explosion at Weehawken, it is instructive to note that neither Cooper's letter nor Burr's request mentioned any specific or clearly libelous statement by Hamilton. To be sure, *despicable* is hardly a compliment. But precisely what it referred to, or what Hamilton allegedly said about Burr, is unidentified. The core of the complaint was hollow. Therefore, all Hamilton had to do at this propitious moment was deny having said anything that could possibly fit that description, then express his personal regret that such slanderous insinuations had been attributed to him in the press. Burr would have had little choice but to accept his explanation.

Hamilton, however, chose to pursue another course. In effect, he used the inherent ambiguity of the offensive statement to evade any direct response to Burr. He could not, he explained, "without manifest impropriety, make the avowal or disavowal you seem to think necessary." What's more, the crucial word "admits of infinite shades, from the very light to very dark. How am I to judge of the degree intended?" After delivering a brief lecture on the vagaries of grammar and syntax, calculated to irritate Burr, Hamilton went on the offensive. He felt obliged to object "on principle, to consent to be interrogated as to the justness of *inferences,* which may be drawn by *others,* from whatever I have said of a political opponent in the course of a fifteen year competition." Burr's own letter, therefore, was a gross insult in its arrogant insistence "upon a basis so vague as that which you have adopted." Hamilton was certain that, once Burr recovered his wits and sense, "you will see the matter in the same light as me." If not, then "I can only regret the circumstances, and must abide the consequences." If Burr's intention was to threaten him with the possibility of a duel, Hamilton was not disposed to submit passively to such threats. He would issue his own.[19]

Hamilton's fate was effectively sealed once he sent this letter. Not only did he miss the opportunity to disown the offensive characterization of Burr; he raised the rhetorical stakes with his dismissive tone and gratuitously defiant counterthreat. Burr's response was incisively curt: "having Considered it attentively," he wrote, "I regret to find in it nothing of that sincerity and delicacy which you profess to Value." Then he raised the verbal game to yet a higher level of insult: "I relied with unsuspecting faith that from the frankness of a Soldier and the Candor of a gentleman I might expect an ingenuous declaration." But such expectations were obviously too much for such a duplicitous character as Hamilton, who lacked "the Spirit to Maintain or the Magnanimity to retract" his own words.[20]

Moreover, Hamilton's complaint—that he could hardly be expected to remember everything he had said over "the course of a fifteen year competition"—inadvertently opened up a whole new and much larger field of conflict. In his instructions to Van Ness, who had become his designated representative in the exchange, Burr explained that the Cooper letter was merely the most recent libel against him by Hamilton. While Burr claimed that he had always restrained himself when criticized by his political enemies, "in regard of Mr. H there has been no reciprocity—for several years his name has been lent to the support of Slanders." Two years earlier, in fact, Burr had claimed to have confronted Hamilton with a personal complaint about incessant vilifications of his character, and Hamilton had acknowledged his indiscretion. Despite the apology and apparent promise to stop, Hamilton had then resumed his back-stabbing campaign. According to Burr, the immediate incident only proved that Hamilton's libelous ways were incorrigible. Now, however, "these things must have an end."[21]

As a result, the form of satisfaction Burr now demanded expanded beyond one single utterance reported in an Albany newspaper. Van Ness relayed the new terms on June 25, 1804: "Col: Burr required a General disavowal of any intention on the part of Genl Hamilton in his various conversations to convey impressions derogatory to the honor of M. Burr." Burr was now demanding a general apology for all past indiscretions. He acknowledged that this represented an escalation, but given Hamilton's arrogant evasiveness, "more will now be required than would have been asked at first."[22]

By now Pendleton had entered the negotiations as Hamilton's representative. He attempted to exercise his influence, as in fact the etiquette of the *code duello* required, to find a way out of the impasse. Under Pendleton's prodding, Hamilton agreed to a statement disclaiming any recollection of the conversation as recounted by Cooper. That conversation, as Hamilton now remembered it, "consisted of comments on the political principles and views of Col. Bur . . . without reference to any instance of past conduct, or to private character." Hamilton saw fit to repeat his main point, "that the conversation to which Doctr Cooper alluded turned wholly on political topics and did not attribute to Colo Burr, any instance of dishonorable conduct, nor relate to his private character."[23]

Strictly speaking, Hamilton's concession should have been the end of it. Affairs of honor were supposed to involve only *personal* charges. Political or ideological disagreements, no matter how deep, lay outside the field of honor on which a gentleman could demand satisfaction. Hamilton's distinction between personal and political criticism was designed to change the dispute with Burr from an affair of honor to a political difference of opinion. Technically, given the rules of the *code duello,* Burr should have felt obliged to accept Hamilton's explanation as the equivalent of an apology.

Except that Burr's blood was now up. If Hamilton had presented his distinction between personal and political criticism earlier, the affair would most probably have ended before it began. Now, however, Burr would be satisfied with nothing less than a wholesale and unqualified apology for all previous remarks about his personal and political character: "No denial or declaration will be satisfactory," Van Ness explained, "unless it be general, so as to wholly exclude the idea that rumors derogatory to Col. Burr's honor have originated with Genl Hamilton or have been fairly inferred from anything he has said." There must be no room in which Hamilton could maneuver; it must be a blanket apology. "A retraction or denial therefore of all such declarations or a disavowal of any intention to impeach Col Burr without reference to time and place," Van Ness concluded, "is the only reparation that can be made." Later on, when this part of the correspondence between the two sides was published, that eccentric Virginia statesman and veteran of multiple duels, John Randolph, observed that Hamilton came off as "a sinking fox," while Burr was "a vigorous old hound" resolutely determined to hunt down his prey with "an undeviating pursuit . . . not to be eluded or baffled."[24]

Just as most duels in this era did not end in death or serious injury, most negotiations over matters of honor did not end in duels. The Burr-Hamilton affair was destined to prove an exception on both counts. Once Burr extended his demands to cover their entire public careers, and then also refused to recognize the traditional distinction between personal and political criticism, Hamilton was truly trapped. Several more letters were exchanged, as Pendleton groped for an honorable exit. He protested that Burr's terms "have greatly changed and extended the original ground of inquiry," requiring Hamilton to assume responsibility for "any *rumours* which may be afloat . . . through the whole period of his acquaintance with Col Burr." But Burr did not budge, repeating his accusation that "secret whispers traducing his fame and impeaching his honor" over more than a decade demanded an unqualified apology, and that Hamilton's insistence on distinctions and qualifications "are proofs that he has done the injury specified." On June 27, 1804, Burr's patience ran out: "The length to which this correspondence has extended only tending to prove that the satisfactory redress . . . cannot be obtained," Van Ness explained, "he deems it useless to offer any proposition except the simple Message which I shall now have the honor to deliver." It was the invitation for "the interview at Weehawken."[25]

Hamilton requested a brief delay so that he could complete some pending legal business and put his personal affairs in order. Both men prepared their wills and left sufficient evidence to piece together some, albeit hazy, picture of what was on their minds. Burr wrote his beloved daughter Theodosia and her husband, extracting a promise that she would be allowed to pursue her study of Latin, Greek, and the classics. Then, in a typically bizarre act of Burrish dash, he requested that, if anything unforeseen should befall him, his daughter and son-in-law convey his respects to one of his former paramours, now a married woman living in Cuba.[26]

On July 4, at the annual Independence Day dinner held by the Society of the Cincinnati, Burr and Hamilton actually sat together at the same table. The artist John Trumbull, who was also present, recorded the scene: "The singularity of their manner was observed by all, but few had any suspicion of the cause. Burr contrary to his wont, was silent, gloomy, sour; while Hamilton entered with glee into the gaiety of a convivial party, and even sung an old military song." The tune that Hamilton sang, called "General Wolfe's Song," was supposedly written by the great British general on the eve of his glorious death on the Plains of Abraham outside Quebec in 1759. It was, therefore, an eerily prophetic song, especially the stanza that went:

> *Why, soldiers, why*
> *Should we be melancholy, boys?*
> *Why, soldiers, why?*
> *Whose business is to die!*
> *What! Sighing? fie!*
> *Damn fear, drink on, be jolly, boys!*
> *'Tis he, you, or I.*[27]

Hamilton's last days contained several other incidents of equivalent poignancy, though they were only recognizable when viewed through the knowledge of the looming duel. On July 3, the day before the Society of the Cincinnati dinner, he had a dinner party of his own at his new country house, the Grange. The list of guests included William

Short, formerly Thomas Jefferson's personal secretary in Paris and a lifelong Jefferson protégé. Also invited were Abigail Adams Smith and her husband, the daughter and son-in-law of John and Abigail Adams. Since Jefferson was Hamilton's primal political enemy, and since Adams was his bitterest opponent within the Federalist party, a man whom Hamilton had publicly described as mentally deranged and unfit for the presidency, the choice of guests suggests that Hamilton was making some kind of statement about separating political and personal differences. About this same time, he drafted a "Thesis on Discretion" for his eldest surviving son. It singled out discretion as "if not a splendid . . . at least a very useful virtue," then went on to offer an obviously autobiographical warning: "The greatest abilities are sometimes thrown into the shade by this defect or are prevented from obtaining the success to which they are entitled. The person on whom it is chargeable [is] also apt to make and have numerous enemies and is occasionally involved . . . in the most difficulties and dangers."[28]

All of which suggests that the impending duel with Burr was prompting some second thoughts on Hamilton's part about the sheer intensity of his past political disagreements, as well as about his own periodic lack of discretion in these highly personalized debates. Those predisposed to detect hints of suicidal intentions during Hamilton's last days might wish to speculate at great length on such tidbits. The main outline of the visible and available evidence, however, reveals a man questioning his own characteristic excesses, which had somehow put him on a course that led to the current impasse. Hamilton did not believe that in going to Weehawken to meet Burr he was most probably going to meet his Maker. But the looming threat of possible injury and perhaps even death did tend to focus his mind on the downside of his swashbuckling style. He was less suicidal than regretful, less fatalistic than meditative.

The regrets and meditations, however, did not spread as far as Aaron Burr. The evidence here does not require inspired conjecture or nuanced analysis. Hamilton wrote out his "Statement on the Impending Duel" to answer those critics who wondered how a statesman of his maturity and distinction could allow himself to be goaded into a juvenile exchange of shots at ten paces. "There were intrinsick difficulties in the thing," Hamilton explained in his statement, rooted in the reality "not to be denied, that my animadversions on the political principles, character and views of Col Burr" had been extremely severe, "to include very unfavourable criticisms on particular instances of the private conduct of the Gentleman." In other words, Burr's allegation that Hamilton had made a practice of vilifying him for many years was essentially correct. For that reason, "the disavowal required of me by Col Burr, in a general and indefinite form, was out of my power." He could not apologize without lying. What ultimately blocked any prospect of an apology or retraction was Hamilton's abiding conviction that his libels of Burr were all true: "I have not censured him on light grounds," Hamilton concluded, "or from unworthy inducements. I certainly have had strong reasons for what I may have said."[29]

The answer, then, to the salient question—What were these two prominent American statesmen doing on that ledge beneath the plains of Weehawken?—is reasonably clear. Burr was there because Hamilton had been libeling him throughout their crisscrossing careers in public life. Despite earlier promises to cease this practice, Hamilton had persisted. Burr's patience had simply worn out.

Hamilton was there because he could not honestly deny Burr's charges, which he sincerely believed captured the essence of the man's character. What's more, Hamilton also believed, as he put it, that his own "ability to be in future useful, whether in resisting mischief or effecting good, in those crises of public affairs, which seem likely to happen, would probably be inseparable from a conformity with public prejudice in this particular." In other words, if he did not answer Burr's challenge, he would be repudiating his well-known convictions, and in so doing, he would lose the respect of those political colleagues on whom his reputation depended. This would be tantamount to retiring from public life. And he was not prepared to do that. If Burr went to Weehawken out of frustration, Hamilton went out of a combination of ambition and insecurity.[30]

WHAT DID IT mean? For those at the time it meant that Hamilton became a martyr to the dying cause of Federalism and Burr became the most despised national leader since Benedict Arnold. Indeed, less than a year after the duel, Burr made secret contact with British officials for the purpose of seizing some substantial portion of the trans-Mississippi territory and placing it under British control, presumably with Burr himself as governor. Perhaps Burr reasoned that, since he was being treated as a new Benedict Arnold, he might as well enjoy the fruits of a similar treason.[31]

Meanwhile, clergymen, college presidents, and other self-appointed spokesmen for communal standards of morality seized upon the Burr-Hamilton encounter to launch a crusade against dueling throughout most of the northern states. What had once seemed an honorable if illegal contest of wills, bathed in a mist of aristocratic glamour and clad in the armor of medieval chivalry, came to be regarded as a pathological ritual in which self-proclaimed gentlemen shot each other in juvenile displays of their mutual insecurity. Though the practice of dueling survived in the South, and in its more democratic blaze-away version on the frontier of the West, the stigma associated with the Burr-Hamilton duel put the *code duello* on the defensive as a national institution. Not that it would ever die out completely, drawing as it did on irrational urges whose potency defies civilized sanctions, always flourishing in border regions, criminal underworlds, and ghetto communities where the authority of the law lacks credibility. Nevertheless, the Burr-Hamilton duel helped turn the tide against the practice of dueling by providing a focal point for its critics and serving as a dramatic object lesson of its self-destructive character. One of the reasons the Burr-Hamilton duel became legendary as the most famous duel in American history is its cautionary role as the most memorable example of how not to do it.[32]

The chief reason, however, for its legendary status, and the main reason why we can call it "The Duel" without much fear of being misunderstood, is the relative prominence of the two participants. Burr was the second-ranking official in the federal government. Hamilton was, after George Washington, the most powerful figure in the Federalist party and, his advocates would have added, the intellectual wellspring for all the political energy that Washington merely symbolized. Their fatal encounter represented a momentary breakdown in the dominant pattern of nonviolent conflict within the American revolutionary generation.

In the wake of other national movements—the French, Russian, and Chinese revolutions, as well as the multiple movements for national independence in Africa, Asia, and Latin America—the leadership class of the successful revolution proceeded to decimate itself in bloody reprisals that frequently assumed genocidal proportions. But the conflict within the American revolutionary generation remained a passionate yet bloodless affair in which the energies released by national independence did not devour its own children. The Burr-Hamilton duel represented the singular exception to this rule. Perhaps this is what Henry Adams had in mind when, in his inimitable style, he described the moment at Weehawken with its "accessories of summer-morning sunlight on rocky and wooded heights, tranquil river, and distant sky, and behind [it] all . . . moral gloom, double treason, and political despair," calling it "the most dramatic moment in the early politics of the Union."[33]

What made it truly dramatic, in the Henry Adams sense, was not the sad consequences of a merely personal feud, but, rather, the underlying values of the political culture that made the encounter simultaneously so poignant and so symbolic. The full meaning of the duel, in other words, cannot be captured without recovering those long-lost values of the early American republic, which shaped the way Burr and Hamilton so mistrusted and even hated each other. More was at stake, much more, than the throbbing egos of two ambitious statesmen vying for personal honor. Hamilton believed—and he had a good deal of evidence to support his belief—that the very survival of the infant American nation was at stake. Understanding why he entertained such hyperbolic thoughts is the key to the core meaning of the duel.

When Burr first demanded an apology, Hamilton refused to comply, complaining that he could not possibly be expected to recall all his remarks about Burr over a fifteen-year period of interaction. Actually, Burr and Hamilton had known each other almost twice that long, from their youthful days as officers in the Continental Army. But Hamilton's reference to "fifteen years" turned out to be a precise estimate of their history as political antagonists. The hostility began in 1789, when Burr accepted the office of attorney general in New York from Governor George Clinton after campaigning for Hamilton's candidate, who lost. Burr's facile shift in his allegiance, the first in what would be several similarly agile switches during his career, captured Hamilton's attention and produced his first recorded anti-Burr remarks, questioning Burr's lack of political principle.

If the first crack appeared in 1789, the real break occurred two years later. In 1791 Burr defeated Philip Schuyler, Hamilton's wealthy father-in-law, in the race for the United States Senate, when several rival factions within the clannish, even quasi-feudal, politics of New York united to unseat the incumbent, who was generally perceived as a Hamilton supporter. It was all downhill from there. Burr used his perch in the Senate to oppose Hamilton's fiscal program, then to decide a disputed (and probably rigged) gubernatorial election in New York against Hamilton's candidate. Hamilton, in turn, opposed Burr's candidacy for the vice presidency in 1792 and two years later blocked his nomination as American minister to France. The most dramatic clash came in 1800, when Burr ran alongside Jefferson in the presidential election—his reward for delivering the bulk of New York's electoral votes, which made Jefferson's victory possible. The election was thrown into the House of Representatives because of the quirk in the electoral college—subsequently corrected by the Twelfth Amendment—which gave Burr and Jefferson the same number of votes without specifying which candidate headed the ticket. Hamilton lobbied his Federalist colleagues in the House to support Jefferson over Burr for the presidency, a decision that probably had a decisive effect on the eventual outcome. Finally, in 1804, in the campaign for governor of New York, which actually produced the remarks Burr cited in his challenge, Hamilton opposed Burr's candidacy for an office he was probably not going to win anyway.[34]

This brief review of the Burr-Hamilton rivalry provides a helpful sense of context, but to fully appreciate Burr's eventual charges, and Hamilton's private acknowledgment that they were justified, one needs to know, specifically, what Hamilton said about Burr. Throughout this same period, Hamilton made a host of political enemies about whom he had extremely critical things to say (and vice versa). Indeed, Jefferson, rather than Burr, was Hamilton's chief political enemy, followed closely behind by Adams. This made logical as well as political sense, since Jefferson was the titular leader of the Republican opposition and Adams was the leader of the moderate wing of the Federalists, a group that found Hamilton's policies sometimes excessive and his flamboyant style always offensive. But within this Hamiltonian rogues' gallery, Burr was always the chief rogue, and what Hamilton said about him was truly distinctive.

Whereas Hamilton's central charge against Jefferson was that he was a utopian visionary with a misguided set of political principles, his core criticism of Burr was that he was wholly devoid of any principles at all. Burr was "unprincipaled, both as a public and private man," Hamilton claimed, "a man whose only political principle is, to mount at all events to the highest political honours of the Nation, and as much further as circumstances will carry him." Sporadic attacks on Burr's character along the same lines—"unprincipaled in private life, desperate in his fortune," "despotic in his ordinary demeanor," "beyond redemption"—are littered throughout Hamilton's correspondence in the 1790s, and they probably reflect a mere fraction of his unrecorded comments to Federalist colleagues.[35]

The full and better-recorded salvo came late in 1800 and early in 1801, during the debate in the House of Representatives over the presidential deadlock between Burr and Jefferson. Since everyone knew that Jefferson was Hamilton's implacable political enemy, the kind of elusive target who seemed to be put on earth by God to subvert Hamilton's visionary plans for a powerful federal government, Hamilton's strong endorsement of Jefferson as "by far not so dangerous a man," who possessed "solid pretensions to character," only served to underline his contempt for Burr. "As to Burr there is nothing in his favour," Hamilton observed, then went on: "His private character is not defended by his most partial friends. He is bankrupt beyond redemption except by the plunder of his country. His public principles have no other spring or aim than his own aggrandizement. . . . If he can he will certainly disturb our institutions to secure himself *permanent power* and with it *wealth*. He is truly the Catiline of America."[36]

This mention of Catiline is worth a momentary pause, in part because the reference is so unfamiliar to modern ears as to seem meaningless, and also because it was so familiar to the leaders of the revolutionary generation as to require no further explanation. By accusing Burr of being Catiline, Hamilton was making the ultimate accusation, for Catiline was the treacherous and degenerate character whose scheming nearly destroyed the Roman Republic and whose licentious ways inspired, by their very profligacy, Cicero's eloquent oration on virtue, which was subsequently memorized by generations of American schoolboys. No one in the political leadership of the early American republic needed to be reminded who Catiline was. He was the talented but malevolent destroyer of republican government. If each member of the revolutionary generation harbored secret thoughts about being the modern incarnation of a classical Greek or Roman hero—Washington was Cato or Cincinnatus, Adams was Solon or Cicero—no one aspired to be Catiline.

Did Burr fit the role? Put differently, were Hamilton's accusations of Burr true? It is an intriguing question, and given Burr's matchless skill at concealing his motives, covering his tracks, and destroying much of his private correspondence, unambiguous answers are not a realistic prospect. The recurrent pattern in Burr's political behavior that caught Hamilton's eye, however, made him eminently vulnerable to the Catiline charge. Whether in the labyrinthine politics of New York or the emerging party wars between Federalists and Republicans at the national level, Burr possessed an absolute genius at positioning himself amid competing factions so as to make himself readily available to the side most desperate for his services.

The presidential election of 1800 is the most politically significant and most illustrative example of the pattern: Burr allowed the voting between him and Jefferson to go on for thirty-six ballots in the House of Representatives without ever indicating his principled recognition that the mass of the electorate had clearly intended to designate Jefferson as president. In his own defense, Burr might have pointed out that he never actively sought Federalist support. But he never repudiated it either. His enigmatic silence, however, unquestionably had mischievous consequences, for it prolonged the scheming in the House and, somewhat ironically, convinced Jefferson that Burr could never be trusted.[37]

His knack for injecting himself into the cracks between warring political factions might have been interpreted as a sign of his independence. Like Washington, so his defenders might have argued, Burr refused to place his own political convictions at the service of any party. But while Washington attempted to transcend the ideological wars of the 1790s, Burr seemed disposed to tunnel beneath the warring camps, then pop up on the side promising him the bigger tribute. If Washington was the epitome of the virtuous leader who subordinated personal interest to the public good, Burr was a kind of anti-Washington, who manipulated the public interest for his own inscrutable purposes.[38]

At least so it appeared to Hamilton. As if to demonstrate that his questionable behavior in the presidential crisis of 1801 was no aberration, Burr repeated the pattern in 1804 during the campaign for governor of New York. Although still serving as vice president under Jefferson, Burr realized that the Republicans intended to drop him from the ticket when Jefferson ran for his second term. And so when Federalist leaders from New York approached him as a prospective candidate for the gubernatorial race, he indicated a willingness to switch party affiliations and run in his home state as a Federalist. This was the decision that caused Hamilton to repeat his earlier characterizations of Burr as the unprincipled American Catiline, which in turn generated the newspaper reports containing the offensive word "despicable."

But that was only half the story. For the Federalist leaders in New England were interested in recruiting Burr as part of a larger scheme that aimed at nothing less than the dismemberment of the American republic. (This was really what Henry Adams was referring to by the phrase "the most dramatic moment in the early politics of the Union.") Their plan envisioned the secession of New England in the wake of Jefferson's reelection and the simultaneous capture of New York, which would then join the secessionist movement to create a Federalist-controlled confederacy of northern states. Burr, true to form, refused to make any promises to deliver New York to the secessionists, but he also would not repudiate the conspiracy.[39]

Hamilton was aware of the Federalist plot, which was no half-baked scheme hatched by marginal figures, involving as it did several Federalist senators from New England and Timothy Pickering, the former secretary of state. "I will here express but one sentiment," Hamilton warned his Federalist colleagues, "which is, the Dismemberment of our Empire will be a clear sacrifice . . . without any counterballancing good." When apprised that the leading New England Federalists were waiting to hear that their old chief was committed to the secessionist plot, Hamilton made clear his opposition: "Tell them from ME, at MY request, for God's sake, to cease these conversations and threatenings about a separation of the Union. It must hang together as long as it can be made to." The last letter that Hamilton ever wrote, composed the night before the duel, was devoted to squelching the still-lingering Federalist fantasies of a separate northeastern confederation, a dream that refused to die until the moribund effort at the Hartford Convention in 1815 exposed it as a fiasco.[40]

What Hamilton seemed to see in Burr, then, was a man very much like himself in several respects: ambitious, energetic, possessing an instinctive strategic antenna and a willingness to take political risks. Hamilton understood the potency of Burr's influence because he felt those same personal qualities throbbing away inside himself. Both men also shared a keen sense of the highly fluid and still-fragile character of the recently launched American republic. The hyperbolic tone of Hamilton's anti-Burr comments derived not so much from intense personal dislike *per se* as from his intense fear that the precarious condition of the infant nation rendered it so vulnerable to Burr's considerable talents. Burr embodied Hamilton's daring and energy run amok in a political culture still groping for its stable shape.

The kernel of truth in Hamilton's distinction between personal and political criticism of Burr resides here. In a sense it was an accurate statement of Hamilton's assessment. Burr's reputation as a notorious womanizer or as a lavish spender who always managed to stay one step ahead of his creditors did not trouble Hamilton. What did worry him to no end was the ominous fit between Burr's political skills and the opportunities for mischief so clearly available in a nation whose laws and institutions were still congealing.[41]

The problem with Hamilton's distinction, however, was that the putative barrier between personal and political criticism, or private and public behavior, kept getting overwhelmed by real choices. Personal character was essential in order to resist public temptations. In Burr's case, for example, the decision to support or betray Jefferson in 1801; or to conspire with Federalists promoting a northern secession in 1804; or, a few years later, to detach the American Southwest from the United States. Character counted in each of these choices, because the temptations being served up by the political conditions in this formative phase of the American republic put the moral fiber of national leadership to a true test.

It was Burr's unique distinction, at least as Hamilton saw it, to fail every such test. Whereas no one else in the revolutionary generation wanted the role of Catiline, Burr seemed to be auditioning for the part at every opportunity. To put it somewhat differently, if the dispute between Burr and Hamilton had been settled in the courts rather than on the dueling grounds, and if one admitted the legal principle that truth constituted a legitimate defense against charges of libel (a principle, intriguingly, that Hamilton insisted on in the last case he ever argued), Hamilton would almost certainly have won.[42]

It is difficult for us to fathom fully the threat that Burr represented to Hamilton because we know that the American experiment with republican government was destined to succeed. We know that a nation so conceived and so dedicated could and did endure, indeed flourish, to become the longest-lived republic in world history. Not only was such knowledge unavailable to Hamilton and his contemporaries, the political landscape they saw around themselves was a dangerously fluid place, where neither the national laws nor institutions had yet hardened into permanent fixtures. Or if one wished to think biologically rather than architecturally, the body politic had yet to develop its immunities to the political diseases afflicting all new nations. What seems extravagant and hyperbolic in Hamilton's critical description of Burr, then, was not a symptom of Hamilton's paranoia so much as a realistic response to the genuine vulnerability of the still-tender young plant called the United States. So much seemed to be at stake because, in truth, it was.[43]

Our search for the full meaning of the duel has led us backward, past the purely personal jealousies, through the only partially resolvable mysteries of what happened beneath the plains of Weehawken on the fateful day, and beyond the history of dueling as a dying institution. It has become an excursion into the highly problematic political world of the newborn American republic, a place where real and not just imagined conspiracies were prevalent, where the endurance of the political entity called the United States was still very much up in the air. As is more or less true about any famous event that is deeply imbedded in the historical soil of a particularly fertile time and place, the real significance of the duel lies beyond the specific parameters of the event itself, beyond that narrow ledge above the Hudson River. It expands to encompass an entire but still-emerging world that Burr threatened and Hamilton believed himself to be defending.

Oliver Wendell Holmes once observed that "a great man represents a strategic point in the campaign of history, and part of his greatness consists of his being there." Both Burr and Hamilton thought of themselves as great men who happened to come of age at one of those strategic points in the campaign of history called the American revolutionary era. By the summer of 1804, history had pretty much passed them by. Burr had alienated Jefferson and the triumphant Republican party by his disloyalty as a vice president and had lost by a landslide in his bid to become a Federalist governor of New York. Hamilton had not held national office for nine years and the Federalist cause he had championed was well on its way to oblivion. Even in his home state of New York, the Federalists were, as John Quincy Adams put it, "a minority, and of that minority, only a minority were admirers and partisans of Mr. Hamilton." Neither man had much of a political future.[44]

But by being there beneath the plains of Weehawken for their interview, they managed to make a dramatic final statement about the time of their time. Honor mattered because character mattered. And character mattered because the fate of the American experiment with republican government still required virtuous leaders to survive. Eventually, the United States might develop into a nation of laws and established institutions capable of surviving corrupt or incompetent public officials. But it was not there yet. It still required honorable and virtuous leaders to endure. Both Burr and Hamilton came to the interview because they wished to be regarded as part of such company.

CHAPTER TWO

The Dinner

THOMAS JEFFERSON'S version of the story follows a plotline that illustrates the natural and almost nonchalant way that history happens in an ideal Jeffersonian world. One day in mid-June of 1790, he encountered Alexander Hamilton by chance as the two members of President Washington's cabinet—Jefferson was secretary of state and Hamilton was secretary of treasury—waited outside the presidential office. Hamilton was not his customarily confident and resplendent self. Jefferson thought he looked "sombre, haggard, and dejected beyond comparison." Even his manner of dress appeared "uncouth and neglected." He was, at least as Jefferson described him, a beaten man.

While they stood in the street outside Washington's residence, Hamilton confided that his entire financial plan for the recovery of public credit, which he had submitted to Congress in January, was trapped within a congressional gridlock. Southern congressmen, led by James Madison, had managed to block approval of one key provision of the Hamilton proposal, the assumption of state debts by the federal government, thereby scuttling the whole Hamiltonian scheme for fiscal reform. Hamilton was simultaneously fatalistic and melodramatic. If his financial plan were rejected, as now seemed certain, then "he could be of no use, and was determined to resign." And without his plan and his leadership—these two items seemed inextricably connected in his own mind—the government and inevitably the national union itself must collapse.

Jefferson suggested that perhaps he could help. "On considering the situation of things," he recalled, "I thought the first step towards some conciliation of views would be to bring Mr. Madison and Colo. Hamilton to a friendly discussion of the subject." Though he was still suffering from the lingering vestiges of a migraine headache that had lasted for over a month, and though he had only recently moved into his new quarters at 57 Maiden Lane in New York City, Jefferson offered to host a private dinner party where the main players could meet alone to see if the intractable political obstacles might melt away under the more benign influences of wine and gentlemanly conversation.

Jefferson's version of what occurred that evening, most probably Sunday, June 20, contains some misleading and self-serving features, but since it is the only account that has survived in the historical record, and since Jefferson's justifiably famous way with words possesses a charming simplicity that embodies nicely the elegant atmosphere of the dinner party itself, it deserves our extended attention:

> They came. I opened the subject to them, acknoleged that my situation had not permitted me to understand it sufficiently but encouraged them to consider the thing together. They did so. It ended in Mr. Madison's acquiescence in a proposition that the question [i.e., assumption of the state debts] should be again brought before the house by way of amendment from the Senate, that he would not vote for it, nor entirely withdraw his opposition, yet he would not be strenuous, but leave it to its fate. It was observed, I forget by which of them, that as the pill would be a bitter one to the Southern states, something should be done to soothe them; and the removal of the seat of government to the Patowmac was a just measure, and would probably be a popular one with them, and would be a proper one to follow the assumption.

In other words, Jefferson brokered a political bargain of decidedly far-reaching significance: Madison agreed to permit the core provision of Hamilton's fiscal program to pass; and in return Hamilton agreed to use his influence to assure that the permanent residence of the national capital would be on the Potomac River. If true, this story deserves to rank alongside the Missouri Compromise and the Compromise of 1850 as one of the landmark accommodations in American politics. And, without much question, what we might call "The Compromise of 1790" would top the list as the most meaningful dinner party in American history.[1]

But is it true? The verdict of history, or at least the reigning judgment of most historians, is that the story is *essentially* true. Hamilton and Madison did meet at Jefferson's quarters in late June of 1790. On July 9 the House passed the Residence Bill, locating the permanent national capital on the Potomac after a ten-year residence in Philadelphia, all this decided by a vote of 32 to 29. On July 26 the House passed the Assumption Bill by a nearly identical vote of 34 to 28, Madison voting against but, in keeping with Jefferson's version of the bargain, not leading the opposition in his previously "strenuous" fashion. Moreover, several different political observers and newspaper editors of the day clearly believed that some kind of secret deal had been made to effect the switching of votes necessary to break the long-standing deadlock on both issues. A disgruntled New York editor, for example, was quite explicit: "The true reason of the removal of Congress from this city will be explained to the people in the course of a very few days. To the lasting disgrace of the majority in both houses it will be seen, that the Pennsylvania and Patowmack interests have been purchased with *twenty-one and one-half million dollars,*" which just happened to be the size of the assumed state debts.[2]

What's more, on the very day that the bargain was struck, Jefferson wrote a long letter to James Monroe, his loyal Virginian disciple, preparing him for news of precisely the kind of compromise that eventually occurred. Monroe, like Madison and most Virginians, adamantly opposed assumption. Jefferson assured him that he too found the measure repulsive: "But in the present instance I see the necessity of yielding for this time . . . for the sake of the union, and to save us from the greatest of all Calamities." He even spelled out what he meant by such alarming words. The congressional debate over Hamilton's financial plan and the location of the national capital had produced total legislative paralysis. If this was the first test of the viability of the new federal government under the Constitution, the government was failing miserably. Without some kind of breakthrough, the entire experiment with republican government at the national level would "burst and vanish, and the states separate to take care of everyone of itself." Either the peaceful dissolution of the United States or a civil war would occur unless some sort of political bargain was struck. "Without descending to talk about bargains," Jefferson wrote— suggesting that making such deals work required not talking about them publicly—a negotiation was in the works that would make assumption more palatable to Virginians of Monroe's persuasion: a trade of assumption for the Potomac location of the permanent capital. "If this plan of compromise does not take place," Jefferson warned, "I fear one infinitely worse." Upon receiving Jefferson's letter, Monroe responded immediately with a warning of his own. The political deal Jefferson described would never go down in Virginia, where assump- tion was regarded as a "fatal poison" and the Potomac location "of but little importance" in comparison.[3]

Two years later Jefferson himself concluded that Monroe had been right. In 1792 he told Washington that the bargain made that evening with Hamilton was the greatest political mistake of his life. In fact, Jef- ferson's version of the dinner-table bargain dates from that later time, probably 1792, when he deeply regretted his complicity. "It was unjust," he had by then decided, "and was acquiesced in merely from a fear of disunion, while our government was still in its infant state." The ever-agile Hamilton had outmaneuvered him to support assumption, which had then become "a principal ground whereon was reared up that Speculating phalanx," which had subsequently conspired so insidiously, as Jefferson put it, "to change the political complexion of the government of the U.S." Perhaps a final reason to accept the credi- bility of Jefferson's version of the story, then, is that he was not boasting about his political influence, but confessing his profound regret. Why fabricate a tale in which one comes off as a self-confessed dunce?[4]

Any attempt to answer that question would carry us into the labyrinthine corridors of Jefferson's famously elusive mind. Suffice to say that there is a core of truth to Jefferson's account of the dinner-table bargain, though it vastly oversimplifies the history that was happening at that propitious moment. Which is to say that several secret meetings were occurring at the same time; and the political corridors were even more labyrinthine than Jefferson's imperfect memory of events. Most importantly, the conversation at Jefferson's quarters was merely one part of an ongoing and larger conversation in which the very survival and subsequent shape of the American republic seemed at stake. The more one looks at the chief characters in this scene and listens to their voices, the more the salient question changes. It is not: Was Jefferson telling the truth? It is, instead: Why were such otherwise-sensible statesmen as Jefferson, Madison, and Hamilton all convinced that the newly established government of the United States was so precarious and problematic? Why was the passage of assumption so threatening? Why was the Potomac so symbolic? Jefferson's version of the story to the contrary notwithstanding, what was going on here?

As MIGHT BE expected, the answer the various participants gave to such an overarching question depended a great deal on the ground on which they were standing. And this, in turn, meant that Hamilton, Jefferson, and Madison arrived at the dinner with different agendas, different experiences, and different stories to tell. Within this formidable trio, it makes most sense to start with Madison.

He was the most centrally situated, having led the debate over both assumption and the residence question in the House. He also enjoyed the reputation as both a preeminent nationalist and favored son of Virginia and had already become famous at the tender age of thirty-nine as the shrewdest and most politically savvy veteran of the tumultuous constitutional battles of the 1780s. Indeed, in 1790 Madison had just completed what turned out to be the most creative phase of his entire career as an American statesman, which several historians would subsequently describe as the most creative contribution to political science in all of American history.[5]

Distressed by the political disarray in the state governments in the 1780s and the congenital weakness of the Articles of Confederation, Madison had helped mobilize the movement for the Constitutional Convention. His arguments for a fortified national government became the centerpiece around which all the compromises and revisions of the eventual document congealed, giving him the honorary title of "Father of the Constitution." He had then joined forces with Hamilton (with a modest assist from John Jay) to write *The Federalist Papers,* which was instantly recognized as an American classic, most especially in its ingenious insistence that republican government would prove more stable when extended over a large landmass and diverse population. In the Virginia ratifying convention he had outmaneuvered the apparently unbeatable opposition led by Patrick Henry, prompting John Marshall, his fellow Virginian Federalist, to observe that Henry might be the all-time oratorical champion in his capacity to persuade; but that Madison was his superior in his capacity to convince. Then, to top it off, he had drafted and ushered the Bill of Rights through the First Congress. In 1790, in short, Madison was at the peak of his powers and, after George Washington and Benjamin Franklin (who died that year), was generally regarded as the most influential political leader in the new nation.[6]

He did not look the part. At five feet six and less than 140 pounds "little Jemmy Madison" had the frail and discernibly fragile appearance of a career librarian or schoolmaster, forever lingering on the edge of some fatal ailment, overmatched by the daily demands of ordinary life. When he left his father's modest-sized plantation at Montpelier in Virginia to attend Princeton in 1769—Aaron Burr was a classmate—the youthful Madison had confessed to intimations of imminent mortality, somewhat morbidly predicting his early death. (As it turned out, he survived longer than all the leaders of the revolutionary generation, observing near the end, "Having outlived so many of my contemporaries, I ought not to forget that I may be thought to have outlived myself.") Not only did he look like the epitome of insignificance— diminutive, colorless, sickly—he was also paralyzingly shy, the kind of guest at a party who instinctively searched out the corners of the room.[7]

Appearances, in Madison's case, were not just massively deceptive; they actually helped to produce his prowess. Amid the flamboyant orators of the Virginia dynasty, he was practically invisible and wholly unthreatening, but therefore the acknowledged master of the inoffensive argument that just happened, time after time, to prove decisive. He seemed to lack a personal agenda because he seemed to lack a personality, yet when the votes were counted, his side almost always won. His diffidence in debate was disarming in several ways: He was so obviously gentle and so eager to give credit to others, especially his opponents, that it was impossible to unleash one's full fury against him without seeming a belligerent fool; he was so reserved that he conveyed the off-putting impression of someone with an infinite reservoir of additional information, all hidden away, the speaker not wishing to burden you with excessively conspicuous erudition; but, if you gave permission, fully prepared to go on for several more hours; or until your side voluntarily surrendered. His physical deficiencies meant that a Madisonian argument lacked all the usual emotional affectations and struck with the force of pure, unencumbered thought. Or as one observer put it later, "Never have I seen *so much mind in so little matter.*" His style, in effect, was not to have one.[8]

It is customary to think of Madison as Jefferson's loyal lieutenant, the junior member of what has been called "the great collaboration." Certainly in later years, when Madison served as Jefferson's political point man in the party wars of the 1790s, then as his secretary of state, then his successor as president, there is much to be said for his characterization. The later pattern was for Jefferson to provide the sweeping vision while Madison managed the messier particulars. (If God was in the details, so the saying went, Madison was usually there to greet Him upon arrival.) Even then, however, Madison's habitual shyness and his willingness to remain within Jefferson's shadow probably concealed the extent of his independent influence on the partnership. The fairest assessment is that the collaboration worked so well because questions of primacy never occurred to Madison. Or, as John Quincy Adams described the seamless character of the partnership, it was "a phenomenon, like the invisible and mysterious movements of the magnet in the physical world."[9]

However, in 1790, if one wished to talk about "the great collaboration," the presumption would have been that one was referring to Madison and Hamilton. After all, while Jefferson was serving as America's minister in Paris from 1784 to 1789, the team of Madison and Hamilton had led the fight for a vastly expanded national government with sovereign power over the states. Their collaboration as "Publius" in *The Federalist Papers* was every bit as seamless as the subsequent alliance between the two Virginians. When Hamilton began to draft his *Report on the Public Credit* in September of 1789, Madison was one of the first persons he consulted for advice. At that very time, Jefferson was writing Madison from France with expressions of great doubt about the powers granted the federal government over domestic affairs, powers that Madison had championed more effectively than anyone else at the Constitutional Convention.[10]

Jefferson had also shared with Madison his intriguingly utopian suggestion that each generation was sovereign, so that the laws made for one generation should expire after about twenty years. Madison had responded in his gentle, unassuming, but logically devastating fashion to suggest that, yes, this was a fascinating notion, but if taken seriously, it was a recipe for anarchy and ran directly counter to the whole thrust of his own political effort to establish a stable constitutional settlement that compelled the trust and abiding veneration of present and future generations of Americans. Knowing as we do that Madison would soon become one of the most ardent and potent Jeffersonians of all time, it is all the more instructive to note that, prior to 1790, they had drifted to different sides of the constitutional divide.[11]

During the six months prior to the dinner at Jefferson's quarters, Madison went through a conversion process, or perhaps a reconversion, from the religion of nationalism to the old revolutionary faith of Virginia. It is tempting to explain the switch in exclusively personal terms: Jefferson returned from France, recalled his old colleague to the colors of the true cause, and together they marched forward into history. Except that it was not that simple. Madison possessed the subtlest and most intellectually sophisticated understanding of the choices facing the new American republic of any member of the revolutionary generation. No crude explanation of the decisions he made can do justice to the multiple loyalties he felt, or the almost Jamesian way he thought about and ultimately resolved them.[12]

If we give chronology the decent respect it is due, it is clear that Madison's thinking began to change before Jefferson returned to the scene. The precipitant was Hamilton's *Report on the Public Credit,* forwarded to Congress in January of 1790. (Jefferson did not arrive in New York until March.) The fiscal goals Hamilton proposed were synonymous with the national vision Madison had advocated at the Constitutional Convention and in *The Federalist Papers.* The total debt of the United States, according to Hamilton's calculations, had reached the daunting (at least then) size of $77.1 million. Of this total, $11.7 million was owed to foreign governments; $40.4 million was domestic debt, most of which dated from the American Revolution; and $25 million was state debt, also largely a legacy of the war. What began to trouble Madison, then terrify him, was not Hamilton's goal—the recovery of public credit—but the way he proposed to reach it.[13]

The first symptom of the trouble appeared when Madison studied Hamilton's proposal for the funding of the domestic debt. On the one hand, Hamilton's recommendation looked straightforward: All citizens who owned government securities should be reimbursed at par—that is, the full value of the government's original promise. But many original holders of the securities, mainly veterans of the American Revolution who had received them as pay for their service in the war, had then sold them at a fraction of their original value to speculators. What's more, the release of Hamilton's plan produced a purchasing frenzy, as bankers and investors aware of the funding proposal bought up the securities in expectation of a tidy profit. Madison observed the buying frenzy and complained that unscrupulous speculators "are still exploring the interior & distant parts of the Union in order to take advantage of the holders." The picture that began to congeal in his mind was the essence of injustice: battle-worn veterans of the war for independence being cheated out of their just rewards by mere moneymen. Benjamin Rush, the prominent Philadelphia physician and permanently incandescent revolutionary, urged Madison to stop this betrayal of the spirit of '76: "Never have I heard more rage expressed against the Oppressors of our Country during the late War," Rush fumed, "than I daily hear against the men who . . . are to reap all the benefits of the revolution, at the expense of the greatest part of the Virtue & property that purchased it."[14]

Hamilton was both surprised and mystified when Madison came out against his funding scheme. On February 11, Madison delivered a long speech in the House, denouncing the Hamilton proposal as a repudiation of the American Revolution and recommending his own plan for payment, which he called "discrimination." It was a vintage Madisonian performance: utterly reasonable, flawlessly logical, disarmingly temperate. The original holders of the securities had justice on their side, he noted, and justice must be honored. The current holders had the obligations of contracts on their side, and such obligations must be observed. The options then revealed themselves with lawyerlike precision: "one of three things must be done; either pay both, reject wholly one or the other, or make a composition between them on some principle of equity." (In the twentieth century students of this mode of reasoning within policy-making circles called it "the Goldilocks principle" and later "triangulation.") Madison, of course, favored the third option. But the House voted 36 to 13 against his motion. It was his first major legislative defeat after a long string of triumphs.[15]

It was not just that Madison hated to lose. (Unlike Jefferson, he could be genuinely gracious in defeat.) It was instead that an ominous picture was congealing in his mind of patriot soldiers being fleeced by an army of speculators whose only loyalty was to their own profit margins. Or perhaps it was a slightly different picture, this one of the nascent national government, which he had visualized as an exalted arena where only the ablest and most intellectually talented officials would congregate, the finest fruits plucked from the more motley state governments, now replaced by an obnoxious collection of financiers and money changers, the kind of social parasites whom Jesus had symbolically driven from the temple. The promise of the American Revolution, at least as Madison understood it, was falling into enemy hands.

The debate over assumption, which followed on the heels of the vote on funding, only intensified the sense of betrayal and made matters worse. Again, on the face of it, Hamilton's proposal looked seductively simple. The federal government would take on—which is to say, assume—all the accumulated debts of the states, most of which had their origins during the war. Instead of thirteen separate ledgers, there would be but one, thereby permitting the fiscal policy of the new nation to proceed with a coherent sense of its financial obligations and the revenues required to discharge them. On February 24 Madison rose from his seat in the House to suggest that the matter was a good deal more complicated than it might appear at first glance, and that this apparently sensible proposal called "assumption" struck him as an alarmingly sinister idea.

If you read Madison's speeches against assumption in the House during the spring of 1790, you get the impression that his core objections were economic. Most of the southern states, Virginia among them, had paid off the bulk of their wartime debts. The assumption proposal therefore did them an injustice, by "compelling them, after having done their duty, to contribute to those states who have not equally done their duty." A subsidiary theme, also economic in character but implying grander suspicions, called for what he termed "settlement" to precede assumption. As Madison expressed it, "I really think it right and proper that we should be possessed of the ways and means by which we should be most likely to encounter the debt before we undertake to assume it." In other words, there needed to be an official estimate of the specific amount each state would have "assumed" and then be obliged to pay in federal taxes *before* the vote on assumption occurred. According to his own rough calculations, Virginia would transfer about $3 million of debt to the federal government, then be charged about $5 million in new taxes. Like the failure to compensate the original holders of government securities, this was unfair.[16]

If you read Madison's correspondence during this same time, you get the strong impression that the problem went much deeper than any shuffling of account books could ever satisfy. The economic injustice toward Virginia and most of the southern states—South Carolina was the exception, since it had not retired much of its debt—was bad enough. But assumption was symptomatic of malevolent tendencies that transcended mere dollars and cents. It was about power. Under the guise of doing the states a favor by assuming their debts, the federal government was implicitly, even covertly, assuming sovereign authority over the economies of all the states. As Madison put it to Jefferson in his most typically elliptical style, assumption "would be peculiarly hard on Virginia," but was "further objectionable as augmenting a trust already sufficiently great for the virtue and number of the federal Legislature." Virginia, in short, was being asked to trust its fate to the collective wisdom and virtue of the central government. Assumption, as Madison came to regard it, was not primarily about money. It was about control, about trust, about independence.[17]

These were all major chords in a revolutionary melody that most Virginians knew by heart. Henry Lee, for example, apprised Madison that the assumption debate reminded him of those glorious days of yesteryear, when the Virginia Assembly refused to recognize Parliament's right to tax colonies. "It seems to me," Lee wrote, "that we southern people must be slaves in effect, or cut the Gordion knot at once." The radical rhetoric of the 1760s and 1770s, now hallowed by its association with the successful war for independence, came pouring out of Madison's correspondents in Virginia, equating assumption with the Stamp Act, the federal Congress with Parliament, the so-called "fixed insolent northern majority" with Great Britain. "How do you feel?" Lee asked Madison rhetorically: "Is your love for the constitution so ardent . . . that it should produce ruin to your native country?" By "native country," Lee meant Virginia.[18]

The entire atmosphere surrounding the assumption debate had become electromagnetic. And Madison, who had a justifiable reputation for making himself the calm center in the midst of all political storms, was being buffeted by shrill accusations from both sides. Northern congressmen, led by Fisher Ames of Massachusetts, accused him of threatening the survival of the republic by blocking the centerpiece of Hamilton's fiscal program, without which, they believed, the union would dissolve. Southerners, chiefly Virginians, were telling him that assumption demonstrated how prophetic the Antifederalist enemies to the Constitution now looked, and how his previous assurances in the Virginia ratifying convention and *The Federalist Papers,* assurances that the Constitution would prove a culmination rather than a betrayal of the American Revolution, now seemed like false promises.

The word that captured the essence of the Virginians' political mentality was *consolidation,* as in "the dreaded consolidation that was denied by the friends of the new government, when it was under consideration." The term conveyed the political fear, so potent among the Antifederalist critics of the constitutional settlement of 1788, that the states would be absorbed by the new federal government. It echoed the ideological fear, so effective as a weapon against the taxes imposed by Parliament and decrees of George III, that once arbitrary power was acknowledged to reside elsewhere, all liberty was lost. And at a primal level it suggested the unconscious fear of being swallowed up by a larger creature, the terror of being completely consumed, eaten alive. If Madison had ever managed to convince himself that these historically sanctioned fears had been banished with the creation of the new national government, the debate over assumption demonstrated that they were still very much alive. Indeed, because of their historical and rhetorical association with the successful war against British imperialism, they were the most potent forces in the entire political culture.[19]

What Madison actually thought about the most frantic expressions of Virginian mistrust is difficult to know. Along with John Adams, Madison was America's most astute student of the role of the passions as a political force. But, unlike Adams, Madison's mastery of his own passions took the form of total suppression. His letters back home to Virginia tended to endorse the legitimacy of the threat posed by assumption, but also to counsel patience, to urge, as much by their tone as the content, a less apocalyptic attitude. Hamilton's fiscal program was certainly a menacing shadow over the new federal edifice. But talk of secession was premature and counterproductive. After all, with Washington as president, Jefferson as secretary of state, Edmund Randolph as attorney general—he might have added Madison as dominant presence in the Congress—Virginia's interests were hardly unrepresented in the capital. As for the threatening insults from their northern brethren in the government, pay them little attention. "We shall risk their prophetic menaces," he noted confidently, "if we should continue to have a majority." For on assumption, unlike the earlier debate over funding, Madison had the votes. Assumption would never pass.[20]

IT GOES WITHOUT saying that Alexander Hamilton's understanding of the issues raised by his fiscal program, and the Virginia-writ-large squadrons that were mobilizing south of the Potomac to oppose it, was blissfully free of all the Madisonian ambiguities. Once Hamilton encountered a major obstacle to the advancement of any cause in which he believed, he instinctively hurled himself onto the offensive, never looked back, and waited for no stragglers. Whether the objective was a British parapet at Yorktown, the admiration of the legal and merchant elite in New York, or the ratification of the Constitution, Hamilton's pattern was the same: to unleash his formidable energies in great bursts of conspicuous productivity; imposing his own personality on events in an ostentatious, out-of-my-way style that was precisely the opposite of Madison's preference for stealth; irritating more modest and cautious colleagues with his casual presumption that both his overall vision and his mastery of the details were self-evidently superior; irritating them even more when events generally proved him right.

Critics of his take-charge temperament and his dashing Hamilton-to-the-rescue demeanor would make a plausible case that they were excessive compensations for his lowly (indeed bastardly) origins. Some biographers, pursuing the same interpretive line, have suggested that his deep-rooted insecurities drove him onto the plains of Weehawken and then into the fatal gaze of Aaron Burr. But if insecurity was the primal source of Hamilton's incredible energy, one would have to conclude that providence had conspired to produce at the most opportune moment perhaps the most creative liability in American history.[21]

Like Madison in 1790, Hamilton was at the peak of his powers. He wrote the forty thousand words of his *Report on the Public Credit* in a three-month surge and with the same kind of desperate speed he had turned out his fifty-one contributions to *The Federalist Papers*. Scholars on the lookout for the theoretical sources that may have shaped his thinking have invariably discovered multiple influences: Adam Smith, Jacques Necker, Malachai Postlethwayt, and David Hume top the list, with Hume a particularly forceful influence on the contours of his thinking about the dynamics of economic growth (much as Hume influenced Madison's thinking about the dynamics of political stability). It is also well established that Hamilton's intense dedication to a centralized solution to the fiscal problems facing the new government emerged, again like Madison's, out of his frustrating experience with the inadequate and hopelessly divided authority of the Confederation government in the 1780s. Finally, the historic significance of Hamilton's *Report* has attracted the attention of specialists in sufficient number to inject a technical dimension into the appraisal—familiarity with sinking funds, tontines, floating rates of interest, and liquidity has become essential for a full appreciation of his economic proficiency.[22]

All well and good, but for our purposes these otherwise-valuable insights are mere subplots almost designed to carry us down side trails while blithely humming a tune about the rough equivalence of forests and trees. What Hamilton thought he was doing was essentially simple: The economy of the United States was a tangled mess of foreign and domestic debt that he was determined to unravel, then place on firm fiscal footing by restoring public credit. All this was to be achieved with a keen and shrewd appreciation for the dynamic potential of America's latent commercial energies, but unencumbered by even the slightest concern with how the resultant system might appear to those not sharing his nationalist vision.

On the question of funding the domestic debt, for example, Hamilton regarded Madison's proposal to distinguish between original and present holders of government securities as naïve and mischievous. To be sure, some injustice might be done the wartime veterans. But who was Madison to lecture him about the venerable sacrifice made by American soldiers, Madison having never fired a shot in anger, now wrapping himself in some rhetorical rendition of the bloodstained uniform he had never worn? More to the point, the original holders had not been coerced to sell. They had done so freely and for an infinite variety of reasons. Sorting out the multiple transactions, prices, and motives would be an administrative nightmare. Indeed, anyone proposing such a course must come under suspicion as a devotee of paralysis. The whole point of the funding scheme was to move past such ambiguous entanglements, to establish the kind of clear and discernible reimbursement policy that inspired trust, and to concentrate the debt in those hands most likely to use it in the interests of the community's productivity and growth.[23]

On the question of assuming the state debts, Madison's opposition struck Hamilton as even more illogical and blatantly sinister. Had not Madison himself advocated the assumption of state debts on several occasions in the 1780s? Had not they locked arms together as "Publius" to justify the need for a national government with sovereign power over the states? Indeed, had not Madison been the most ardent advocate at the Constitutional Convention for a clear assertion of federal sovereignty? Of course there were massive accounting problems in calculating the different state debts, not the least of the difficulties being sloppy records kept by several southern states, with Virginia topping the list for administrative disarray. But the final numbers were hardly set in stone. If Virginia wanted to negotiate these calculations, well, it was the kind of thing that could always be worked out among friends.

But friends did not make ominous charges that the whole assumption proposal was a plot to lure the states into some Faustian bargain in which they lost the political semblance of childlike innocence, an innocence in fact already abandoned, wisely so, when the Constitution was ratified. Assumption was not a plot to destroy the political integrity of the states; it was a plan to consolidate their debts and nationalize the economy for the benefit of all. Hamilton simply took it for granted that the new government created by the Constitution was, as he phrased it in his *Report,* "cloathed with powers competent to calling for the resources of the community"; and he, as the officer responsible for fiscal policy, was simply the chosen instrument to implement this collective effort.[24]

Therein lay the problem, and not just because Madison and his Virginia constituents heard such words as *consolidate* and *nationalize* like alarm bells in the night; or, as one of Hamilton's fondest biographers put it, because the secretary of the treasury was "more adept at meeting financial crises than mending political fences." The real difficulty was that Hamilton's plan was very much a projection of his own audacious personality. In fact, once one steps back from the specific provisions for calculating and funding the various state and federal debts, perhaps the best way to understand the grand design of Hamilton's *Report*, and the implicit presumptions that animated its visionary sense of where the new American republic was heading, is to see it as Hamilton's distinctive temperament and cast of mind superimposed on the fluid conditions of an emergent nation.[25]

First, there is the implication, floating between the lines of the entire *Report*, that an authoritative new presence has appeared on the scene and taken charge. The command ethos went beyond matters of personality (though Hamilton was certainly auditioning for the part), and it even went beyond questions of constitutionality (though the *Report* certainly announced the unequivocal sovereignty of the federal government). More sweepingly, it suggested that the enormous but latent potential of the American economy required more than mere release to achieve its full potential. Hamilton was hardly unique in his recognition that the vast resources of the North American continent constituted a repository of riches that, once unlocked, offered prospects of unparalleled prosperity and national destiny. He was, however, distinctive for his sense that the mobilization of these resources required abiding management and strategic orchestration at the national level. Madison, and to an even greater extent Jefferson, seemed to think that economic policy consisted of getting out of the way to allow the natural laws of economic recovery and growth to proceed. But Hamilton thought the conditions for economic development needed to be created, then enduringly overseen. His model was England, with its national bank, regulated commerce, and powerful finance ministers. From the perspective south of the Potomac, of course, these were the institutions and symbols the American Revolution had supposedly repudiated forever.

Second, there is the Hamiltonian confidence that the concentration of political and economic power was a dynamic force; it was not a threatening cluster of invasive corruption, but a synergistic fusion of developmental energies. Hamilton was tone-deaf to the familiar refrains in the republican song about the inherent evil of aggregated power, a tune that the emerging chorus of dissenters in Virginia was replaying under the new label of "consolidation." For Hamilton, consolidation was a wonderful idea. While Madison's frame of reference was instinctively political, and idealized the dispersal of power naturally checked by the inherent diversity of diffused interest groups, Hamilton's cast of mind was instinctively economic. He visualized the concentration of capital in the hands of a select few as the essential precondition for commercial investment and economic growth. One of the reasons he did not mind if original holders of government securities sold out to speculators was that he preferred to see the money in fewer hands. When money was spread out, it was only money. When concentrated, it was capital. And the main reason he welcomed the enlargement of the federal debt produced by assuming the state debts was that, once properly funded, it enlarged the pool of government credit for investment purposes by the wealthy few who held the notes. In this limited sense at least, Hamilton regarded the national debt as "a national blessing," for it permitted the clustering of resources in the hands of a small group of enterprising men who would invest and not just spend it. For Madison, on the other hand, "a Public Debt is a Public curse," and "in a Representative Government greater than in any other."[26]

Finally, there is Hamilton's enshrinement of the urban elite—the merchants, bankers, and business leaders—as the central figures in the emergent American society. These were the kind of men who had rescued him from obscurity in the tropics as a youth and then, once he had displayed his brilliance, welcomed him into the inner circles of New York society. Hamilton himself was a kind of Horatio Alger hero who aspired to fame more than fortune, but he understood the world of banking, investing, and speculating from within. He wrote no idyllic testimonials to merchants and moneymen comparable to Jefferson's hymns to the bucolic splendor of America's yeomen farmers, but his entire financial plan was an implicit endorsement of commerce as America's economic lifeblood and of men of trade and commerce as its chief beneficiaries and silent heroes. Hamilton did not design his system, as his critics frequently claimed, primarily to enrich the commercial elite. He designed it to channel their talent and resources into productive activities that served the public interest. Nor did his insider knowledge of interest rates ever tempt him to take personal advantage: "But you remember the saying with regard to Caesar's Wife," he wrote to Henry Lee. "I think the spirit of it applicable to every man concerned in the administration of the finances of a Country." Nevertheless, he was excessively trusting of some of his speculator friends; and he only fired his assistant in the Treasury Department, William Duer, after Duer's mixing of personal and public funds reached criminal proportions. Duer was the epitome of the enterprising speculator whom he trusted and who ultimately proved untrustworthy.[27]

To Virginians like Madison and Jefferson, on the other hand, Duer was not the exception, but the rule. The Virginia gentry were psychologically incapable of sharing Hamilton's affinity with men who made their living manipulating interest rates. Land, not fluid forms of capital, was their ultimate measure of wealth. Investment bankers and speculators, as they saw it, made no productive contribution to society. All they did was move paper around and adjust numbers. At the nub, the issue was not rich versus poor or the few versus the many, since the planter class of Virginia was just as much an elite minority as the wealthy merchants of New York or Boston. The issue was agrarian versus commercial sources of wealth.

Nor did it help that a significant percentage of Virginia's landed class, Jefferson among them, were heavily in debt to British and Scottish creditors, who were compounding their interest rates faster than the profit margins in tobacco and wheat could match. One cannot help but suspect that the beleaguered aristocracy of Virginia saw in Hamilton and his beloved commercial elite of the northern cities the American replicas of British bankers who were bleeding them to death. The more one contemplates the mentality of the Virginia planters—the refusal to bring their habits of consumption and expenditure into line with the realities of their economic predicament, the widespread pattern of denial right up to the declaration of bankruptcy—the more likely it seems that an entrenched and even willful ignorance of the economic principles governing the relationship between credit and debt had become a badge of honor in their world. These were simply not the kind of concerns that a gentleman of property should take seriously. In a sense, they took considerable pride in not having the dimmest understanding of what Hamilton was talking about.[28]

THE THIRD participant in the dinner-table bargain, and the host for the occasion, was Thomas Jefferson. He was not being characteristically diplomatic when he claimed that Madison and Hamilton both understood the issues at stake more fully than he did. After all, he had only returned from his five-year tour of duty in France six months earlier and had just taken up his post as secretary of state in March. His mind was also on other things: the recent marriage of his eldest daughter, Martha; finding suitable quarters in New York; drafting a lengthy report on weights and measures; reading dispatches from Paris on the ongoing French Revolution. The onset of his chronic migraine headache had also incapacitated him for much of May. In fact, Jefferson's headache coincided with a veritable plague that seemed to descend on the leadership of the Virginia dynasty. Madison was laid up with dysentery, Edmund Randolph remained in Virginia to care for his wife, who had nearly died delivering a stillborn baby, and, most ominously of all, George Washington came down with the flu and developed pulmonary complications that the physicians considered life-threatening. "You cannot conceive the public alarm on this occasion," Jefferson reported to William Short, his former secretary in Paris, adding that Washington's demise would in all probability have meant the abrupt end of the whole national experiment.[29]

Slightly above six feet two, Jefferson towered over both Madison and Hamilton, and at forty-seven he was sufficiently their senior to enjoy the kind of respect accorded an older brother. Neither his physical stature nor his age, however, could compensate for his lengthy absence abroad throughout the great constitutional reforms of the late 1780s. Madison had kept him apprised of the debates at the Constitutional Convention (no better source existed on the planet), and Madison had also beaten down the rumors circulating in the Virginia ratifying convention that Jefferson was at best lukewarm on the constitutional settlement itself. The rumors were in fact true, though on all constitutional questions Jefferson deferred to Madison's superior judgment, so he could accept the offer to become America's first secretary of state without political reservations. It also helped that foreign policy was the one area where he believed the nation should speak with one voice. Beyond that elemental level, his views on federal power were unknown, in part because he had not been involved in the great debates of 1787–1788, and in part because his own mind did not operate at Madisonian levels of specificity and legalistic clarity. "I am not a Federalist," he declared in 1789, "because I never submitted the whole system of my opinions to the creed of any party of men whatever. . . . If

I could not go to heaven but with a party, I would not go there at all."
The temporary capital in New York was hardly heaven, but he had
agreed to go there in the spring of 1790 with his allegiances undeclared
and his own lofty political principles uncontaminated by the kind of
infighting that Madison and Hamilton had perfected to an art.[30]

He had come reluctantly. This was part of a lifelong pattern of reti-
cence, dating back to the prerevolutionary years in Virginia, when he
had first emerged from the mists of the Blue Ridge Mountains to
attend William and Mary, study law with George Wythe, and win marginal acceptance by the Tidewater elite. He gained his reputation as an
effective writer against British encroachments but was a reclusive non-
presence in debates. In the Continental Congress, John Adams had
described him as a staunch advocate of independence who never
uttered more than two or three sentences, even in committees. His lasting fame, indeed immortality, derived from his authorship of the Declaration of Independence in June of 1776, but few Americans knew
about that role in 1790. The Declaration was still regarded as a product
of the whole Continental Congress, not the work of one man, and
had yet to achieve the symbolic significance it would in the nineteenth
century.[31]

His service as wartime governor of Virginia had ended disastrously
when British troops burned the capital as Jefferson galloped off and
into official disgrace. Though later cleared of any wrongdoing, he
vowed never to accept public office again. The hurly-burly of politics
did not suit his temperament, which was only comfortable when
ensconced on his mountaintop and redesigning his mansion at Monticello. Always poised for retirement, he had accepted the diplomatic
post in Paris to escape the painful memories of his wife's premature
death in childbirth, had performed his duties ably, and had even gained
a semblance of fame in France as Franklin's successor as the Gallic
embodiment of the archetypal American in Paris. His protestations
when offered a position in the new government in 1789 were utterly
sincere, but Madison had been his usually persuasive self and, more
to the point, America's only indispensable figure had suggested that
Jefferson was also indispensable. One did not turn down George
Washington.

The dinner invitation he had extended to the embattled Madison
and Hamilton was perfectly in keeping with his character. Put simply,

Jefferson could not abide personal conflict. One of the reasons he was so notoriously ineffective in debate was that argument itself offended him. The voices he heard inside himself were all harmonious and agreeable, reliable expressions of the providentially aligned universal laws that governed the world as he knew it, so that argument struck him as dissonant noise that defied the natural order of things. Madison, who knew him better than any man alive, fully realized that there was an invisible line somewhere in Jefferson's mind above which lay his most cherished personal and political ideals. Cross that line and you set off explosions and torrents of unbridled anger of the sort that got spewed at George III in the Declaration of Independence. (Jefferson did not regard such occasions as arguments, but rather as holy wars to the death.) But short of that line, he was endlessly polite and accommodating, genuinely pained at the presence of partisan politics. This was clearly his posture in June of 1790.

There were also practical reasons why he wanted to broker a compromise. As a former foreign minister now serving as secretary of state, Jefferson required no instruction on the international implications of America's debtor status. Until her foreign debts were paid and her credit with the Dutch bankers in Amsterdam restored, the United States would simply not be taken seriously in Europe's capitals. Jefferson had learned this the hard way during his Paris phase. He therefore felt even more sharply than Madison that the fiscal goals of Hamilton's plan were absolutely essential. Without credit, the new nation would remain a laughingstock in foreign eyes. And therefore when those same frenzied Virginians who were writing Madison about the fatal curse of assumption also wrote him, he was even less supportive, though characteristically elusive. "It appears to me one of those questions which present great inconveniences whichever way it is decided," he wrote his new son-in-law. Or when Henry Lee flooded him with apocalyptic premonitions if assumption somehow were to pass, he counseled patience and greater trust in the wisdom of Congress. "In the meanwhile," he observed rather elliptically, "the voice of the nation will perhaps be heard." While vague, the intended effect of the Jeffersonian message was to calm his fellow Virginians. "My duties prevent me from mingling in these questions," he explained to George Mason just a week before the dinner: "I do not pretend to be very competent to their decision. In general I think it necessary to give as well as take in a government like ours."[32]

THE GIVING and the taking on the location of the permanent national capital had been positively fierce ever since the question had come before Congress in September of 1789. The Constitution had provided for Congress to identify a "seat of government" not to exceed one hundred square miles in size to be purchased from the proximate states. The question was where. From the start, the prospect of congressional representatives reaching an easy consensus on the location was problematic at best. One newspaper editor had sagely, if cynically, observed that "the usual custom is for the capital of new empires to be selected by the whim or caprice of a despot." While this was obviously not the republican way, perhaps an exception was justified. Since George Washington, as the editor observed, "has never given bad advice to his country," did it not make practical sense to "let him point to a map and say 'here'?"[33]

What became known as the "residency question" was a logistic nightmare. All the regional voting blocs—New England, the Middle Atlantic, and the South—could cite plausible reasons for claiming primacy. And each of the twelve states—Rhode Island did not show up in the Congress until June of 1790—could imagine schemes whereby the capital fell within its borders or the support for another location promised collateral benefits to be negotiated at a price. The crisscrossing patterns of regional and state bargaining were further complicated by two political considerations almost guaranteed to preclude consensus: First, legislation had to pass both the Senate and the House, so as soon as an apparently victorious option made its way through one branch of the Congress, the opposition mobilized against it in the other; second, early on a decision was made to choose a temporary location, which would serve as the capital for ten to twenty years, then a permanent location, which would presumably require the extra time to ready itself for the federal occupation. This distinction played havoc with congressional debate by creating doubt that the temporary location, once chosen, would ever be abandoned. As a result, by the time Jefferson had arrived in New York in March, sixteen possible sites had been proposed but had failed to muster a majority. The leading candidates (in alphabetical order) were: Annapolis, Baltimore, Carlisle, Frederick, Germantown, New York, Philadelphia, the Potomac, the Susquehanna, and Trenton. Given its geographic centrality, some location in Pennsylvania appeared to have the edge.[34]

"The business of the seat of Government is become a labyrinth," Madison reported back to a fellow Virginian, "for which the votes printed furnish no clue, and which it is impossible in a letter to explain to you." The political wheeling and dealing inside the Congress and out had reached such epidemic proportions that Madison was given the unofficial title "Big Knife" for cutting deals: "If the Big Knife would give up Potowmack the Matter would be easily settled," one Pennsylvania man reported to Jefferson. "But that you will say is as unreasonable as it would be to expect a Pennsilvanian to surrender at Discretion to New York. It therefore amuses me to see the Arguments our grave politicians bring forward when I know it will be determined by local Interests." While the Virginians were not accustomed to thinking of their interests as merely local, by the eve of the dinner at Jefferson's the prospects for a Potomac site had faded and Madison's formidable skills as a political negotiator had assumed a wholly defensive posture—coordinating opposition to a Pennsylvania victory.[35]

The case Madison had tried to make for the Potomac was simultaneously crafty and driven by romantic illusions about its prowess that were shared by Jefferson, Washington, and most members of the Virginia dynasty. In the crafty vein, Madison was ingenious at contesting the strongest argument for a Pennsylvania location, which was its geographic centrality. (The Pennsylvanians were not devoid of craft either, arguing that the Susquehanna River was destined to become the center of the United States because the trans-Mississippi West would never enter the union and eastern Canada almost surely would.) Madison countered that centrality could be measured demographically as well as geographically, so they should await the results of the census of 1790 before deciding. Then he argued that a purely geographic measure on a north-south axis revealed that the exact midpoint between northern Maine and southern Georgia was not just the Potomac; it was Washington's estate at Mount Vernon, a revelation calculated to carry providential overtones.[36]

The more romantic case for the Potomac entered the debate during

Madison's initial speech against the Susquehanna site. He seemed to argue, contrary to common sense and the visual evidence provided by all maps, that the Potomac was actually farther west than the Susquehanna. What he seemed to mean was that the upper reaches of the Potomac near the Maryland-Pennsylvania border, where the Conococheague Creek emptied into the Potomac, was nearly as far west as the Susquehanna and—here was the grand Virginian illusion—afforded the only direct water route to the Ohio Valley and through its river system to the Mississippi itself. The mention of Conococheague Creek provoked waves of sarcasm from incredulous congressmen: "Enquiries will be made," observed one Massachusetts member, "where in the name of common sense is Connogochque?" (And, he might have added, how does one spell it?) The consensus outside Virginia seemed to be that "not one person in a thousand in the United States knows that there is such a place on earth," and those few who did were all Indians. Madison's preferred location for the national capital was a "wigwam place" suitable for hunting parties and hermits.[37]

While Madison was probably stretching the truth for his Potomac-driven political purposes, it was nevertheless a truth that he and many Virginians sincerely believed. For nearly a decade, Jefferson and Washington had corresponded about making navigation improvements in the Potomac on the presumption that it afforded a direct link between the vast American interior and the Chesapeake Bay. The misconception drew its inspiration from the same combination of soaring hope and geographic ignorance that subsequently led Jefferson to believe that the Lewis and Clark expedition would discover a water route across the North American continent where none existed. One could trace the illusory properties of the Potomac's waters all the way back to John Smith, who first explored the mouth of what the Algonquin Indians had named "Petomek," meaning "trading place," in 1608. For Virginians of the revolutionary generation, the myth of the Potomac probably derived its credibility from the colonial era, when the lack of any border to Virginia's western provinces—theoretically and legally, Virginia extended to either the Mississippi or the Pacific Ocean—caused a habit of mind to develop within the Old Dominion that it was America's gateway to the West. Once established, the myth developed a rather hilarious life of its own, to include publications like *Potomac Magazine,* in which the Potomac was described as the Thames, the

Seine, and the Rhine rolled into one and the confluence of the Potomac and the Anacostia was thought the world's most perfect harbor, where "10,000 ships the size of Noah's ark" could comfortably dock.[38]

Unfortunately for Madison, the Potomac mythology was largely confined to Virginians. Fisher Ames of Massachusetts spoke for those congressmen denied the vision when he said that the customarily sensible Madison had obviously come under some biblical spell and had confused the Potomac with "a Euphrates flowing through paradise." The Virginians were certainly free to dream their provincial Potomac dreams, but meanwhile the Congress should proceed to the serious business of selecting a national capital located in this world rather than in Madison's imagination. By June of 1790, Madison himself had just about given up hope. "If any arrangement should be made that will answer our wishes," he confessed, "it will be the effect of a coincidence of causes as fortuitous as it will be propitious." And this, of course, is where the fortuitous prospect of a bargain entered the picture.[39]

WE CANNOT know how many secret meetings and political dinners occurred in New York during the late spring and early summer of 1790. We do know that Jefferson's famous dinner was not, as he implied, the only such occasion. First, Hamilton's chief assistant in the Treasury Department, Tench Coxe, met with Jefferson and Madison on June 6, presumably to discuss Virginia's debt and the impact of assumption on the state's balance of payments to the federal government; second, around the same time Hamilton met with members of the Pennsylvania delegation to negotiate a trade of their support for assumption—Hamilton's overwhelming priority—in return for the location of both the temporary and permanent capital in their state, a trade that never materialized because Hamilton could not deliver the votes to assure Pennsylvania's victory in the residency sweepstakes; third, and most significantly, delegates from Virginia and Pennsylvania met on June 15 and agreed on a political alliance whereby Philadelphia would become the temporary capital and—a major triumph for the Virginians—the Potomac site was resurrected as the permanent residence, a compromise the Pennsylvania delegates probably accepted out of the conviction that, once the capital moved from New York to Philadelphia, it would never move again. Doubtless there were several additional dinners, clandestine meetings, and secret sessions that have escaped the historical record. But the ones we do know about demonstrate conclusively that the compromise reached over Jefferson's dinner table was really the final chapter in an ongoing negotiation that came together because the ground had already been prepared.[40]

More specifically, Jefferson's account of the dinner-table conversation distorts the truth by conveniently eliminating the preliminary negotiations, thereby giving the story a more romantic gloss by implying that three prominent leaders could solve an apparently intractable national problem by establishing the proper atmospherics. The Potomac location for the permanent capital had, in fact, already been secured. Hamilton did not need to deliver any votes on that score, though there is some evidence he agreed to help seal the Potomac deal by urging his friends in New York and Massachusetts not to spoil it. Madison did need to come up with at least three votes on assumption—here Jefferson's account is accurate—and eventually four members switched their votes, all of them congressmen from districts bordering on the Potomac. The major business of the evening, in all likelihood, was an agreement to recalculate Virginia's debt and corresponding share of the enlarged federal debt. In effect, Madison got what he had always demanded: settlement before assumption. And Hamilton did what he had unofficially implied he would do all along: manipulate the numbers to make the Virginians more comfortable with assumption.[41]

This last dimension of the deal was not terribly attractive, so Jefferson left it out of his account altogether. But he immediately sent out letters to his Virginia friends, confiding that the new version of the Assumption Bill would reduce the state's total obligation so that the debt assumed and the federal taxes owed would turn out, rather miraculously, exactly equal ($3.5 million). "Being therefore to receive exactly what she is to pay," he observed triumphantly, "she will neither win nor lose by the measure." Assumption, in effect, would be a wash. The total financial package, moreover, once the Potomac location was factored into the equations, should make most Virginians smile. For the proximity of the new capital, Jefferson predicted, "will vivify our agriculture and commerce by circulating thro' our state an additional sum every year of half a million dollars." Jefferson was only guessing, of course, and the larger significance of the Potomac site transcended any merely economic forecast, but his initial gloss on the bargain had substantive merit: It was a three-sided deal—residence, revised assumption, and settlement—and Virginia won on each score.[42]

But would the bargain actually hold? Jefferson and Madison made their greatest contribution, not during the dinner itself, but in the months afterward, when they assured that the answer to that question remained resolutely positive. The sudden victory of the Potomac location had surprised almost everybody, since it had fallen to the bottom of the list in the spring of 1790, then somehow bobbed to the top again without any congressional debate. As a result, despite the passage of the Residency Bill in July, there was a widespread skepticism about a capital, as one New York wag put it, "Where the houses and kitchens are yet to be framed / The trees to be felled, and the streets to be named." The Philadelphia press was particularly incredulous, declaring that it was "abhorrent to common sense to suppose they are to have a place dug out of the rocky wilderness, for the use of Congress only four months in the year and all the rest of the time to be inhabited by wild beasts." The consensus in Congress was clear that, once ensconced in Philadelphia, the capital would never move to some deserted and wholly hypothetical place: "It will be generally viewed . . . as a mere political maneuver," observed one congressman. "You might as well induce a belief that you are in earnest by inserting Mississippi, Detroit, or Winnipiprocket Pond as Connogocheque."[43]

The strategy that Jefferson and Madison adopted was elegantly effective and thoroughly imperialistic. One senses Madison's matchless political savvy at work throughout the process, but also a preview of Jefferson's defiantly bold behavior thirteen years later in pushing through the Louisiana Purchase. The key strategic insight was that the residency question must never again be allowed to come before Congress, where it was certain to fall victim to the political version of death by a thousand cuts. Jefferson was particularly clear on this point: "if the present occasion of securing the Federal seat on the Patowmack should be lost, it could never more be regained [and therefore] it would be dangerous to rely on any aids from Congress or the assemblies of Virginia or Maryland, and that therefore measures should be adopted to carry the residence bill into execution without recourse to those bodies." But how could one do that, since the funds to purchase the land, the selection of the specific site, the appointment of an architect, and a host of unforeseeable but inevitable practicalities would seem to require legislative approval? The answer recalled the earliest advice half-jokingly offered by a newspaper editor when the residency question had first appeared on the national agenda: Give the decision to George Washington. Jefferson proposed in August of 1790 that the entire series of subsequent decisions about the location, size, and shape of the capital be made a matter of executive discretion, that is "subject to the President's direction in every point."[44]

While congressmen continued to make sarcastic jokes about the uncertain location of the theoretical Potomac site—why not put the new capital on wheels and roll it from place to place?—Jefferson and Madison were tramping up and down the Maryland and Virginia countryside assessing the terrain. Washington listened to their report, then made the decision in January of 1791—the hundred-square-mile area stretching east from Georgetown to the mouth of the Potomac. Jefferson noticed that Washington seemed "unusually reticent" about his choice, probably because Mount Vernon adjoined the site and Washington also owned considerable acreage within its borders. He might also have felt somewhat uncomfortable knowing that this easternmost option contradicted the impression that Madison had created in the earlier debates—namely, that a more western location near the Pennsylvania border was preferred. (The Pennsylvanians, who had conceded the Potomac choice on the presumption of its proximity, were surely disappointed. Perhaps naming the central street in the new capital Pennsylvania Avenue was Washington's gesture of accommodation.) At any rate, the decision was made. And it was final. And no one in America was prepared to question a decision made by Washington, at least publicly, when rendered so summarily.[45]

Every step in the decade-long process of designing and building the city predestined to carry his name was supervised by Washington. Like a military operation, it had many troops but only one commander. In late fall of 1790, Jefferson wrote Washington about the political urgency of starting construction as soon as possible: "Mr. Madison and myself have endeavored to press . . . the expediency of their undertaking to build ten good private dwellings a year, for ten years, in the new city. . . . Should they do this . . . it will be one means of ensuring the removal of government thither." Once the buildings were up, in other words, Philadelphia's hopes would collapse. In a speech delivered as the Residency Bill was being passed in the House, Madison had noted that many observers fully expected the Potomac choice to be repealed and the capital to remain at Philadelphia: "But what more can we do than pass a law for this purpose?" he asked rhetorically, since "A repeal is a thing against which no provision can be made." Then he concluded, "But I flatter myself that some respect will be paid to the public interest, and to the plighted faith of the government." By making the implementation an executive action headed by Washington, Jefferson and Madison demonstrated that, "plighted faith" notwithstanding, they were taking no chances.[46]

On the other side of the dinner-table bargain, however, they had already taken a calculated risk by betting that more favorable financial terms, plus the capture of the permanent capital, would undermine Virginia's powerful aversion to assumption. Several friends south of the Potomac had warned them that the widespread hostility toward Hamilton's financial plan defied compromise of any sort. "The Assumption under any Modification will I fear be Considered as a Bitter pill in this State," ran one typical account, and "Arguments of Accommodation will have but little Avail." The old Antifederalist coalition that Madison had opposed so effectively at the Virginia ratifying convention in 1788 believed with some justification that their cause had never really been defeated, merely outmaneuvered. Under the renewed leadership of Patrick Henry, with an able assist from Henry Lee, this powerful group mobilized against assumption in the fall of 1790 and pushed a resolution through both branches of the Virginia legislature in December. It brought together the old revolutionary rhetoric, even deploying some familiar Jeffersonian language, with all the oppositional energy of the Whig tradition, then hurled it at assumption as the new incarnation of foreign domination. Like the previous attempts by Parliament, assumption was described as a threat to Virginia's independence and "a measure which . . . must in the course of human events, produce one or other of two evils, the prostration of agriculture at the feet of commerce, or a change in the present form of federal government, fatal to the existence of American liberty."[47]

As Jefferson and Madison arrived in Philadelphia for the first session of Congress in the new but merely temporary capital, the newspapers were filled with caustic commentary on the defiant tone of the Virginia resolution:

> The resolution of the Virginia Assembly respecting the Assumption of the State Debts . . . exhibits a very curious phenomenon in the history of the United States. The majority who voted in favor of the resolution, it seems, fell asleep in September 1787, (just before the rising of the Federal Convention) and did not awake till a few weeks ago; during which time the Federal Government was adopted and established throughout all the States. Their vote therefore must be ascribed to *ignorance* of what passed during their long sleep. The *Resolution* is calculated only for those years of anarchy, which preceded the general ratification of the present HAPPY NATIONAL GOVERNMENT. It is now nugatory and ridiculous.[48]

Hamilton also took note of the implicit secessionist threat contained in Virginia's statement. It was, he warned, "the first symptom of a spirit which must either be killed or will kill the constitution of the United States." Back in September of 1787, just as the Constitutional Convention was completing its business, Hamilton had made a prediction: The newly created federal government would either "triumph altogether over the state governments and reduce them to an entire subordination," he surmised, or "in the course of a few years . . . the contests about the boundaries of power between the particular governments and the general government . . . will produce a dissolution of the Union." Virginia's posture toward assumption was now making his prophecy look prescient. Hamilton shared his ominous sense of the situation with John Jay, his part-time collaborator as "Publius" in *The Federalist Papers*. But he said nothing to Madison, his full-time collaborator, since it was no longer clear where Madison stood. Was he a Virginian or an American? Did he think the truly founding moment for the new nation was 1776 or 1787? These dramatic questions, as much as the location of the capital on the Potomac, were the residual legacies of the dinner at Jefferson's.[49]

For the next seventy years, until the outbreak of the Civil War in 1861, the essence of political wisdom in the emergent American republic was to insist that such choices did not have to be made. But the recognition that these were the competing options, the contested versions, if you will, of what the core legacy of the American Revolution truly meant, first became visible in the summer of 1790. The Constitution did not resolve these questions; it only provided an orderly framework within which the arguments could continue. Nor would it be historically correct to regard the issues at stake as exclusively or even primarily constitutional. Legalistic debates over federal versus state sovereignty were just the most accessible handles to grab, the safest and most politically suitable ways to talk about alternative national visions.

The Compromise of 1790 is most famous for averting a political crisis that many statesmen of the time considered a threat to the survival of the infant republic. But it also exposed the incompatible expectations concerning America's future that animated these same statesmen. In a sense, it is a very old story, which has been rendered even more familiar by the violent dissolution of revolutionary regimes in modern-day emergent nations: Bound together in solidarity against the imperialistic enemy, the leadership fragments when the common enemy disappears and the different agenda for the new nation must confront its differences. Securing a revolution has proven to be a much more daunting assignment than winning one. The accommodation that culminated in the agreement reached over Jefferson's dinner table provides a momentary exposure of the sharp differences dividing the leadership of the revolutionary generation: sectional versus national allegiance; agrarian versus commercial economic priorities; diffusion versus consolidation as social ideals; an impotent versus a potent federal government. The compromise reached did not resolve these conflicts so much as prevent them from exploding when the newly created government was so vulnerable; it bought time during which the debate could continue.[50]

Thanks to the efforts of Jefferson and Madison, the ongoing debate would have a decidedly southern accent. In some vaguely general fashion, they understood this, regarding the construction of the District of Columbia on the Potomac as a statement of Virginia's enduring influence over the federal government. Although the Virginia-writ-large view of the United States they harbored had an arrogant and provincial odor about it, their presumptions did reflect certain demographic and economic realities: Virginia contained one-fifth of the nation's total population and generated one-third of its commerce. What's more, as John Adams so nicely put it, "in Virginia all Geese are Swans," meaning that Virginia's elite genuinely believed that it had almost single-handedly launched and led the war for independence. The Old Dominion was accustomed to thinking of itself as *primus inter pares* in any confederation of states. The geographic location of the new capital played to these pretensions by making it the physical projection of Virginia. It did not matter so much that the Virginia-writ-large vision was mostly an illusion; it was a deeply felt illusion that the location of the new capital somewhat appeased.[51]

Although it never seemed to be part of the conscious intention of either Jefferson or Madison at the time, the isolated location and *de novo* character of the national capital had even deeper political implications. For at the start and for several decades thereafter, it remained a vast and nearly vacant plot of ground. Visitors in those early years who stopped to ask directions to the American capital were often astonished when told they were standing squarely in its center. Anyone apprehensive about the encroaching powers of the federal government must have felt a palpable sense of reassurance that the seat of power was virtually invisible. Or if, like Jefferson, one believed that cities were sores on the body politic, and agrarian values were the mainstay of American virtue, then Washington, D.C., must have seemed the perfect capital for the new republic, since it was really not a city at all. If the clustering together or consolidation of political power touched some primal nerve, conjuring up horrific scenes of courtiers in London or Paris plotting against the rights of ordinary citizens, again the American capital performed visual therapy by lacking courts, corridors, or many public buildings whatsoever. It symbolized the victory of diffusion over consolidation.[52]

Nor were Hamilton's dreaded moneymen likely to find it a particularly hospitable environment. The pervasive emptiness and stultifying summer heat were only minor deterrents when compared with the more elemental consideration that all the banking and commercial institutions were based elsewhere, chiefly in Philadelphia and New York. By selecting the Potomac location, the Congress had implicitly decided to separate the political and financial capitals of the United States. All the major European capitals—Berlin, London, Paris, Rome, Vienna—were metropolitan centers that gathered together the political, economic, and cultural energies of their respective populations in one place. The United States was almost inadvertently deciding to segregate them. The exciting synergy of institutional life in an all-purpose national metropolis was deemed less important than the dangerous corruptions likely to afflict a nexus of politicians and financiers.[53]

And so while Hamilton and his followers could claim that the compromise permitted the core features of his financial plan to win approval, which in turn meant the institutionalization of fiscal reforms with centralizing implications that would prove very difficult to dislodge, the permanent residence of the capital on the Potomac institutionalized political values designed to carry the nation in a fundamentally different direction. It was also symbolic in a personal sense for Jefferson and Madison. For the Compromise of 1790 signaled the resumption of their political partnership after five years of separation. Now "the great collaboration" was truly an alliance worthy of its name.

Many of their closest friends and colleagues in Virginia had urged them to regard Hamilton's program as clinching evidence of a foreign takeover of the national government that fully justified a withdrawal from the union. Jefferson and Madison claimed to share their apprehensions and their political principles, but not their secessionist impulses. Their strategy was different. They would not abandon the government, but capture it. Like the new capital, it would become an extension of Virginia, or at least the Virginia vision of what the American Revolution meant and the American republic was therefore meant to be. Jefferson would oversee and orchestrate this campaign and provide its rhetorical foundation, which enjoyed a privileged association with the spirit of '76. Madison would actually lead the troops and do the necessary political infighting. Though it would not be easy, and would take the remainder of the decade to accomplish, that is pretty much what happened.

CHAPTER THREE

The Silence

JUST A FEW months before Jefferson staged his historic dinner party, something happened in the Congress of the United States that no one had anticipated; indeed, most of the political leadership considered it an embarrassing intrusion. On February 11, 1790, two Quaker delegations, one from New York and the other from Philadelphia, presented petitions to the House calling for the federal government to put an immediate end to the African slave trade. This was considered an awkward interruption, disrupting as it did the critical debate over the assumption and residency questions with an inflammatory proposal that several southern representatives immediately denounced as mischievous meddling. Representative James Jackson from Georgia was positively apoplectic that such a petition would even be considered by any serious deliberative body. The Quakers, he argued, were infamous innocents incessantly disposed to drip their precious purity like holy water over everyone else's sins. They were also highly questionable patriots, having sat out the recent war against British tyranny in deference to their cherished consciences. What standing could such dedicated pacifists enjoy among veterans of the Revolution, who, as Jackson put it, "at the risk of their lives and fortunes, secured to the community their liberty and property?"[1]

William Loughton Smith from South Carolina rose to second Jackson's objection. The problematic patriotism of the Quaker petitioners was, Smith agreed, reprehensible. But his colleague from Georgia need not dally over the credentials of these pathetic eccentrics. The Constitution of the United States, only recently ratified, specifically prohibited the Congress from passing any law that abolished or restricted the slave trade until 1808. (Article 1, Section 9, paragraph 1, read: "The Migration or Importation of such Persons as any of the States now existing shall think proper to admit, shall not be prohibited by the Congress prior to the Year one thousand eight hundred and eight.") Several current members of Congress also happened to have served as delegates to the Constitutional Convention, and they could all testify that the document would never have been approved in Philadelphia or ratified by several of the southern states without this provision. Beyond these still warm memories, the language of the Constitution was unambiguous: The federal government could not tamper with the slave trade during the first twenty years of the nation's existence. The Quaker petitioners, therefore, were asking for something that had already been declared unavailable.[2]

Jackson, however, was not about to be consoled by constitutional protections. He detected even more sinister motives behind the benign smiles of the misnamed Society of Friends. "I apprehend, if through the interference of the general government, the slave-trade was abolished," he observed, "it would evince to the people a general disposition toward a total emancipation." In short, the Quaker petition for an end of the slave trade was really a stalking horse for a more radical and thoroughgoing scheme to end the institution of slavery itself.

James Madison rose to assume his customary role as the vigilant voice of cool reason. His colleague from Georgia was overreacting. Indeed, his impassioned rhetoric, while doubtless sincere, was both misguided and counterproductive. The Quaker petition should be heard and forwarded to a committee "as a matter of course." If, in other words, the matter were treated routinely and with a minimum of fuss, it would quickly evaporate. As Madison put it, "no notice would be taken it out of doors." On the other hand, Jackson's own overwrought opposition, much like airbursts in a night battle, actually called attention to the issues the Quakers wished to raise. If Jackson would only restrain himself, the petition would go away and "never be blown up into a decision of the question respecting the discouragement of the African slave-trade, nor alarm the owners with an apprehension that the general government were about to abolish slavery in all the states."

For, as Madison assured Jackson, "such things are not contemplated by any gentlemen in the congress."[3]

The next day, however, on February 12, Jackson's fearful prophecies seemed to be coming true. For on that day another petition arrived in the House, this one from the Pennsylvania Abolition Society. It urged the Congress to "take such measures in their wisdom, as the powers with which they are invested will authorize, for promoting the abolition of slavery, and discouraging every species of traffic in slaves." Just as Jackson had warned, opposition to the slave trade was now being linked to ending slavery altogether. What's more, this new petition made two additional points calculated to exacerbate the fears of men like Jackson: First, it claimed that both slavery and the slave trade were incompatible with the values for which the American Revolution had been fought, and it even instructed the Congress on its political obligation to "devise means for removing this inconsistency from the Character of the American people." Second, it challenged the claim that the Constitution prohibited any legislation by the federal government against the slave trade for twenty years, suggesting instead that the "general welfare" clause of the Constitution empowered the Congress to take whatever action it deemed "necessary and proper" to eliminate the stigma of traffic in human beings and to "Countenance the Restoration of Liberty for all Negroes." Finally, to top it all off and heighten its dramatic appeal, the petition arrived under the signature of Benjamin Franklin, whose patriotic credentials and international reputation were beyond dispute. Indeed, if there were an American pantheon, only Washington would have had a more secure place in it than Franklin.[4]

Franklin's endorsement of the petition from the Pennsylvania Abolition Society effectively assured that the preferred Madisonian strategy—calmly receiving these requests, then banishing them to the congressional version of oblivion—was not going to work. In fact, the ongoing debate on the assumption and residency questions was set aside for the entire day as the House put itself into committee of the whole to permit unencumbered debate on the petitions. During the course of that debate, which lasted between four and six hours, things were said that had never before been uttered in any public forum at the national level.

Granted, the delegates to the Constitutional Convention had engaged in extensive debates about the slave trade and how to count slaves for the purposes of representation and taxation. But these debates had all occurred behind closed doors and under the strictest code of confidentiality. (Madison's informal record of these debates, the fullest account, was not published in his lifetime.) Granted also that the place of slavery in the new national order had come up in several state ratifying conventions in 1788. But these state-based deliberations quite naturally tended to focus on local or regional interpretations of the Constitution's rather elliptical handling of the forbidden subject. (No specific mention of "slavery," "slaves," or "Negroes" had been permitted into the final draft of the document.) If political leaders who had pushed through the constitutional settlement of 1787–1788 had been permitted to speak, their somewhat awkward conclusion would have been that slavery was too important and controversial a subject to talk about publicly.[5]

This explains the initial reaction of several representatives from South Carolina, who objected to the suggestion that the petitions should be read aloud in the halls of Congress. Aedanus Burke, for example, warned that the petitioners were "blowing the trumpet of sedition" and demanded that the galleries be cleared of all spectators and newspaper reporters. Jackson also heard trumpets blowing, though for him they were "trumpets of civil war." The position of all the speakers from the Deep South seemed to be that the Constitution not only prohibited the Congress from legislating about slavery or the slave trade; it forbade anyone in Congress from even mentioning those subjects publicly. If this was their position, events quickly demonstrated that it was an argument they were destined to lose.[6]

THE DEBATE began when Thomas Scott of Pennsylvania, speaking on behalf of the petitioners, acknowledged that the Constitution imposed restrictions on Congress's power to end the slave trade but said nothing whatsoever about abolishing slavery itself. As Scott put it, "if I was one of the judges of the United States, I do not know how far I might go if these people were to come before me and claim their emancipation, but I am sure I would go as far as I could." Whereupon Jackson commented that any judge rendering such an opinion in Georgia "would be of short duration."[7]

Jackson then launched into a sermon on God's will, which he described as patently proslavery, based on several passages in the Bible and the pronouncements of every Christian minister in Georgia. Alongside the clear preferences of the Almighty, there was the nearly unanimous opinion of every respectable citizen in his state, whose livelihood depended on the availability of slave labor and who shared the elemental recognition, as Jackson put it, "that rice cannot be brought to market without these people." William Loughton Smith preferred to leave the interpretation of God's will to others, but he seconded the opinion of his colleague from Georgia that slavery was an economic precondition for the prosperity of his constituents, noting that "such is the state of agriculture in that country, no white man would perform the tasks required to drain the swamps and clear the land, so that without slaves it must be depopulated."[8]

Smith also led the debate on behalf of the Deep South on that other great text, which was not the Bible but the Constitution. In Smith's version of the story, the framers of the Constitution had recognized that the chief source of conflict among the state delegations was between those dependent on slave labor and those free of such dependency. A sectional understanding had emerged whereby northern states had agreed not to tamper with the property rights of southern states. In addition to the specific provisions of the Constitution, which recognized the slave population as worthy of at least some measure of representation in Congress and the protection of the slave trade for at least another twenty years after ratification, there was also an implicit but broadly shared understanding that the newly created federal government could do nothing to interfere with the existence of slavery in the South. All the southern states had ratified the Constitution with that understanding as a primal precondition: "Upon that reason they acceded to the Constitution," Smith declared. "Unless that part was granted they would not [have] come into the union." His evident distress at these Quaker petitions was rooted in his belief that the current debate represented a violation of that understanding.[9]

Representative Abraham Baldwin of Georgia chimed in to support Smith's version of the federal compact. "Gentlemen who had been present at the formation of this Constitution"—Baldwin himself had been one such gentleman—"could not avoid the recollection of the pain and difficulty which the subject caused in that body." The essential agreement reached at Philadelphia in 1787, Baldwin claimed, was the decision to remove slavery in the southern states from any influence by the northern states. "If gentlemen look over the footsteps of that body," Baldwin observed, "they will find the greatest degree of caution used to imprint them, so as not to be easily eradicated." Any attempt to renegotiate that sectional agreement by the current Congress would result in the disintegration of the national confederation at the very moment of its birth.[10]

Several northern representatives rose to contest the claim that both the Bible and the Constitution endorsed slavery. John Laurance of New York wondered how any Christian could read the Sermon on the Mount and believe it was compatible with chattel slavery. As far as the Constitution was concerned, Laurance acknowledged that certain provisions recognized the existence of slavery and provided temporary protection for those states wishing to import more Africans. But the larger understanding, as Laurance saw it, was that slavery was an anomaly in the American republic, a condition that could be tolerated in the short run precisely because there was a clear consensus that it would be ended in the long run. Scott of Pennsylvania echoed those sentiments, suggesting that the defining text was not the Constitution but the Declaration of Independence, which clearly announced that it was "not possible that one man should have property in person of another."[11]

Elbridge Gerry of Massachusetts attempted to offer conciliatory words to his southern colleagues, though he did so in a decidedly northern accent. His rambling remarks described the predicament of slave owners as truly tragic and not of their own making. They had been "betrayed into the slave-trade by the first settlers." But rather than countenance their unfortunate condition, the chief task of those northern states spared the same fate should be to rescue them from it. This was both a political obligation and a "matter of humanity" toward both the slaves and those who owned them. The Quaker petitions were therefore not treasonable or out of order. They were "as worthy as anything that can come before the house." Gerry then presented his own personal estimate of the revenue required to compensate the slave owners for purchasing their slaves at current market value and came up with the figure of $10 million. How he derived this amount was murky—it was much lower than any realistic estimate—but his thinking about the source for the revenue was clear: Voters would not accept a tax sufficient to cover these costs, so the only plausible course would be to establish a national fund for this purpose created out of the profits from the sale of western lands. As for the slave trade, the sooner that despicable traffic was ended, the better for everybody.[12]

Although the sectional battle lines were clearly drawn in the debate, the position of the Virginia delegation was equivocal. Representative John Page, for example, seemed to offer one of the most ringing endorsements of the petitions. He warned his colleagues from the Deep South that their opposition to the mere mention of an end to slavery and the slave trade was misguided. The real threat was silence. But then Page explained his thinking, which went like this: Reports of this debate would eventually find their way into the slave quarters of the South, and when the slaves learned that Congress would not even consider ways to mitigate their condition or end their misery, they would have no hope. The consequence would be slave insurrections, for "if anything could induce him [a slave] to rebel, it must be a stroke like this."[13]

Madison's thinking was decidedly less eccentric, although still problematic. As befitted the central player in the Constitutional Convention, Madison emphasized the various legal obligations imposed by the compact of 1787. While he thought the Constitution was crystal clear that Congress could not restrict or terminate the slave trade before 1808, it did not prohibit the members of the House from talking about the issue. They could talk about anything they wished, including the gradual abolition of slavery itself, though he felt that Congress was unlikely to take any dramatic action "tending to the emancipation of the slaves." It could, however, opt to "make some regulation respecting the introduction of them [slaves] in the new states, to be formed out of the Western Territory," a matter he thought "well worthy of consideration." On the all-important question of the implicit understanding about the future of slavery itself, whether it was presumed to be on the road to extinction or forever protected where it already existed, Madison did not comment.[14]

Given the sharp sectional divisions in the debate, the vote to refer the petitions to a committee was surprisingly one-sided, 43 to 11; seven of the negative votes came from South Carolina and Georgia. Nor was anyone from either of those two states willing to serve on the committee, which was instructed to report its findings to the full House before the end of the session. Thus ended, at least for the time being, the fullest public exchange of views on the most deep-rooted problem facing the new American republic.[15]

HINDSIGHT PERMITS us to listen to the debate of 1790 with knowledge that none of the participants possessed. For we know full well what they could perceive dimly, if at all—namely, that slavery would become the central and defining problem for the next seventy years of American history; that the inability to take decisive action against slavery in the decades immediately following the Revolution permitted the size of the enslaved population to grow exponentially and the legal and political institutions of the developing U.S. government to become entwined in compromises with slavery's persistence; and that eventually over 600,000 Americans would die in the nation's bloodiest war to resolve the crisis, a trauma generating social shock waves that would reverberate for at least another century.

What is familiar history for us, however, was still the unknown future for them. And while the debate of 1790 reveals that they were profoundly interested in what the future would bring, their arguments were rooted in the past they knew best, which is to say, the recent experience of the successful revolutionary struggle against Great Britain and the even more recent creation of a federal government uniting the thirteen states into a more cohesive nation. The core of the disagreement in the debate of 1790 revolved around different versions of what has come to be called America's "original intentions," more specifically what the Revolution meant for the institution of slavery. One's answer, it turned out, depended a great deal on which founding moment, 1776 or 1787, seemed most seminal. And it depended almost entirely on the geographic and demographic location of the person posing the question.

At least at the rhetorical level, the egalitarian principles on which the American revolutionaries had based their war for independence from Great Britain placed slavery on the permanent defensive and gave what seemed at the time a decisive advantage to the antislavery side of any debate. Jefferson's initial draft of the Declaration of Independence had included language that described the slave trade as the perverse plot of an evil English monarch designed to contaminate innocent colonists. Though the passage was deleted by the Continental Congress in the final draft, it nevertheless captured the nearly rhapsodic sense that the American Revolution was both a triumphant and transformative moment in world history, when all laws and human relationships dependent on coercion would be swept away forever. And however utopian and excessive the natural rights section of the Declaration ("We hold these truths to be self-evident") might appear later on, in the crucible of the revolutionary moment it gave lyrical expression to a widespread belief that a general emancipation of slaves was both imminent and inevitable, the natural consequence and fitting capstone of a glorious liberation from medieval mores historically associated with the very British government that Americans were rejecting. If the Bible were a somewhat contradictory source when it came to the question of slavery, the Declaration of Independence, the secular version of American scripture, was an unambiguous tract for abolition.[16]

In the long run, as we know, the liberal values of the Declaration did indeed win out. But we also need to recognize that in the short run, during and immediately after the war for independence, there was a prevailing consensus that slavery was already on the road to extinction. In 1776, for example, when the Continental Congress voted to repeal the nonimportation agreement of 1774, it chose to retain its prohibition against the importation of African slaves, a clear statement of opposition to the resumption of the slave trade. The manpower needs created by the six-year war generated several emancipation schemes whereby slaves would be freed and their owners compensated in return for enlistment for the duration of the conflict. Though this was really an emergency proposal dictated by the military crisis, and was ultimately rejected by the planter class in South Carolina and Georgia, its very suggestion seemed prophetic. Toward the end of the war, Lafayette, that paragon of the Franco-American alliance who was always eager to join the parade when history was on the march, urged Washington to declare a general emancipation for all slaves in Virginia and resettle them in the western region of the state as tenant farmers.[17]

But these were merely inspirational episodes that never quite lived up to their promise. The most tangible and enduring antislavery effects of the revolutionary mentality occurred in the northern states during and immediately after the war. Vermont (1777) and New Hampshire (1779) made slavery illegal in their state constitutions. Massachusetts declared it unconstitutional in a state Supreme Court decision (1783). Pennsylvania (1780) and Rhode Island (1784) passed laws ending it immediately within their borders. Connecticut (1784) followed suit with a gradual emancipation plan. New York and New Jersey, which contained the largest slave populations north of the Chesapeake, proved more recalcitrant for that very reason. But despite the defeat there of several gradual emancipation schemes in the 1780s, defenders of slavery in the northern states were clearly fighting a losing battle; abolition in the North was more a question of when than whether.[18]

Nor was this all. In 1782 the Virginia legislature passed a law permitting slave owners to free their slaves at their own discretion. By the end of the decade, there were over twelve thousand freedmen in the state. At the same time, Thomas Jefferson was writing *Notes on the State of Virginia,* the only book he ever published, in which he sketched out a plan whereby all slaves born after 1800 would eventually become free. In 1784 Jefferson also proposed a bill in the federal Congress prohibiting slavery in all the western territories; it failed to pass by a single vote. One did not need to be a hopeless visionary to conjure up a mental picture of the American Revolution as a dramatic explosion that had destroyed the very foundation on which slavery rested and then radiated out its emancipatory energies with irresistible force: The slave trade was generally recognized as a criminal activity; slavery was dead or dying throughout the northern states; the expansion of the institution into the West looked uncertain; Virginia appeared to be the beachhead for an antislavery impulse destined to sweep through the South; the time seemed ripe to reconcile America's republican rhetoric with a new postrevolutionary reality.[19]

This uplifting vision, it turned out, was mostly a mirage. In fact, the very presumptiveness of the revolutionary rhetoric served to obfuscate the quite palpable reality that slavery, no matter how anomalous in purely ideological terms, was still deeply imbedded in the very structure of American society at multiple levels or layers that remained impervious to wishful thinking and revolutionary expectations.

The passionate conviction that the Revolution was like a mighty wave fated to sweep slavery off the American landscape actually created false optimism and fostered a misguided sense of inevitability that rendered human action or agency superfluous. (Why bother with specific schemes when history would soon arrive with all the answers?) More-

over, one of the reasons the Revolution proved so successful as a movement for independence was that its immediate and short-run goals
were primarily political: removing royal governors and rewriting state
constitutions that, in fact, already embodied many of the republican
features the Revolution now sanctioned. Removing slavery, however,
was not like removing British officials or revising constitutions. In isolated pockets of New York and New Jersey, and more panoramically in
the entire region south of the Potomac, slavery was woven into the fabric of American society in ways that defied appeals to logic or morality.
It also enjoyed the protection of one of the Revolution's most potent
legacies, the right to dispose of one's property without arbitrary interference from others, especially when the others resided far away or
claimed the authority of some distant government. There were, to be
sure, radical implications latent in the "principles of '76" capable of
challenging privileged appeals to property rights, but the secret of their
success lay in their latency—that is, the gradual and surreptitious ways
they revealed their egalitarian implications over the course of the nineteenth century. If slavery's cancerous growth was to be arrested and the
dangerous malignancy removed, it demanded immediate surgery. The
radical implications of the revolutionary legacy were no help at all so
long as they remained only implications.[20]

The depth and apparent intractability of the problem became much
clearer during the debates surrounding the drafting and ratification of
the Constitution. Although the final draft of the document was conspicuously silent on slavery, the subject itself haunted the closed-door
debates. No less a source than Madison believed that slavery was the
central cause of the most elemental division in the Constitutional Convention: "the States were divided into different interests not by their
difference of size," Madison observed, "but principally from their having or not having slaves. . . . It did not lie between the large and small
States: it lay between the Northern and Southern."[21]

The delegates from New England and most of the Middle Atlantic
states drew directly on the inspirational rhetoric of the revolutionary
legacy to argue that slavery was inherently incompatible with the
republican values on which the American Revolution had been based.
They wanted an immediate end to the slave trade, an explicit statement
prohibiting the expansion of slavery into the western territories as a
condition for admission into the union, and the adoption of a national

plan for gradual emancipation analogous to those state plans already adopted in the North. The most forceful expression of the northern position on the slave trade came, somewhat ironically, from Luther Martin of Maryland, who denounced it as "an odious bargain with sin" that was "inconsistent with the principles of the revolution and dishonorable to the American character." The fullest expression of the northern position on abolition itself came from Gouverneur Morris, a New Yorker, but serving as a delegate from Pennsylvania, who described slavery as "a curse" that actually retarded the economic development of the South and "the most prominent feature in the aristocratic countenance of the proposed Constitution." Morris even proposed a national tax to compensate the slave owners, claiming that he would much prefer "a tax for paying for all the Negroes in the United States than saddle posterity with such a Constitution." In the speeches of Martin and Morris one can discern the clearest articulation of the view, later embraced by the leadership of the abolitionist movement, that slavery was a nonnegotiable issue; that this was the appropriate and propitious moment to place it on the road to ultimate extinction; and that any compromise of that long-term goal was a "covenant with death."[22]

The southern position might more accurately be described as "deep southern," since it did not include Virginia. Its major advocates were South Carolina and Georgia, and the chief burden for making the case in the Constitutional Convention fell almost entirely on the South Carolina delegation. The underlying assumption of this position was most openly acknowledged by Charles Cotesworth Pinckney of South Carolina—namely, that "South Carolina and Georgia cannot do without slaves." What those from the Deep South wanted was open-ended access to African imports to stock their plantations. They also wanted equivalently open access to western lands, meaning no federal restrictions on slavery in the territories. Finally, they wanted a specific provision in the Constitution that would prohibit any federal legislation restricting the property rights of slave owners—in effect, a constitutional assurance that slavery as it existed in the Deep South would be permitted to flourish. The clearest statement of their concerns came from Pierce Butler and John Rutledge of South Carolina. Butler explained that "the security the southern states want is that their Negroes may not be taken from them." Rutledge added that "the people of those States will never be such fools as to give up so important an interest." The implicit but unmistakably clear message underlying their position, which later became the trump card played by the next generation of South Carolinians in the Nullification Crisis in 1832, then more defiantly by the secessionists in 1861, was the threat to leave the union if the federal government ever attempted to implement a national emancipation policy.[23]

Neither side got what it wanted at Philadelphia in 1787. The Constitution contained no provision that committed the newly created federal government to a policy of gradual emancipation, or in any clear sense placed slavery on the road to ultimate extinction. On the other hand, the Constitution contained no provisions that specifically sanctioned slavery as a permanent and protected institution south of the Potomac or anywhere else. The distinguishing feature of the document when it came to slavery was its evasiveness. It was neither a "contract with abolition" nor a "covenant with death," but rather a prudent exercise in ambiguity. The circumlocutions required to place a chronological limit on the slave trade or to count slaves as three-fifths of a person for purposes of representation in the House, all without ever using the forbidden word, capture the intentionally elusive ethos of the Constitution. The underlying reason for this calculated orchestration of noncommitment was obvious: Any clear resolution of the slavery question one way or the other rendered ratification of the Constitution virtually impossible.

Two specific compromises illustrate the tendency to fashion political bargains on slavery that simultaneously disguised the deep moral division within the Convention and framed the compromise solution in terms that permitted each side to claim victory. The first enigmatic bargain concerned the expansion of slavery into the West and actually occurred in the Confederation Congress that was also meeting in Philadelphia. One of the last and most consequential acts of the Congress was to pass the Northwest Ordinance in July of 1787. Article Six of the ordinance forbade slavery in the territory north of the Ohio River, a decision that could plausibly be interpreted as the first step toward a more general exclusion of slavery in all incoming states (the Jefferson proposal of 1784). On the other hand, the ordinance could also be read as a tacit endorsement of slavery in the southwestern region (which eventually proved to be the case). In any event, the passage of the Northwest Ordinance was a blessed event for the delegates at the Constitutional Convention, in part because it removed a potentially divisive issue from their agenda, and in part because the solution it posed could be heard to speak with both a northern and southern accent.[24]

The second bargain can, with considerable justice, be described as the most important compromise reached at the Constitutional Convention, even more so than the "Great Compromise" between large and small states over representation in the Senate and House. It might more accurately be called the "Sectional Compromise." No less an authority than Madison considered it the most consequential of all the secret deals made in Philadelphia: "An understanding on the two subjects of *navigation* and *slavery,*" Madison explained, "had taken place between those parts of the Union." The bargain entailed an exchange of votes whereby New England agreed to back an extension of the slave trade for twenty years in return for support from the Deep South for making the federal regulation of commerce a mere majority vote in the Congress rather than a supermajority of two-thirds. As with the Northwest Ordinance, both sides could declare victory; and the true victors would only become known with the passage of time. (John C. Calhoun would subsequently conclude that if the Deep South had regarded this bargain as a wager on the future, it was a losing bet.)[25]

The debates in the ratifying conventions of the respective states only exposed the irreconcilable differences of opinion that the Constitution had so deftly bundled together. In Massachusetts and Pennsylvania, for example, opponents of the Constitution objected to the implicit acceptance of slavery's persistence, represented by the three-fifths clause and the twenty-year extension of the slave trade. Supporters assured them, however, that these partial and limited concessions only reflected the fading gasps of a dying institution. James Wilson of Pennsylvania predicted that emancipation was inevitable "and though the period is more distant than I could wish, yet it will produce the same kind of gradual change for the whole nation as was pursued in Pennsylvania." As for the western territories, Wilson was certain that Congress "would never allow slaves in any of the new states." Luther Martin, on the other hand, came out against the Constitution on the grounds that the protections afforded slavery "render us contemptible to every *true friend* of liberty in the world." Martin was perhaps the first public advocate of the "covenant with death" interpretation of the

Constitution, as well as the first former delegate to denounce the Sectional Compromise as a corrupt bargain. But in a close vote, his Maryland colleagues rejected his reading of the document as excessively pessimistic.[26]

Meanwhile, down in South Carolina the assurances afforded slavery that so troubled Martin of Maryland struck many delegates as inadequate. Charles Cotesworth Pinckney helped win the day for ratification with his own gloss on the true meaning of the compact:

> We have a security that the general government can never emancipate them, for no such authority is granted and it is admitted, on all hands, that the general government has no powers but which are expressly granted by the Constitution, and that all rights not expressed were reserved by the several states. . . . In short, considering all circumstances, we have made the best terms for the security of this species of property it was in our power to make. We would have made better if we could; but on the whole, I do not think them bad.[27]

The fullest and most intellectually interesting debate occurred in Virginia. As the most populous state with both the largest slave population (292,000) and the largest free-black population (12,000), Virginia's demographic profile looked decidedly southern. Only South Carolina had a higher density of blacks (60 percent to Virginia's 40 percent). But Virginia's rhetorical posture sounded distinctly northern; or perhaps more accurately, the political leadership of the Old Dominion relished its role as the chief spokesman for "the principles of '76," which placed slavery under a permanent shadow and seemed to align Virginia against the Deep South. Jefferson, it must be remembered, had proposed the abolition of slavery in all the western territories. Madison, though he eventually endorsed the three-fifths clause, acknowledged his discomfort with the doctrine, confessing that "it may appear to be a little strained in some points." Most significantly, the Virginians were adamantly opposed to the continuation of the slave trade. Both Madison and his colleague George Mason denounced the Sectional Compromise in the Constitutional Convention that prolonged the trade; and Mason eventually voted against ratification in part for that very reason. On the surface, at least, Virginia seemed the one southern state where the ideological contagion of the American Revolution remained sufficiently potent to dissolve the legacy of slavery.[28]

Upon closer examination, however, Virginia turned out to resemble the fuzzier and more equivocal picture that best describes the nation at large and that the Constitution was designed to mirror. For beneath their apparent commitment to antislavery and their accustomed place in the vanguard of revolutionary principles, the Virginians were overwhelmingly opposed to relinquishing one iota of control over their own slave population to any federal authority. Whether they were living a paradox or a lie is an interesting question. What is undeniably clear is that the Virginia leadership found itself in the peculiar position of acknowledging that slavery was an evil and then proceeding to insist that there was nothing the federal government could do about it. Mason's vehement opposition to the slave trade rested cheek by jowl with his demand for a constitutional guarantee to protect what he described as "the property of that kind which we have already."

Virginia's true position was less principled than it looked. Its plantations were already stocked with slaves, so opposition to the slave trade made economic sense, as did opposition to emancipation. Mason thought that the Constitution had it exactly wrong: "they have done what they ought not to have done"—that is, extended the life of the slave trade—"and have left undone what they ought to have done"—that is, explicitly prohibited federal interference in what he called "our domestic interests." Edmund Randolph made it abundantly clear at the Virginia ratifying convention just what "domestic interests" Mason had in mind. Randolph in his own roundabout way had come over to support ratification, so he needed to counter Mason's apprehensions about slavery. "I might tell you," he apprised his Virginia colleagues, *"that the Southern States, even South Carolina herself, conceived this property to be secure,"* and that except for Mason "not a member of the Virginia delegation had *the smallest suspicion of the abolition of slavery."* Virginia, in short, talked northern but thought southern.[29]

IF ONE WISHED to generalize, then, about the situation that obtained in 1790 at the moment of the congressional debate over the Quaker petitions, the one thing that seemed clear concerning slavery was that nothing was clear at all. The initial debate in February had, in fact, accurately reflected the competing and incompatible presumptions about slavery's fate in the American republic, with one side emphasizing the promissory note to end it purportedly issued in 1776, the other side emphasizing the gentlemen's agreement to permit it reached in 1787, and a middle group, dominated by the Virginians, straddling both sides and counseling moderation lest the disagreement produce a sectional rupture. Both sides could plausibly claim a core strand of the revolutionary legacy as their own. And all parties to the debate seemed to believe that history, as well as the future, was on their side.

Like a lightning flash in the night, the initial exchange on the floor of Congress in February of 1790 had exposed these divisions of opinion before a national audience for the first time. On March 8 the committee was prepared to submit its report, thereby assuring that the controversy would not go away or get buried in some parliamentary graveyard. Representatives from the Deep South rose to express their outrage that the forbidden subject was again being allowed into public view. William Loughton Smith pointed up to the antislavery advocates who had stacked the galleries "like evil spirits hovering over our heads." James Jackson actually made menacing faces at the Quakers in the gallery, called them outright lunatics, then launched into a tirade so emotional and incoherent that reporters in the audience had difficulty recording his words. The gist seemed to be that any decision to receive the committee report was tantamount to the dissolution of the union.[30]

These threatening harangues managed to delay matters, but the Deep South lacked the votes. On March 16 the committee was ready to make its report to the House. First Jackson and then Smith were also prepared with their response, which turned out to be the fullest public exposition of the proslavery position yet presented in the United States. In fact, virtually every argument that southern defenders of slavery would mount during the next seventy years of the national controversy, right up to the eve of the Civil War, came gushing forth over the next two days.[31]

Jackson spoke first and held the floor for about two hours. He could not believe that a dignified body of sober-minded legislators were allowing these "shaking Quakers" with their throbbing consciences to control the national agenda. One of the petitioners, an infamous do-gooder of uncertain sanity named Warner Mifflin, had actually acknowledged that his antislavery vision had come to him after he was struck by lightning in a thunderstorm. The Congress had been elected to steer the ship of state through rough and uncharted waters, not to take aboard a crew of dazed dreamers bent on sailing to the Promised Land but inadvertently destined to sink the ship on its maiden voyage.

Speaking of promises, a "sacred compact" had been made when the nation was founded in 1787, "a compact which brought us together mutually to relinquish a share of our interests to preserve the remainder." Then Jackson described the Sectional Compromise at the Constitutional Convention, whereby "the southern states for this very principle gave into what might be termed the navigation law of the eastern and western states," a concession granted in return for retention of the slave trade for twenty years. The Quaker petitioners were now asking the Congress to break that compact and thereby violate the understanding on which the states of the Deep South had entered the union.

Moreover, there was an even more elemental understanding implicitly codified in Philadelphia but actually predating the Constitutional Convention by many years. It was rooted in the realistic recognition that slavery had been grafted onto the character of the southern states during the colonial era and had become a permanent part of American society south of the Potomac. "If it were a crime, as some assert but which I deny," Jackson explained, "the British nation is answerable for it, and not the present inhabitants, who now hold that species of property in question." Northern posturing on this matter was insufferable, as Jackson saw it, since their oozing arguments transformed a geographic accident and a product of historical circumstance into a willful sin. The incontrovertible truth was that slavery was "one of those habits established long before the Constitution, and could not now be remedied." When the thirteen colonies rebelled against Britain, "no one raised this question." And when the nation was formed into a more unified whole in 1787, "the Union had received them with all the ill habits about them." The implicit but thoroughly understood sectional agreement, which the Sectional Compromise at Philadelphia merely underlined, was that slavery, while anomalous within the framework of republican ideology, was a self-evident reality that had been allowed to coexist alongside Jefferson's self-evident truths. "The custom, the habit of slavery is established," Jackson observed, and all responsible American statesmen had agreed that "the southern states must be left to themselves on this subject." Antislavery idealists might prefer to live in some better world, which like all such places was too good to be true. The American nation in 1790, however, was a real world, laden with legacies like slavery, and therefore too true to be good. Jackson did not go so far as to argue, as did southern apologists two or three generations later, that slavery was "a positive good." But he did insist, in nonnegotiable language, that it was "a necessary evil."

Jackson had several books at his side, and he began to read to his colleagues in order to demonstrate that his opinions were shared by the most respected authorities. The most respected authority of all, the Christian God in the Bible, sanctioned slavery in several passages from the Old Testament. In addition, the most reliable and recent studies of African tribal culture demonstrated that slavery was a long-standing custom among the Africans themselves, so enslaved Africans in America were simply experiencing a condition here that they would otherwise experience, probably in more oppressive fashion, in their mother country.

Then Jackson referred his colleagues to the opinions of "Mr. Jefferson, our secretary of state," and began reading from Jefferson's *Notes on the State of Virginia* on the practical question: "What is to be done with the slaves when freed?" Either they must be incorporated where they are or they must be colonized somewhere else. Jefferson's view of the question was so well known that Jackson claimed he could quote from Jefferson's book from memory: The two races cannot live together on equal terms because of "deep rooted prejudices entertained by the whites—ten thousand recollections by the blacks of the injuries they have sustained—new provocations—the real distinctions that nature has made, and many other circumstances which divide us into parties, and produce convulsions which would never end but with the extermination of one or the other race." Perhaps there were a few whites in the North who did not concur with Mr. Jefferson's sentiments. Perhaps the Quaker petitioners approved of racial mixing and looked forward to "giving their daughters to negro sons, and receiving the negro daughters for their sons." But despite the relatively small size of the black population in the North, the pattern of racial segregation there suggested that most northern whites shared Jefferson's belief that "incorporation" was unlikely. In the South, where the number of blacks was so much larger, it was unthinkable.

Those advocating emancipation, then, need to confront the intractable dilemma posed by the sheer size of an African population that, once freed, must be removed to some other location. Apart from the obvious question of cost, which would prove astronomically high, where could the freed blacks be sent? Those advocating an African solution might profitably study the recent English efforts to establish a black colony in Sierra Leone, where most of the freed blacks died or were enslaved by the local African tribes. Those advocating a location in the American West also needed to think again: "The peoples of America, like an overwhelming torrent, are rapidly covering the earth, and extending their settlements throughout this vast continent, nor is there any spot, however remote, but a short period will settle." Moreover, vast tracts in the West had already been promised to the Indians, whose response to a population of black neighbors was likely to prove uncharitable in the extreme. If anyone had a responsible solution to this problem, Jackson claimed to be receptive. But until such a solution materialized, all talk of emancipation must cease.[32]

No one from outside the Deep South rose to answer Jackson. The next day, March 17, William Loughton Smith held the floor for over two hours without interruption and repeated most of Jackson's points. Whereas Jackson tended toward a more volatile and pulpit-thumping style reminiscent of an itinerant Presbyterian minister in the revivalistic mode, Smith preferred the more measured cadences of the South Carolina aristocrat steeped in Ciceronian formalities. But despite the stylistic differences, the arguments were identical: The Constitution was absolutely clear that the slave trade could not be ended before 1808; there was a sectional compact that recognized slavery's existence where it was already rooted south of the Potomac; any attempt to renegotiate that compact would mean the dissolution of the union; the demographic and racial realities rendered any emancipation scheme impossible, most especially for white southerners who lived amid a sizable black population. Smith also quoted from Jefferson's *Notes on the State of Virginia,* then put his own cast on the racial implications of a large free-black population in America: "If the blacks did not intermarry with the whites, they would remain black until the end of time; for it was not contended that liberating them would whitewash them; if they did intermarry with the whites, then the white race would be extinct, and the American people would all be of the mulatto breed. In whatever light therefore the subject was viewed, the folly of emancipation was manifest."[33]

The full proslavery argument was now out in the open. If one looked forward from this dramatic moment, the speeches by Jackson and Smith became prophetic previews of coming attractions for the southern defense of slavery in the nineteenth century, a defense that would eventually lose on the battlefields of the Civil War. If one looked backward, nothing quite so defiant or systematic had ever been presented before. True enough, the constitutional arguments represented a consolidation of points made in Philadelphia in 1787 and then in several state ratifying conventions. But the brazen claim that slavery must be accepted unconditionally as a permanent feature of the national confederation was, if not wholly new, at least an interpretive clarification never made before in a national forum. And the racial argument, which added the specter of a racially mixed American society as a consequence of emancipation, gave a new dimension to the debate by attempting to transform the sectional disagreement between North and South into a national alliance of whites against blacks.[34]

The novelty of the arguments now pouring forth from the representatives of the Deep South must also be understood in context. The particulars were new, but the attitudes on which they rested were familiar. No responsible statesman in the revolutionary era had ever contemplated, much less endorsed, a biracial American society. In 1776, for example, when the Continental Congress had commissioned John Adams, Benjamin Franklin, and Thomas Jefferson to design a seal for the United States, they produced a national emblem depicting Americans of English, Scottish, Irish, French, German, and Dutch extraction. There were no Africans or Native Americans in the picture. The new proslavery argument, then, drew on assumptions about the white Anglo-Saxon character of the emerging American nation that were latent but long-standing. No explicit articulation of those assumptions had been necessary in a national forum before 1790, because no frontal assault on slavery had been made that required a direct or systematic response.

Those historians who claim that a distinctive racial ideology first came into existence at this time, describing it as a fresh "construction" or "invention" designed to frame the debate over slavery in a more effectively prejudicial way, have a point, or perhaps half a point, in the sense that the challenge to slavery drove the racial (and racist) presumptions to the surface of the debate for the first time. But they had been lurking in the hearts and minds of the revolutionary generation all along. The ultimate legacy of the American Revolution on slavery was not an implicit compact that it be ended, or a gentlemen's agreement between the two sections that it be tolerated, but rather a calculated obviousness that it not be talked about at all. Slavery was the unmentionable family secret, or the proverbial elephant in the middle of the room. What was truly new in the proslavery argument was not really the ideas or attitudes expressed, but the expression itself.[35]

There was yet another new ingredient about to enter the debate in 1790, though it too was more a matter of making visible and self-conscious what had previously hovered in some twilight zone of hazy and unspoken recognition. Perhaps the least controversial decision of the First Congress was passage of legislation that authorized the census of 1790, an essential item because accurate population figures were necessary to determine the size of state delegations in the House. The following information was being gathered, quite literally, while the debate over the Quaker petitions raged:

1790 CENSUS OF THE UNITED STATES*			
STATES	FREE WHITE	ALL OTHER FREE PERSONS	SLAVES	TOTAL
Vermont	85,268	255	16	85,539
New Hampshire	141,097	630	158	141,885
Maine	96,002	538	none	96,540
Massachusetts	373,324	5,463	none	378,787
Rhode Island	64,470	3,407	948	68,825
Connecticut	232,674	2,808	2,764	237,946
New York	314,142	4,654	21,324	340,120
New Jersey	169,954	2,762	11,423	184,139
Pennsylvania	424,099	6,537	3,737	434,373
Delaware	46,310	3,899	8,887	59,094
Maryland	208,649	8,043	103,036	319,728
Virginia	442,117	12,866	292,627	747,610
Kentucky	61,133	114	12,430	73,677
North Carolina	288,204	4,975	100,572	393,751
South Carolina	140,178	1,801	107,094	249,073
Georgia	52,886	398	29,264	82,548
Total	3,140,205	59,150	694,280	3,893,635

* Data excerpted from U.S. Bureau of Census, *First Census of the United States* (Baltimore, 1978), 6–8.

At the most obvious level, these numbers confirmed with enhanced precision the self-evident reality that slavery was a sectional phenomenon that was dying out in the North and flourishing in the South. The exceptions were New York and New Jersey, which, not incidentally, remained the only northern states to resist the passage of gradual emancipation laws. In general, then, there was a direct and nearly perfect correlation between demography and ideology—that is, between the ratio of blacks to whites in the population and the reluctance to consider abolition. When the proslavery advocates of the Deep South unveiled their racial argument—What will happen between the races after emancipation?—the census of 1790 allowed one to predict the response with near precision. Wherever the black population reached a threshold level, slavery remained the preferred means of assuring the segregation of the races.

The only possible exception to this rule was the Upper South, to include the states of Maryland, Virginia, and North Carolina. There the slave populations were large, in Virginia very large indeed, but so were the populations of free blacks ("All Other Free Persons"). From a strictly demographic perspective, Virginia was almost as vulnerable to the specter of postemancipation racial fears as South Carolina, but the growing size of the free-black population accurately reflected the presence of multiple schemes for gradual emancipation within the planter class and the willingness of at least a few slave owners to act in accord with the undeniable logic of the American Revolution. The sheer size of Virginia's total population, amplified by the daunting racial ratio, and then further amplified by the political prowess of its leadership at the national level, all combined to make it the key state. If any national plan for ending slavery was to succeed, Virginia needed to be in the vanguard.

Finally, the census of 1790 provided unmistakable evidence that those antislavery advocates who believed that the future was on their side were deluding themselves. For the total slave population was now approaching 700,000, up from about 500,000 in the year of the Declaration of Independence. Despite the temporary end of the slave trade during the war, and despite the steady march of abolition in the North, the slave population in the South was growing exponentially at the same exploding rate as the American population as a whole, which meant it was doubling every twenty to twenty-five years. Given the political realities that defined the parameters of any comprehensive program for emancipation—namely, compensation for owners, relocation of freed slaves, and implementation over a sufficient time span to permit economic and social adjustments—the larger the enslaved population grew, the more financially and politically impractical any emancipation scheme became. (One interpretation of the Deep South's argument of 1790 was that, at least from their perspective, the numbers already made such a decision impossible.) The census of 1790 revealed that the window of opportunity to end slavery was not opening, but closing. For not only were the numbers becoming wholly unmanageable, but the further one got from 1776, the lower the revolutionary fires burned and the less imperative the logic of the revolutionary ideology seemed. What one historian has called "the perishability of revolutionary time" meant that the political will to act was also racing against the clock. In effect, the fading revolutionary ideology and the growing racial demography were converging to close off the political options. With all the advantage of hindsight, a persuasive case can be made that the Quaker petitioners were calling for decisive action against slavery at the last possible moment, if indeed there was such a moment, when gradual emancipation had any meaningful prospect for success.[36]

THE CHIEF strength of the proslavery argument that emerged from the Deep South delegation in the congressional debate of March 16–17 was its relentless focus on the impractical dimensions of all plans for abolition. In effect, their arguments exposed the two major weaknesses of the antislavery side: First, those ardent ideologues who believed that slavery would die a natural death after the Revolution were naïve utopians proven wrong by the stubborn realities reflected in the census of 1790; second, the gradual emancipation plans implemented in the northern states were inoperative models for the nation as a whole, because the northern states contained only about 10 percent of the slave population; for all those states from Maryland south, the cost of compensation and the logistical difficulties attendant upon the relocation of the freed slaves were simply insurmountable; the numbers, quite simply, did not work.

How correct were these conclusions? From a strictly historical perspective, we can never know the answer to that question. Since no one from the North or the Upper South rose to answer the delegation from the Deep South, and since no national plan for gradual emancipation ever came before the Congress for serious consideration, we are left with a great silence, which itself becomes the principal piece of historical evidence to interpret. And the two overlapping interpretations that then present themselves with irresistible logic are quite clear: First, the arguments of the Deep South were unanswerable because there was sufficient truth in the fatalistic diagnosis to persuade other members of the House that the slavery problem was intractable; and second, whatever shred of possibility still existed to take concerted action against slavery was overwhelmed by the secessionist threat from South Carolina and Georgia, since there could be no national solution to the slavery problem if there were no nation at hand to implement a solution. Perhaps, as some historians have argued, South Carolina and Georgia were bluffing. But the most salient historical fact cannot be avoided: No one stepped forward to call their bluff.

Though we might wish otherwise, the history of what might have been is usually not really history at all, mixing together as it does the messy tangle of past experience with the clairvoyant certainty of our present preferences. That said, even though no formal proposal for a gradual emancipation program came before the Congress in 1790, all the elements for such a program were present in the debates. Moreover, in March of 1790, while the congressional debate was raging, a prominent Virginian by the name of Fernando Fairfax drafted a "Plan for Liberating the Negroes within the United States," which was subsequently published in Philadelphia the following December. Fairfax's plan fleshed out the sketchy outline that Jefferson had provided in *Notes on the State of Virginia*. Another Virginian, St. George Tucker, developed an even fuller version of the same scheme six years later. In short, the historical record itself, and not just our own omniscient imaginations, provides the requisite evidence from which we can reconstruct the response to the proslavery argument. In so doing, we are not just engaging in wishful thinking, are not attempting to rewrite history along more attractive lines, but rather trying to assess the historical viability of a national emancipation policy in 1790. What chance, if any, existed at that propitious moment to put slavery on the road to extinction?[37]

All the plans for gradual emancipation assumed that slavery was a moral and economic problem that demanded a political solution. All also assumed that the solution needed to combine speed and slowness, meaning that the plan needed to be put into action quickly, before the burgeoning slave population rendered it irrelevant, but implemented gradually, so the costs could be absorbed more easily. Everyone advocating gradual emancipation also made two additional assumptions: First, that slave owners would be compensated, the funds coming from some combination of a national tax and from revenues generated by the sale of western lands; second, that the bulk of the freed slaves would be transported elsewhere, the Fairfax plan favoring an American colony in Africa on the British model of Sierra Leone, others proposing what might be called a "homelands" location in some unspecified region of the American West, and still others preferring a Caribbean destination.

As we have seen, the projected cost of compensation was a potent argument against gradual emancipation, and the argument has been echoed in most scholarly treatments of the topic ever since. Estimates vary according to the anticipated price for each freed slave, which ranges between one hundred and two hundred dollars. The higher figure produces a total cost of about $140 million to emancipate the entire slave population in 1790. Since the federal budget that year was less than $7 million, the critics seem to be right when they conclude that the costs were not just daunting but also prohibitively expensive. The more one thought about such numbers, in effect, the more one realized that further thought was futile. There is some evidence that reasoning of just this sort was going on in Jefferson's mind at this time, changing him from an advocate of emancipation to a silent and fatalistic procrastinator.[38]

The flaw in such reasoning, however, would have been obvious to any accountant or investment banker with a modicum of Hamiltonian wisdom. For the chief virtue of a gradual approach was to extend the cost of compensation over several decades so that the full bill never landed at one time or even on one generation. In the scheme that St. George Tucker proposed, for example, purchases and payments would continue for the next century, delaying the arrival of complete emancipation, to be sure, but significantly reducing the impact of the current costs by spreading them into the distant future. The salient question in

1790 was not the total cost but, with an amortized debt, the initial cost of capitalizing a national fund (often called a "sinking fund") for such purposes. The total debt inherited from the states and the federal government in 1790 was $77.1 million. A reasonable estimate of the additional costs for capitalizing a gradual emancipation program would have increased the national debt to about $125 million. While daunting, these numbers were not fiscally impossible. And they became more palatable when folded into a total debt package produced by a war for independence.[39]

The other major impediment, equally daunting as the compensation problem at first glance, even more so upon reflection, was the relocation of the freed slaves. Historians have not studied the feasibility of this feature as much as the compensation issue, preferring instead to focus on the racial prejudices that required its inclusion, apparently fearing that their very analysis of the problem might be construed as an endorsement of the racist and segregationist attitudes prevalent at the time. Two unpalatable but undeniable historical facts must be faced: First, that no emancipation plan without this feature stood the slightest chance of success; and second, that no model of a genuinely biracial society existed anywhere in the world at that time, nor had any existed in recorded history.[40]

The gradual emancipation schemes adopted in the northern states never needed to face this question squarely, because the black population there remained relatively small. South of the Potomac was a different matter altogether, since approximately 90 percent of the total black population resided there. Any national plan for gradual emancipation needed to transform this racial demography by relocating at least a significant portion of that population elsewhere. But where? The subsequent failure of the American Colonization Society and the combination of logistical and economic difficulties in the colony of Liberia exposed the impracticality of any mass migration back to Africa. The more viable option was transportation to the unsettled lands of the American West, along the lines of the Indian removal program adopted over forty years later. In 1790, however, despite the presumptive dreams of a continental empire, the Louisiana Purchase remained in the future and the vast trans-Mississippi region continued under Spanish ownership. While the creation of several black "homelands" or districts east of the Mississippi was not beyond contemplation—it was mentioned in private correspondence by a handful of antislavery advocates—it was just as difficult to envision then as it is difficult to digest now.[41]

More than the question of compensation, then, the relocation problem was perilously close to insoluble. To top it all off, and add yet another layer of armament to the institution of slavery, any comprehensive plan for gradual emancipation could only be launched at the national level under the auspices of a federal government fully empowered to act on behalf of the long-term interests of the nation as a whole. Much like Hamilton's financial plan, any effective emancipation initiative conjured up fears of the much-dreaded "consolidation" that the Virginians, more than anyone else, found so threatening. (Indeed, for at least some of the Virginians, the deepest dread and greatest threat was that federal power would be used in precisely this way.) All the constitutional arguments against the excessive exercise of government power at the federal level then kicked in to make any effort to shape public policy more problematic.

Any attempt to take decisive action against slavery in 1790, given all these considerations, confronted great, perhaps impossible, odds. The prospects for success were remote at best. But then the prospects for victory against the most powerful army and navy in the world had been remote in 1776, as had the likelihood that thirteen separate and sovereign states would create a unified republican government in 1787. Great leadership had emerged in each previous instance to transform the improbable into the inevitable. Ending slavery was a challenge on the same gigantic scale as these earlier achievements. Whether even a heroic level of leadership stood any chance was uncertain because—and here was the cruelest irony—the effort to make the Revolution truly complete seemed diametrically opposed to remaining a united nation.

ONE PERSON stepped forward to answer the challenge, unquestionably the oldest, probably the wisest, member of the revolutionary generation. (In point of fact, he was actually a member of the preceding generation, the grandfather among the fathers.) Benjamin Franklin was very old and very ill in March of 1790. He had been a fixture on the American scene for so long and had outlived so many contemporaries—he had once traded anecdotes with Cotton Mather and was a contemporary of Jonathan Edwards—that reports of his imminent departure lacked credibility; his last act seemed destined to go on forever; he was an American immortal. If a twentieth-century photographer had managed to commandeer a time machine and travel back to record the historic scenes in the revolutionary era, Franklin would have been present in almost every picture: in Philadelphia during the Continental Congress and the signing of the Declaration of Independence; in Paris to draft the wartime treaty with France and then almost single-handedly (assist to John Adams) conclude the peace treaty with Great Britain; in Philadelphia again for the Constitutional Convention and the signing of the Constitution. Even without the benefit of photography, Franklin's image—with its bemused smile, its bespectacled but twinkling eyes, its ever-bald head framed by gray hair flowing down to his shoulders—was more famous and familiar to the world than the face of any other American of the age.

What Voltaire was to France, Franklin was to America, the symbol of mankind's triumphal arrival at modernity. (When the two great philosopher-kings embraced amid the assembled throngs of Paris, the scene created a sensation, as if the gods had landed on earth and declared the dawning of the Enlightenment.) The greatest American scientist, the most deft diplomat, the most accomplished prose stylist, the sharpest wit, Franklin defied all the categories by inhabiting them all with such distinction and nonchalant grace. Over a century before Horatio Alger, he had invented the role and called it Poor Richard, the original self-taught, homespun American with an uncanny knack for showing up where history was headed and striking a folksy pose that then dramatized the moment forever: holding the kite as the lightning struck; lounging alongside Jefferson and offering witty consolations as the Continental Congress edited out several of Jefferson's most cherished passages; wearing a coonskin cap for his portrait in Paris; remarking as the delegates signed the Constitution that, yes, the sun that was carved into the chair at the front of the room did now seem to be rising.[42]

In addition to seeming eternal, ubiquitous, protean, and endlessly quotable, Franklin had the most sophisticated sense of timing among all the prominent statesmen of the revolutionary era. His forceful presence at the defining moment of 1776 had caused most observers to forget that, in truth, Franklin was a latecomer to the patriot cause, the man who had spent most of the 1760s in London attempting to obtain, of all things, a royal charter for Pennsylvania. He had actually lent his support to the Stamp Act in 1765 and lobbied for a position within the English government as late as 1771. But he had leapt back across the Atlantic and onto the American side of the imperial debate in the nick of time, a convert to the cause, who, by the dint of his international reputation, was quickly catapulted into the top echelon of the political leadership. Sent to France to negotiate a wartime alliance, he arrived in Paris just when the French ministry was ready to entertain such an idea. He remained in place long enough to lead the American delegation through the peace treaty with England, then relinquished his ministerial duties to Jefferson in 1784, just when all diplomatic initiatives on America's behalf in Europe bogged down and proved futile. (When asked if he was Franklin's replacement, Jefferson had allegedly replied that he was his successor, but that no one could replace him.) He arrived back in Philadelphia a conquering hero and in plenty of time to be selected as a delegate to the Constitutional Convention.[43]

This gift of exquisite timing continued until the very end. In April of 1787, Franklin agreed to serve as the new president of the revitalized Pennsylvania Abolition Society and to make the antislavery cause the final project of his life. Almost sixty years earlier, in 1729, as a young printer in Philadelphia, he had begun publishing Quaker tracts against slavery and the slave trade. Throughout the middle years of the century and into the revolutionary era, he had lent his support to Anthony Benezet and other Quaker abolitionists, and he had spoken out on occasion against the claim that blacks were innately inferior or that racial categories were immutable. Nevertheless, while his antislavery credentials were clear, at one point Franklin had owned a few household slaves himself, and he had never made slavery a priority target or thrown the full weight of his enormous prestige against it.

Starting in 1787, that changed. At the Constitutional Convention he intended to introduce a proposal calling for the inclusion of a statement of principle, condemning both the slave trade and slavery, thereby making it unequivocally clear that the founding document of the new American nation committed the government to eventual emancipation. But several northern delegates, along with at least one officer in the Pennsylvania Abolition Society, persuaded him to withdraw his proposal on the grounds that it put the fragile Sectional Compromise, and therefore the Constitution itself, at risk. The petition submitted to the First Congress under his signature, then, was essentially the same proposal he had wanted to introduce at the Convention. With the Constitution now ratified and the new federal government safely in place, Franklin resumed his plea that slavery be declared incongruous with the revolutionary principles on which the nation was founded. The man with the impeccable timing was choosing to make the anomaly of slavery the last piece of advice he would offer his country.[44]

Though his health was declining rapidly, newspaper accounts of the proslavery speeches in the House roused him for one final appearance in print. Under the pseudonym "Historicus," he published a parody of the speech delivered by James Jackson of Georgia. It was a vintage Franklin performance, reminiscent of his bemused but devastating recommendations to the English government in 1770 about the surest means to take the decisive action guaranteed to destroy the British Empire. This time, he claimed to have noticed the eerie similarity between Jackson's speech on behalf of slavery and one delivered a century earlier by an Algerian pirate named Sidi Mehemet Ibrahim.

Surely the similarities were inadvertent, he suggested, since Jackson was obviously a virtuous man and thus incapable of plagiarism. But the arguments and the very language were identical, except that Jackson used Christianity to justify enslavement of the Africans, while the African used Islam to justify enslavement of Christians. "The Doctrine, that Plundering and Enslaving the Christians is unjust, is at best *problematical*," the Algerian had allegedly written, and when presented with a petition to cease capturing Europeans, he had argued to the divan of Algiers "that it is in the Interest of the State to continue the Practice; therefore let the Petition be rejected." All the same practical objections to ending slavery were also raised: "But who is to indemnify their Masters for the Loss? Will the State do it? Is our Treasury sufficient . . . ? And if we set our Slaves free, what is to be done with them . . . ? Our people will not pollute themselves by intermarrying with them." Franklin then had the Algerian argue that the enslaved Christians were "better off with us, rather than remain in Europe where they would only cut each other's throats in religious wars." Franklin's pointed parody was reprinted in several newspapers from

Boston to Philadelphia, though nowhere south of the Potomac. It was his last public act. Three weeks later, on April 17, the founding grandfather finally went to his Maker.[45]

Prior to his passing, however, the great weight of Franklin's unequivocal endorsement made itself felt in the congressional debate and emboldened several northern representatives to answer the proslavery arguments of the Deep South with newfound courage. Franklin's reputation served as the catalyst in an exchange, as Smith of South Carolina attempted to discredit his views by observing that "even great men have their senile moments." This prompted rebuttals from the Pennsylvania delegation: "Instead of proving him superannuated," Franklin's antislavery views showed that "the qualities of his soul, as well as those of his mind, are yet in their vigour"; only Franklin still seemed able "to speak the language of America, and to call us back to our first principles"; critics of Franklin, it was suggested, only exposed the absurdity of the proslavery position, revealing clearly that "an advocate for slavery, in its fullest latitude, at this stage of the world, and on the floor of the American Congress too, is *a phenomenon in politics*. . . . They defy, yea, mock all belief." William Scott of Pennsylvania, his blood also up in defense of Franklin, launched a frontal assault on the constitutional position of the Deep South: "I think it unsatisfactory to be told that there was an understanding between the northern and southern members, in the national convention"; the Constitution was a written document, not a series of unwritten understandings; where did it say anything at all about slavery? Who were these South Carolinians to instruct us on what Congress could and could not do? "I believe," concluded Scott, "if Congress should at any time be of the opinion that a state of slavery was a quality inadmissible in America, they would not be barred . . . of prohibiting this baneful quality." He went on for nearly an hour. It turned out to be the high-water mark of the antislavery effort in the House.[46]

In retrospect, Franklin's final gesture at leadership served to solidify his historic reputation as a man who possessed in his bones a feeling for the future. But in the crucible of the moment, another quite plausible definition of leadership was circulating in the upper reaches of the government. John Adams, for example, though an outspoken enemy of slavery who could match his revolutionary credentials with anyone, concurred from his perch as presiding officer of the Senate when that body refused to permit the Quaker petitions to be heard. Alexander Hamilton, who was a founding member of the New York Manumission Society and a staunch antislavery advocate, also regretted the whole debate in the House, since it stymied his highest priority, which was approval of his financial plan. And George Washington, the supreme Founding Father, who had taken a personal vow never to purchase another slave and let it be known that it was his fondest wish "to see some plan adopted, by which slavery in this country may be abolished by slow, sure, and imperceptible degrees," also concurred that the ongoing debate in the House was an embarrassing and dangerous nuisance that must be terminated. Jefferson probably agreed with this verdict, though his correspondence is characteristically quiet on the subject. The common version of leadership that bound this distinguished constellation together was a keen appreciation of the political threat that any direct consideration of slavery represented in the still-fragile American republic. And the man who stepped forward to implement this version of leadership was James Madison.[47]

If Franklin's great gift was an uncanny knack for levitating above political camps, operating at an altitude that permitted him to view the essential patterns and then comment with great irony and wit on the behavior of those groveling about on the ground, Madison's specialty was just the opposite. He lived in the details and worked his magic in the context of the moment, mobilizing those forces on the ground more adroitly and with a more deft tactical proficiency than anyone else. Taken together, he and Franklin would have made a nearly unbeatable team. But in 1790, they were on different sides.

Madison's position on slavery captured the essence of what might be called "the Virginia straddle." On the one hand, he found the blatantly proslavery arguments "shamefully indecent" and described his colleagues from South Carolina and Georgia as "intemperate beyond all example and even all decorum." Like most of his fellow Virginians, he wanted it known that he preferred an early end to the slave trade and regarded the institution of slavery "a deep-rooted abuse." He claimed to be genuinely embarrassed at the stridently proslavery rhetoric of the delegates from the Deep South and much more comfortable on the high moral ground of his northern friends.[48]

But a fault line ran through the center of his thinking, a kind of mysterious region where ideas entered going in one direction but then emerged headed the opposite way. For example, when urged by Benjamin Rush, the Philadelphia physician and abolitionist, to support the Quaker petitions in the House, Madison responded, "Altho I feel the force of many of your remarks, I can not embrace the idea to which they lead." When pressed to explain the discrepancy between his hypothetical antislavery position and his actual dedication to self-imposed paralysis, he tended to offer several different answers. Sometimes it was a matter of his Virginia constituents: "Those from whom I derive my public station," he explained, "are known by me to be greatly interested in that species of property, and to view the matter in that light." Sometimes it was a matter of timing: He concurred with the progressive segment of Virginia's planter class that "slavery is a Moral, and political Evil, and that Whoever brings forward in the Respective States, some General, rational and Liberal plan, for the Gradual Emancipation of Slaves, will deserve Well of his Country—yet I think it was very improper, at this time, to introduce it in Congress."[49]

Any effort to locate the core of Madison's position on slavery, therefore, misses the point, which is that there was no core, except perhaps the conviction that the whole subject was taboo. Like Jefferson and the other members of the Virginia dynasty, he regarded any explicit defense of slavery in the mode of South Carolina and Georgia as a moral embarrassment. On the other hand, he regarded any effort to end slavery as premature, politically impractical, and counterproductive. As a result, he developed a way of talking and writing about the problem that might be described as "enlightened obfuscation." For example, consider the following Madisonian statement, written during the height of the debate in the House: "If this folly did not reproach the public councils, it ought to excite no regret in the patrons of Humanity & freedom. Nothing could hasten more the progress of these reflections & sentiments which are secretly undermining the institution which this mistaken zeal is laboring to secure agst. the most distant approach of danger." The convoluted syntax, multiple negatives, indefinite antecedents, and masterful circumlocutions of this statement defy comprehension. What begins as a denunciation of those defending slavery somehow doubles back on itself and ends up in worrisome confusion that the matter is being talked about at all. What is meant to sound like an antislavery argument transforms itself in midpassage into a verbal fog bank that descends over the entire subject like a cloud.[50]

In the midst of this willful confusion, one Madisonian conviction shone through with his more characteristic clarity—namely, that slavery was an explosive topic that must be removed from the political agenda of the new nation. It was taboo because it exposed the inherent contradictions of the Virginia position, which was much closer to the position of the Deep South than Madison wished to acknowledge, even to himself. And it was taboo because, more than any other controversy, it possessed the political potential to destroy the union. Franklin wanted to put slavery onto the national agenda before it was too late to take decisive action in accord with the principles of the Revolution. Madison wanted to take slavery off the national agenda because he believed that decisive action would result in the destruction of either the Virginia planter class or the nation itself. (In the minds of many Virginians, the two items were synonymous.) "The true policy of the Southern members," he explained to a fellow Virginian, "was to let the affair proceed with as little noise as possible." The misguided representatives of the Deep South had spoiled that strategy. Now Madison resolved to seize the opportunity created by their threats of secession to put Congress on record as rejecting any constitutional right by the federal government to end slavery. It was the South Carolina solution achieved in the Virginia style.[51]

THE ESSENCE of that style was indirection. Madison was its master, so deft behind the scenes and in unrecorded conversations that his most significant political achievements, including his impact on the eventual shape of the Constitution and his enduring influence on the thought and behavior of Thomas Jefferson, remain forever hidden, visible only in the way that one detects the movement of iron filings within a magnetic field. The Madisonian influence revealed itself in the House debate of March 23 when the committee report came up for a vote.

Something had changed. Several northern members, who had previously sided with the Quaker petitioners, now expressed their regret that the matter had gotten out of hand. Fisher Ames of Massachusetts wondered out loud why the House had allowed itself to be drawn into a debate over "abstract propositions" and now urged that the committee report be tabled. Jackson rose to thank Ames and his northern colleagues for seeing the light and recovering the old conciliatory spirit that had once permitted northern and southern interests to cooperate. One of the Quaker petitioners in the gallery, John Pemberton, noted in his diary that some kind of sectional bargain had obviously been struck: "It was a matter of scratch me and I will scratch thee." (Pemberton surmised that a secret deal had been arranged whereby Massachusetts would align itself with the Deep South on the slavery issue in return for southern support on assumption. If so, Jefferson's dinner party the following June was the culmination of an even more complicated sectional negotiation than previously realized.) But all claims about what had gone on behind the scenes are conjectural. Madison seldom left footprints.[52]

The goal of the Deep South, now with support from Massachusetts and Virginia, was to have the committee report tabled, again threatening that further debate would risk disunion, which William Loughton Smith likened to "heaving out an anchor to windward." Madison, however, wanted more than just an end to the debate. He wished to establish a precedent that clarified the constitutional ambiguities concerning the power of Congress over slavery. Therefore he welcomed the positive vote (29 to 25) to accept the committee report (details of which forthcoming), because he had resolved to use the occasion to establish a constitutional precedent. In the twentieth century, what Madison aimed to achieve would have required a decision by the Supreme Court. But in 1790 the Supreme Court was a woefully weak third branch of the federal government and the principle of judicial review had yet to be established. Madison wanted to use the vote on the committee report to create the equivalent of a landmark decision prohibiting any national scheme for emancipation.[53]

It happened just as he desired. The committee report consisted of seven resolutions that addressed this salient question: What are "the powers vested in Congress, under the present constitution, relating to the abolition of slavery"? The first resolution was designed to appease the Deep South by confirming that the Constitution prohibited any federal legislation limiting or ending the slave trade until 1808. The fourth was a gesture toward the northern interests, authorizing Congress to levy a tax on slave imports designed to discourage the practice without prohibiting it. The seventh was a nod toward the Quaker petitioners, declaring that "in all cases, to which the authority of Congress extends, they will exercise it for the humane objects of the memorialists, so far as they can be promoted on the principles of justice, humanity and good policy." But what did this deliberately vague promise mean? Specifically, how far did the authority of Congress extend? The implicit answer was in the second resolution. It read: "That Congress, by a fair construction of the Constitution, are equally restrained from interfering in the emancipation of slaves, who already are, or who may, within the period mentioned, be imported into, or born within any of the said States."[54]

This was the key provision. In keeping with the compromise character of the committee report, it gave the Deep South the protection it had demanded by denying congressional authority to pass any gradual emancipation legislation. But it also set a chronological limit to this moratorium. The prohibition would only last "within the period mentioned"—that is, until 1808. In effect, the committee report extended the deadline for the consideration of emancipation to bring it into line with the deadline for the end of the slave trade. The Deep South would get its way, but only for a limited time. After 1808, Congress possessed the authority to do what it wished; then all constitutional restraints would lapse.

At this decisive moment, the Madisonian magic worked its will. The House went into committee of the whole to revise the language of the report. In parliamentary maneuverings of this sort, Madison had no peer. The Virginia delegation had already received its marching orders to mobilize behind an amended version of the report. And several northern delegations, chiefly those of Massachusetts and New York, had clearly been lobbied to support the amendments, though no one will ever know what promises were made. In the end, the seven resolutions were reduced to three. The tax on the slave trade was dropped altogether, as was the seventh resolution, with its vague declaration of solidarity with the benevolent goals of the Quaker petitioners. The latter gesture had become irrelevant because of the new language of the second resolution. It now read: "The Congress have no authority to interfere in the emancipation of slaves, or in the treatment of them within any of the States; it remaining with the several States alone to provide any regulation therein, which humanity and true policy may require." During the debate over this language, Madison provided the clearest gloss on its fresh meaning by explaining that, instead of imposing an eighteen-year moratorium on congressional action against slavery, the amendment made it unconstitutional "to attempt to manumit them at any time." The final report passed by the House in effect placed any and all debate over slavery as it existed in the South out of bounds forever. What had begun as an initiative to put slavery on the road to extinction had been transformed into a decision to extinguish all federal plans for emancipation. By a vote of 29 to 25 the House agreed to transcribe this verdict in the permanent record. A relieved George Washington wrote home to a Virginia friend that "the slave business has at last [been] put to rest and will scarce awake."[55]

As usual, Washington was right. Congress had moved gradual emancipation off its political agenda; its decision in the spring of 1790 became a precedent with the force of common law. In November of 1792, for example, when another Quaker petition came forward under the sponsorship of Fisher Ames, William Loughton Smith referred his colleague to the earlier debate of 1790. The House had then decided never again to allow itself to become inflamed by the "mere rant and rhapsody of a meddling fanatic" and had argued "that the subject would never be stirred again." The petition was withdrawn. Over forty years later, in 1833, Daniel Webster cited the same precedent: "My opinion of the powers of Congress on the subject of slaves and slavery is that Congress has no authority to interfere in the emancipation of slaves. This was so resolved by the House in 1790 . . . and I do not know of a different opinion since."[56]

Whatever window of opportunity had existed to complete the one glaring piece of unfinished business in the revolutionary era was now closed. As noted earlier, perhaps the window, if in fact there ever was a window, had already closed by 1790, so the debate and decision in the House merely sealed shut what the formidable combination of racial demography, Anglo-Saxon presumptions, and entrenched economic interests had already foreclosed. Over two hundred years after the event, it is still not possible to demonstrate conclusively that Madison's understanding of the political priorities was wrong, or that the pursuit of Franklin's priorities would not have dismembered the American republic at the moment of its birth. Perhaps it was inevitable, even preferable, that slavery as a national problem be moved from the Congress to the churches, where it could come under scrutiny as a sin requiring a national purging, rather than as a social dilemma requiring a political solution. That, in any event, is what happened.

One can only speculate on what thought and feelings went streaking through the conscience of James Madison after the fleeting moment passed. Madison understood better than most what was at stake in the debate over slavery. He knew what the American Revolution had promised, that slavery violated that promise, and that Franklin had gone to his Maker reminding all concerned that silence was a betrayal of the revolutionary legacy. During the memorial service in Franklin's honor on April 22, Madison rose to deliver the final tribute of the House:

> The House being informed of the decease of BENJAMIN FRANKLIN, a citizen whose native genius was not more an ornament to human nature, than his various exertions of it have been precious to science, to freedom, and to his country, do resolve, as mark of the veneration due to his memory, that the members wear the customary badge of mourning for one month.[57]

The symbolism of the scene was poignant, dramatizing as it did the passing of the prototypical American and the cause of gradual emancipation. Whether they knew it or not, the badge of mourning the members of the House agreed to wear also bore testimony to the tragic and perhaps intractable problem that even the revolutionary generation, with all its extraordinary talent, could neither solve nor face.

CHAPTER FOUR

The Farewell

THROUGHOUT THE first half of the 1790s, the closest approximation to a self-evident truth in American politics was George Washington. A legend in his own time, Americans had been describing Washington as "the Father of the Country" since 1776—which is to say, before there was even a country. By the time he assumed the presidency in 1789—no other candidate was even thinkable—the mythology surrounding Washington's reputation had grown like ivy over a statue, effectively covering the man with an aura of omnipotence, rendering the distinction between his human qualities and his heroic achievements impossible to delineate.[1]

Some of the most incredible stories also happened to be true. During Gen. Edward Braddock's ill-fated expedition against the French outside Pittsburgh in 1755, a young Washington had joined with Daniel Boone to rally the survivors, despite having two horses shot out from under him and multiple bullet holes piercing his coat and creasing his pants. At Yorktown in 1781, he had insisted on standing atop a parapet for a full fifteen minutes during an artillery attack, bullets and shrapnel flying all about him, defying aides who tried to pull him down before he had properly surveyed the field of action. When Washington spoke of destiny, people listened.[2]

If there was a Mount Olympus in the new American republic, all the lesser gods were gathered farther down the slope. The only serious contender for primacy was Benjamin Franklin, but just before his

death in 1790, Franklin himself acknowledged Washington's supremacy. In a characteristically Franklinesque gesture, he bequeathed to
Washington his crab-tree walking stick, presumably to assist the general in his stroll toward immortality. "If it were a sceptre," Franklin
remarked, "he has merited it and would become it."[3]

In the America of the 1790s, Washington's image was everywhere, in
paintings, prints, lockets; on coins, silverware, plates, and household
bric-a-brac. And his familiarity seemed forever. His commanding presence had been the central feature in every major event of the revolutionary era: the linchpin of the Continental Army throughout eight
long years of desperate fighting from 1775 to 1783; the presiding officer
at the Constitutional Convention in 1787; the first and only chief
executive of the fledgling federal government since 1789. He was the
palpable reality that clothed the revolutionary rhapsodies in flesh and
blood, America's one and only indispensable character. Washington
was the core of gravity that prevented the American Revolution from
flying off into random orbits, the stable center around which the revolutionary energies formed. As one popular toast of the day put it, he
was "the man who unites all hearts." He was the American Zeus,
Moses, and Cincinnatus all rolled into one.[4]

Then, all of a sudden, on September 19, 1796, an article addressed to
"the PEOPLE of the United States" appeared on the inside pages of the
American Daily Advertiser, Philadelphia's major newspaper. The conspicuous austerity of the announcement was matched by its calculated
simplicity. It began: "Friends, and Fellow Citizens: The period for a
new election of a Citizen, to Administer the Executive government of
the United States, being not far distant . . . it appears to me proper,
especially as it may conduce to a more distinct expression of the public
voice, that I should now apprise you of the resolutions I have formed,
to decline being considered among the number of those, out of whom
a choice is to be made." It ended, again in a gesture of ostentatious
moderation, with the unadorned signature: "G. Washington, United
States."[5]

Every major newspaper in the country reprinted the article over the
ensuing weeks, though only one, the *Courier of New Hampshire,* gave it
the title that would echo through the ages—"Washington's Farewell
Address." Contemporaries began to debate its contents almost immediately, and a lively (and ultimately silly) argument soon ensued about

whether Washington or Hamilton actually wrote it. Over a longer stretch of time, the Farewell Address achieved transcendental status, ranking alongside the Declaration of Independence and the Gettysburg Address as a seminal statement of America's abiding principles. Its Olympian tone made it a perennial touchstone at those political occasions requiring platitudinous wisdom. And in the late nineteenth century the Congress made its reading a mandatory ritual on Washington's birthday. Meanwhile, several generations of historians, led by students of American diplomacy, have made the interpretation of the Farewell Address into a cottage industry of its own, building up a veritable mountain of commentary around its implications for an isolationist foreign policy and a bipartisan brand of American statecraft.[6]

But in the crucible of the moment, none of these subsequent affectations or interpretations mattered much, if at all. What did matter, indeed struck most readers as the only thing that truly mattered, was that George Washington was retiring. The constitutional significance of the decision, of course, struck home immediately, signaling as it did Washington's voluntary surrender of the presidency after two terms, thereby setting the precedent that held firm until 1940, when Franklin Delano Roosevelt broke it. (It was reaffirmed in 1951 with passage of the Twenty-second Amendment.) But even that landmark precedent, so crucial in establishing the republican principle of rotation in office, paled in comparison to an even more elemental political and psychological realization.

For twenty years, over the entire life span of the revolutionary war and the experiment with republican government, Washington had stood at the helm of the ship of state. Now he was sailing off into the sunset. The precedent he was setting may have seemed uplifting in retrospect, but at the time the glaring and painful reality was that the United States without Washington was itself unprecedented. The Farewell Address, as several commentators have noted, was an oddity in that it was not really an address; it was never delivered as a speech. It should, by all rights, be called the Farewell Letter, for it was in form and tone an open letter to the American people, telling them they were now on their own.[7]

INSIDERS HAD suspected that this was coming for about six months. In February of 1796, Washington had first approached Alexander Hamilton about drafting some kind of valedictory statement. Shortly thereafter, the gossip network inside the government had picked up the scent. By the end of the month, James Madison was writing James Monroe in Paris: "It is pretty certain that the President will not serve beyond his present term." On the eve of the Farewell Address, the Federalist leader from Massachusetts, Fisher Ames, predicted that Washington's looming announcement would constitute "a signal, like dropping a hat, for the party races to start," but in fact they had been going on unofficially throughout the preceding spring and summer. In May, for example, Madison had speculated—correctly, it turned out—that in the first contested election for president in American history, "Jefferson would probably be the object on one side [and] Adams apparently on the other." By midsummer, Washington himself was apprising friends of his earnest desire to leave the government when his term was up, "after which no consideration under heaven that I can foresee shall again with draw me from the walks of private life." He had been dropping hints, in truth, throughout his second term, describing himself as "on the advanced side of the grand climacteric" and too old for the rigors of the job, repeating his familiar refrain about the welcome solace of splendid isolation beneath his "vine and fig tree" at Mount Vernon.[8]

But did he mean it? Lamentations about the tribulations of public life, followed by celebrations of the bucolic splendor of retirement to rural solitude, had become a familiar, even formulaic, posture within the leadership class of the revolutionary generation, especially within the Virginia dynasty. Everyone knew the classical models of latter-day seclusion represented by Cincinnatus and described by Cicero and Virgil. Declarations of principled withdrawal from the hurly-burly of politics to the natural rhythms of one's fields or farms had become rhetorical rituals. If Washington's retirement hymn featured the "vine and fig tree," Jefferson's idolized "my family, my farm, and my books." The motif had become so commonplace that John Adams, an aspiring Cicero himself, claimed that the Virginians had worn out the entire Ciceronian syndrome: "It seems the Mode of becoming great is to retire," he wrote Abigail in 1796. "It is marvellous how political Plants grow in the shade." Washington had been threatening to retire even before he was inaugurated as president in 1789, and he had repeated the threat in 1792 prior to his reelection. While utterly sincere on all occasions, his preference for a virtuous retirement had always been trumped by a more public version of virtue, itself reinforced by the unanimous judgment of his political advisers that he and he alone was indispensable. Why expect a different conclusion in 1796?[9]

The short answer: age. Throughout most of his life, Washington's physical vigor had been one of his most priceless assets. A notch below six feet four and slightly above two hundred pounds, he was a full head taller than his male contemporaries. (John Adams claimed that the reason Washington was invariably selected to lead every national effort was that he was always the tallest man in the room.) A detached description of his physical features would have made him sound like an ugly, misshapen oaf: pockmarked face, decayed teeth, oversized eye sockets, massive nose, heavy in the hips, gargantuan hands and feet. But somehow, when put together and set in motion, the full package conveyed sheer majesty. As one of his biographers put it, his body did not just occupy space; it seemed to organize the space around it. He dominated a room not just with his size, but with an almost electric presence. "He has so much martial dignity in his deportment," observed Benjamin Rush, "that there is not a king in Europe but would look like a valet de chambre by his side."[10]

Not only did bullets and shrapnel seem to veer away from his body in battle, not only did he once throw a stone over the Natural Bridge in the Shenandoah Valley, which was 215 feet high, not only was he generally regarded as the finest horseman in Virginia, the rider who led the pack in most fox hunts, he also possessed for most of his life a physical constitution that seemed immune to disease or injury. Other soldiers came down with frostbite after swimming ice-choked rivers. Other statesmen fell by the wayside, lacking the stamina to handle the relentless political pressure. Washington suffered none of these ailments. Adams said that Washington had "the gift of taciturnity," meaning he had an instinct for the eloquent silence. This same principle held true on the physical front. His medical record was eloquently empty.[11]

The inevitable chinks in his cast-iron constitution began to appear with age. He fell ill just before the Constitutional Convention in 1787 and almost missed that major moment. Then in 1790, soon after assuming the presidency, he came down with influenza, then raging in New York, and nearly died from pulmonary complications. Jefferson's statements about Washington were notoriously contradictory and unreliable, as we shall see, but he dated Washington's physical decline from this moment: "The firm tone of his mind, for which he had been remarkable, was beginning to relax; a listlessness of labor, a desire for tranquillity had crept on him, and a willingness to let others act, or even think, for him." In 1794, while touring the terrain around the new national capital that would bear his name, he badly wrenched his back while riding. After a career of galloping to hounds, and a historic reputation as America's premier man on horseback, he was never able to hold his seat in the saddle with the same confidence. As he moved into his mid-sixties, the muscular padding around his torso softened and sagged, his erect bearing started to tilt forward, as if he were always leaning into the wind, and his energy flagged by the end of each long day. Hostile newspaper editorials spoke elliptically of encroaching senility. Even his own vice president, John Adams, conceded that Washington seemed dazed and wholly scripted at certain public ceremonies, like an actor reading his lines or an aging athlete going through the motions.[12]

Perhaps age alone would have been sufficient to propel Washington down the road from Philadelphia to Mount Vernon one last time. Surely if anyone deserved to spend his remaining years relaxing under his "vine and fig tree," it was Washington. Perhaps, in that eerily instinctive way in which he always grasped the difference between the essential and the peripheral, he literally felt in his bones that another term as president meant that he would die in office. By retiring when he did, he avoided that fate, which would have established a precedent that smacked of monarchical longevity by permitting biology to set the terminus of his tenure. Our obsession with the two-term precedent obscures the more elemental principle established by Washington's voluntary retirement—namely, that the office would routinely outlive the occupant, that the American presidency was fundamentally different from a European monarchy, that presidents, no matter how indispensable, were inherently disposable.

But advancing age and sheer physical fatigue were only part of the answer. Perhaps the most succinct way to put it is that Washington was leaving office not just because he was hearing whispers of mortality, but also because he was wounded. What no British bullet could do in the revolutionary war, the opposition press had managed to do in the political battles during his second term. In the wake of his Farewell Address, for example, an open letter appeared in Benjamin Franklin Bache's *Aurora*, in which the old firebrand Tom Paine celebrated Washington's departure, actually prayed for his imminent death, then predicted that "the world will be puzzled to decide whether you are an apostate or an impostor, whether you have abandoned good principles, or whether you ever had any."[13]

Some of the articles were utterly preposterous, like the charge, also made in the *Aurora*, that recently obtained British documents from the wartime years revealed that Washington was secretly a traitor who had fully intended to sell out the American cause until Benedict Arnold beat him to the punch. His critics, it should also be noted, were a decided minority, vastly outnumbered by his countless legions of supporters. The rebuttals to Paine's open letter, for example, appeared immediately, describing Paine as "that noted sot and infidel," whose efforts to despoil Washington's reputation "resembled the futile efforts of a reptile infusing its venom into the Atlantic or ejecting its filthy saliva towards the Sun." Paine's already-questionable reputation, in fact, never recovered from this episode. Taking on Washington was the fastest way to commit political suicide in the revolutionary era.[14]

Nevertheless, the attacks had been a persistent feature of his second term, and despite his customarily impenetrable front, Washington was deeply hurt by them: "But these attacks, unjust and unpleasant as they are, will occasion no change in my conduct; nor will they work any other effect in my mind," he postured. Although Washington was not, like Adams or Jefferson, a prodigious reader of books, he was an obsessive reader of newspapers. (He subscribed to ten papers at Mount Vernon.) His pose of utter disregard was just that, a pose: "Malignity therefore may dart her shafts," he explained, "but no earthly power can deprive me of the consolation of knowing that I have not . . . been guilty of willful error, however numerous they may have been from other causes." This outwardly aloof but blatantly defensive tone seemed to acknowledge, in its backhanded way, that his critics had struck a nerve.[15]

The main charge levied against Washington was that he had made himself into a quasi king: "We have given him the powers and prerogatives of a King," claimed one New York editorial. "He holds levees like a King, receives congratulations on his birthday like a King, employs his old enemies like a King, shuts himself up like a King, shuts up other people like a King, takes advice of his counsellors or follows his own opinions like a King." Several of these charges were patently false. The grain of truth in them, on the other hand, involved Washington's quite conspicuous embodiment of authority. He had no compunction about driving around Philadelphia in an ornate carriage drawn by six cream-colored horses; or, when on horseback, riding a white stallion with a leopard cloth and gold-trimmed saddle; or accepting laurel crowns at public celebrations that resembled coronations. It also did not help that when searching for a substitute for the toppled statue of George III in New York City, citizens chose a wooden replica of Washington, encouraging some critics to refer to him as George IV.[16]

In a sense, it was a problem of language. Since there had never been a republican chief executive, there was no readily available vocabulary to characterize such a creature, except the verbal traditions that had built up around European courts and kings. In another sense, it was a problem of personality. Washington was an inherently stiff and formal man who cultivated aloofness and possessed distancing mechanisms second to none. This contributed to his sense of majesty, true enough, but pushed an increment further, the majestic man became His Majesty.

Beyond questions of appearance or language or personal style, the larger problem was imbedded within the political culture of postrevolutionary America itself. The requirements of the American Revolution, in effect, cut both ways at once. To secure the Revolution and stabilize its legacy on a national level required a dominant leader who focused the energies of the national government in one "singular character." Washington had committed himself to that cause, and in so doing, he had become the beneficiary of its political imperatives, effectively being cast in the role of a "republican king" who embodied national authority more potently and more visibly than any collective body like Congress could possibly convey.[17]

At the very core of the revolutionary legacy, however, was a virulent hatred of monarchy and an inveterate suspicion of any consolidated version of political authority. A major tenet of the American Revolution—Jefferson had given it lyrical expression in the Declaration of Independence—was that all kings, and not just George III, were inherently evil. The very notion of a republican king was a repudiation of the spirit of '76 and a contradiction in terms. Washington's presidency had become trapped within that contradiction. He was living the great paradox of the early American republic: What was politically essential for the survival of the infant nation was ideologically at odds with what it claimed to stand for. He fulfilled his obligations as a "singular character" so capably that he seemed to defy the republican tradition itself. He had come to embody national authority so successfully that every attack on the government's policies seemed to be an attack on him.

This is the essential context for grasping Washington's motives for leaving public office in 1796. By resigning voluntarily, he was declaring that his deepest allegiances, like those of his critics, were thoroughly republican. He was answering them, not with words, but with one decisive, unanswerable action. And this is also the proper starting point for understanding the words he left as his final valedictory, the Farewell Address. Washington was making his ultimate statement as America's first and last benevolent monarch. Whatever the Farewell Address has come to mean over the subsequent two centuries of its interpretive history, Washington intended it as advice to his countrymen about how to sustain national unity and purpose, not just without him, but without a king.

THE MAIN themes of the Farewell Address are just as easy to state succinctly as they are difficult to appreciate fully. After declaring his irreversible intention to retire, Washington devoted several paragraphs to the need for national unity. He denounced excessive partisanship, most especially when it took the form of political parties pursuing a vested ideological agenda or sectional interest groups oblivious to the advantages of cooperation. The rest of the Farewell Address was then devoted to foreign policy, calling for strict American neutrality and diplomatic independence from the tangled affairs of Europe. He did not use the phrase "entangling alliances" so often attributed to him—Jefferson actually coined it in his First Inaugural Address (1801)—but Washington's message of diplomatic independence from Europe preceded Jefferson's words to the same effect. Taken together, his overlapping themes lend themselves to easy summary: unity at home and independence abroad. It was that simple.

The disarming simplicity of the statement, combined with its quasi-Delphic character, has made the Farewell Address a perennial candidate for historical commentary. Throughout the nineteenth and most of the twentieth centuries, the bulk of attention focused on the foreign policy section, advocates of American isolationism citing it as the classic statement of their cause, others arguing that strict isolation was never Washington's intention, or that America's emergence as a world power has rendered Washington's wisdom irrelevant. More recently, the early section of the Farewell Address has been rediscovered, its plea for a politics of consensus serving as a warning against single-issue political movements, or against the separation of America into racial, ethnic, or gender-based constituencies. Like the classic it has become, the Farewell Address has demonstrated the capacity to assume different shapes in different eras, to change color, if you will, in varying shades of light.[18]

Although Washington's own eyes never changed color and were set very much on the future, he had no way of knowing (much less influencing) the multiple meanings that future generations would discover in his words. The beginning of all true wisdom concerning the Farewell Address is that Washington's core insights were firmly grounded in the lessons he had learned as America's premier military and civilian leader during the revolutionary era. Unless one believes that ideas are like migratory birds that can fly unchanged from one century to the next, the only way to grasp the authentic meaning of his message is to recover the context out of which it emerged. Washington was not claiming to offer novel prescriptions based on his original reading of philosophical treatises or books; quite the opposite, he was reminding his countrymen of the venerable principles he had acquired from personal experience, principles so obvious and elemental that they were at risk of being overlooked by his contemporaries; and so thoroughly grounded in the American Revolution that they are virtually invisible to a more distant posterity.

First, it is crucial to recognize that Washington's extraordinary reputation rested less on his prudent exercise of power than on his dramatic flair at surrendering it. He was, in fact, a veritable virtuoso of exits. Almost everyone regarded his retirement of 1796 as a repeat performance of his resignation as commander of the Continental Army in 1783. Back then, faced with a restive and unpaid remnant of the victorious army quartered in Newburgh, New York, he had suddenly appeared at a meeting of officers who were contemplating insurrection; the murky plot involved marching on the Congress and then seizing a tract of land for themselves in the West, all presumably with Washington as their leader.[19]

He summarily rejected their offer to become the American Caesar and denounced the entire scheme as treason to the cause for which they had fought. Then, in a melodramatic gesture that immediately became famous, he pulled a pair of glasses out of his pocket: "Gentlemen, you will permit me to put on my spectacles," he declared rhetorically, "for I have not only grown gray but almost blind in service to my country." Upon learning that Washington intended to reject the mantle of emperor, no less an authority than George III allegedly observed, "If he does that, he will be the greatest man in the world." True to his word, on December 22, 1783, Washington surrendered his commission to the Congress, then meeting in Annapolis: "Having now finished the work assigned me," he announced, "I now retire from the great theater of action." In so doing, he became the supreme example of the leader who could be trusted with power because he was so ready to give it up.[20]

Second, when Washington spoke about the need for national unity in 1796, his message resonated with all the still-fresh memories of his conduct during the revolutionary war. Although he actually lost more battles than he won, and although he spent the first two years of the war making costly tactical mistakes that nearly lost the American Revolution at its very start, by 1778 he had reached an elemental understanding of his military strategy; namely, that captured ground—what he termed "a war of posts"—was virtually meaningless. The strategic key was the Continental Army. If it remained intact as an effective fighting force, the American Revolution remained alive. The British army could occupy Boston, New York, and Philadelphia, and it did. The British navy could blockade and bombard American seaports with impunity, and it did. The Continental Congress could be driven from one location to another like a covey of pigeons, and it was. But as long as Washington held the Continental Army together, the British could not win the war, which in turn meant that they would eventually lose it.[21]

Like all of Washington's elemental insights, this one seems patently obvious only in retrospect. A score of genuinely brilliant military leaders who also confronted a superior enemy force—Hannibal, Robert E. Lee, and Napoléon come to mind—were eventually defeated because they presumed that victory meant winning battles. Washington realized it meant sustaining the national purpose as embodied in the Continental Army. Space and time were on his side if he could keep the army united until the British will collapsed. And that is precisely what happened.

Third, when Washington talked about independence from foreign nations, his understanding of what American independence entailed cut much deeper than the patriotic veneer customarily suggested by the term. Once again, the war years shaped and hardened his convictions on this score, though the basic attitudes on which they rested were in place long before he assumed command of the Continental Army. Simply put, Washington had developed a view of both personal and national independence that was completely immune to sentimental attachments or fleeting ideological enthusiasms. He was a rock-ribbed realist, who instinctively mistrusted all visionary schemes dependent on seductive ideals that floated dreamily in men's minds, unmoored to the more prosaic but palpable realities that invariably spelled the difference between victory and defeat. At its psychological nub, Washington's inveterate realism was rooted in his commitment to control, over himself and over any and all events with the power to determine his fate. At its intellectual core, it meant he was the mirror image of Jefferson, for whom ideals were the supreme reality and whose inspirational prowess derived from his confidence that the world would eventually come around to fit the pictures he had in his head. Washington, however, regarded all such pictures as dangerous dreams.

In 1778, for example, at a time when patriotic propagandists were churning out tributes to the superior virtue of the American cause, Washington confided to a friend that, though virtue was both a wonderful and necessary item, it was hardly sufficient to win the war: "Men may speculate as they will," he wrote, "they may draw examples from ancient story, of great achievements performed by its influence; but whoever builds upon it, as a sufficient basis for conducting a long and bloody War, will find themselves deceived in the end. . . . For a time it may, of itself, be enough to push Men to Action; to bear much, to encounter difficulties; but it will not endure unassisted by Interest."[22]

Another example: In 1780 Maj. John André was captured while attempting to serve as a British spy in league with Benedict Arnold to produce a major strategic debacle on the Hudson River at West Point. By all accounts, André was a model British officer with impeccable manners, who had the misfortune to be caught doing his duty. Several members of Washington's staff, including Hamilton, pleaded that André's life be spared because of his exceptional character. Washington dismissed the requests as sentimental, pointing out that if André had succeeded in his mission, it might very well have turned the tide of the war. The staff then supported André's gallant request that he be shot like an officer rather than hanged as a spy. Washington also rejected this request, explaining that André, regardless of his personal attractiveness, was no more and no less than a spy. He was hanged the next day.[23]

A final example: Shortly after the French entry into the war in 1778, several members of the Continental Congress began to lobby for a French invasion of Canada, arguing that the likelihood of French military success was greater because Canada was populated mainly by Frenchmen. Washington opposed the scheme on several grounds, but confided his deepest reasons to Henry Laurens, president of the Continental Congress. He feared "the introduction of a large body of French troops into Canada, and putting them in possession of the capital of that Province, attached to them by all the ties of blood, habits, manners, religion and former connexions of government." The French were America's providential allies, to be sure, but once they were ensconced in Canada, it would be foolish to expect them to withdraw: "I fear this would be too great a temptation to be resisted by any power actuated by the common maxims of national policy." He went on to offer his advice to the Congress in one of his clearest statements about the motives governing nations: "Men are very apt to run into extremes," he explained, "hatred to England may carry some into an excess of Confidence in France. . . . I am heartily disposed to entertain the most favourable sentiments of our new ally and to cherish them in others to a reasonable degree; but it is a maxim founded on the universal experience of mankind, that no nation is to be trusted farther than it is bound by its interest; and no prudent statesman or politician will venture to depart from it." There was no such thing as a permanent international alliance, only permanent national interests.[24]

The clearest statement Washington ever made on America's national interest came in his Circular Letter of 1783, the last of his annual letters to the state governments as commander in chief. He projected a panoramic and fully continental vision of an American empire and he expressed his vision in language that, at least for one moment, soared beyond the usually prosaic boundaries of his subdued style: "The Citizens of America, placed in the most enviable condition, as the sole Lords and Proprietors of a vast Tract of Continent, comprehending all the various soils and climates of the World, and abounding with all the necessaries and conveniences of life, are now by the late satisfactory pacification, acknowledged to be possessed of absolute freedom and Independency; They are, from this period, to be considered as Actors on a most conspicuous Theatre, which seems to be peculiarly designated by Providence for the display of human greatness and felicity."[25]

The breathtaking sweep of this vision is remarkable. Washington had spent his young manhood fighting with the British to expel the French from North America. With the victory in the American Revolution, the English had then been expelled. The entire continent was now a vast American manor, within which the people could expand unrestricted by foreign opposition. (Presumably the Native Americans would be assimilated or conquered; and the Spanish west of the Mississippi, Spain being Spain, would serve as a mere holding company until the American population swept over them.) Within the leadership of the revolutionary generation, Washington was, if not unique, at least unusual, for never having traveled or lived in Europe. (His only foreign excursion was to Barbados as a young man.) His angle of vision for the new American nation was decidedly western. The chief task facing the next several generations was to consolidate control of the North American continent. Anything that impaired or deflected that central mission was to be avoided at all costs.

In the same Circular Letter, he laid down the obligations and opportunities implicit in his national vision, again in some of the most poetic language he ever wrote: "The foundation of our Empire was not laid in the gloomy age of Ignorance and Suspicion, but at an Epoch when the rights of mankind were better understood and more clearly defined, than at any former period." He then went on to specify the treasure trove of human knowledge that had accumulated over the past two centuries—it was about to be called the Enlightenment—and which constituted a kind of intellectual or philosophical equivalent of the nearly boundless natural resources waiting to be developed in the West. It was the fortuitous conjunction of these two vast reservoirs of philosophical and physical wealth that defined America's national interest and made it so special. "At this auspicious period," he wrote, "the United States came into existence as a Nation, and if their Citizens should not be completely free and happy, the fault will be intirely their own."[26]

The modern British philosopher Isaiah Berlin once described the different perspectives that political leaders bring to the management of world affairs as the difference between the hedgehog and the fox: The hedgehog knows one big thing and the fox knows many little things. Washington was an archetypal hedgehog. And the one big thing he knew was that America's future as a nation lay to the West, in its development over the next century of a continental empire. One of the reasons he devoted so much time and energy to planning the construction of canals, and shared in the misguided belief of his fellow Virginians that the Potomac constituted a direct link to the river system of the interior, was that he knew in his bones that the energy of the American people must flow in that direction. Europe might contain all the cultural capitals and current world powers, but in terms of America's national interest, it was a mere sideshow and distraction. The future lay in those forests he had explored as a young man. All this he understood intuitively by the time of his first retirement in 1783.[27]

GRAND VISIONS, even ones that prove as prescient as Washington's, must nevertheless negotiate the damnable particularities that history in the short run tosses up before history in the long run arrives to validate the vision. In Washington's case, the most obvious corollary to his view of American national interest was the avoidance of a major war during the gestative phase of national development. It so happened, however, that England and France were engaged in a century-old struggle for dominance of Europe and international supremacy, a struggle in which both the French and Indian War and the American Revolution were merely peripheral sideshows, and which would only end with

Napoleon's defeat at Waterloo in 1815. Washington's understanding of the proper American response to this global conflict was crystal clear: "I trust that we shall have too just a sense of our own interest to originate any cause that may involve us in it," he wrote in 1794, "and I ardently wish we may not be forced into it by the conduct of other nations. If we are permitted to improve without interruption, the great advantages which nature and circumstances have placed within our reach, many years will not revolve before we may be ranked not only among the most respectable, but among the happiest people on earth."[28]

The linchpin of his foreign policy as president, it followed naturally, was the Proclamation of Neutrality (1793), which declared America an impartial witness to the ongoing European conflict. His constant refrain throughout his presidency emphasized the same point, even offering an estimate of the likely duration of America's self-imposed alienation from global politics: "Every true friend to this Country must see and feel that the policy of it is not to embroil ourselves with any nation whatsoever; but to avoid their disputes and politics; and if they will harass one another, to avail ourselves of the neutral conduct we have adopted. Twenty years peace with such an increase of population and resources as we have a right to expect; added to our remote situation from the jarring powers, will in all probability enable us in a just cause to bid defiance to any power on earth." In a sense, it was a fresh application of the same strategic lesson he had learned as head of the Continental Army—namely, to avoid engagement with a superior force until the passage of time made victory possible, what we might call "the strategy of enlightened procrastination." In retrospect, and with all the advantages of hindsight, Washington's strategic insights as president were every bit as foresighted as his strategic insights as commander in chief during the American Revolution, right down to his timing estimate of "twenty years," which pretty much predicted the outbreak of the War of 1812.[29]

Since Washington's seminal insight was also the core piece of foreign policy wisdom offered in the Farewell Address, and since every major American statesman of the era also embraced the principle of neutrality as an obvious maxim, the meaning of the Farewell Address would seem to be incontrovertible, its message beyond controversy. But that was not at all how the message was heard at the time; in part because there was a deep division within the revolutionary generation that Washington was trying to straddle over just what a policy of American neutrality should look like; and in part because there was an alternative vision of the national interest circulating in the higher reaches of the political leadership, another opinion about where history was headed that could also make potent claims on the legacy of the American Revolution. All this had come to a head in Washington's second term in the debate over Jay's Treaty, creating the greatest crisis of Washington's presidency, the most virulent criticism of his monarchical tendencies, and the immediate context for every word he wrote in the Farewell Address.[30]

Jay's Treaty was a landmark in the shaping of American foreign policy. In 1794, Washington had sent Chief Justice John Jay to London to negotiate a realistic bargain that avoided a war with England at a time when the United States was ill prepared to fight one. Jay returned in 1795 with a treaty that accepted the fact of English naval and commercial supremacy and implicitly endorsed a pro-English version of American neutrality. It recognized England's right to retain tariffs on American exports while granting English imports most-favored status in the United States; it implicitly accepted English impressment of American sailors. It also committed the United States to compensate English creditors for outstanding pre-revolutionary debts, most of which were owed by Virginia's planters. In return for these concessions, the English agreed to submit claims by American merchants for confiscated cargoes to arbitration and to abide by the promise made in the Treaty of Paris (1783) to evacuate its troops from their posts on the western frontiers. In effect, Jay's Treaty was a repudiation of the Franco-American alliance of 1778, which had been so instrumental in gaining French military assistance for the winning of the American Revolution.[31]

While the specific terms of the treaty were decidedly one-sided in England's favor, the consensus reached by most historians who have studied the subject is that Jay's Treaty was a shrewd bargain for the United States. It bet, in effect, on England rather than France as the hegemonic European power of the future, which proved prophetic. It recognized the massive dependence of the American economy on trade with England. In a sense, it was a precocious preview of the Monroe Doctrine (1823), for it linked American security and economic development to the British fleet, which provided a protective shield of incalculable value throughout the nineteenth century. Mostly, it postponed war with England until America was economically and politically more capable of fighting one.

The long-term advantages of Jay's Treaty, however, were wholly invisible to most Americans in the crucible of the moment. Sensing the unpopularity of the pact, Washington attempted to keep its terms secret until the Senate had voted. But word leaked out in the summer of 1795 and then spread, as Madison put it, "like an electric velocity to every part of the Union." Jay later claimed that the entire eastern seaboard was illuminated each evening by protesters burning him in effigy. In New York Hamilton was struck in the head by a rock while attempting to defend the treaty to a crowd. John Adams recalled that Washington's house in Philadelphia was "surrounded by an innumerable multitude, from day to day buzzing, demanding war against England, cursing Washington, and crying success to the French patriots and virtuous Republicans." Any concession to British economic and military power, no matter how strategically astute, seemed a betrayal of the very independence won in the Revolution. Washington predicted that after a few months of contemplation, "when passion shall have yielded to sober reason, the current may possibly turn," but in the meantime "this government, in relation to France and England, may be compared to a ship between the rocks of Sylla and Charybdis."[32]

To make matters worse, the debate over the treaty prompted a constitutional crisis. Perhaps the most graphic illustration of the singular status that Washington enjoyed was the decision of the Constitutional Convention to deposit the minutes of its secret deliberations with him for safekeeping. He therefore had exclusive access to the official record of the convention and used it to argue that the clear intent of the framers was to vest the treaty-making power with the executive branch, subject to the advice and consent of two-thirds of the Senate. Madison, however, had kept his own extensive "Notes on the Debates at the Constitutional Convention" and carried them down to share with Jefferson, who was in retirement at Monticello.

Although a careful reading of Madison's "Notes on the Debates" revealed that Washington was correct, and indeed that Madison himself had been one of the staunchest opponents of infringements on executive power over foreign policy at the Convention, Jefferson managed to conclude that the House was intended to be an equal partner in approving all treaties, going so far as to claim that that body was the sovereign branch of the government empowered to veto any treaty it wished, thereby "annihilating the whole treaty making power" of the executive branch. "I trust the popular branch of our legislature will disapprove of it," Jefferson wrote from Monticello, "and thus rid us of this infamous act, which is really nothing more than a treaty of alliance between England and the Anglomen of this country against the legislatures and people of the United States."[33]

The actual debate in the House in the fall and winter of 1795 proceeded under Madison's more cautious leadership and narrower interpretation of the Constitution. (Jefferson's position would have re-created the hapless and hamstrung conditions that he himself had decried while serving as minister to France under the Articles of Confederation, essentially holding American foreign policy hostage to congressional gridlock and the divisive forces of domestic politics.) Madison instead argued that the implementation of Jay's Treaty required the approval of the House for all provisions dependent on funding. This achieved the desired result, blocking the treaty, while avoiding a frontal assault on executive power.[34]

Madison served as the floor leader of the opposition in the House during the debate that raged throughout the winter and spring of 1796. At the start, he enjoyed an overwhelming majority and regarded his position as impregnable. But as the weeks rolled on, he experienced firsthand the cardinal principle of American politics in the 1790s: whoever went face-to-face against Washington was destined to lose. The majority started to melt away in March. John Adams observed bemusedly that "Mr. Madison looks worried to death. Pale, withered, haggard." When the decisive vote came in April, Madison attributed his defeat to "the exertions and influence of Aristocracy, Anglicism, and mercantilism" led by "the Banks, the British Merchts., the insurance Comps." Jefferson was more candid. Jay's Treaty had passed, he concluded, because of the gigantic prestige of Washington, "the one man who outweighs them all in influence over the people." Jefferson's sense of frustration had reached its breaking point a few weeks earlier when, writing to Madison, he quoted a famous line from Washington's favorite play, Joseph Addison's *Cato,* and applied it to Washington himself: "a curse on his virtues, they've undone his country."[35]

WHAT COULD Jefferson's extreme reaction possibly mean? After all, from our modern perspective Washington's executive leadership throughout the debate over Jay's Treaty was nothing less than we would expect from a strong president, whose authority to shape foreign policy is taken for granted. We also know the course he was attempting to steer, a middle passage between England and France that required tacking back and forth to preserve American neutrality and avoid war, turned out to be the correct policy. But in this instance, hindsight does not make us clairvoyant so much as blind to the ghosts and goblins that floated above the political landscape in the 1790s. What we might describe as admirably strong executive leadership struck Jefferson and his Republican followers as the arbitrary maneuverings of a monarch. And what appears in retrospect like a prudent and farsighted vision of the national interest looked to Jefferson like a betrayal of the American Revolution.

For Jefferson also had a national vision and a firm conviction about where American history was headed, or at least where it ought to be headed. The future he felt in his bones told him that the true spirit of '76, most eloquently expressed in the language he had drafted for the Declaration of Independence, was a radical break with the past and with all previous versions of political authority. Like Voltaire, Jefferson longed for the day when the last king would be strangled with the entrails of the last priest. The political landscape he saw in his mind's eye was littered with the dead bodies of despots and corrupt courtiers, a horizon swept clean of all institutions capable of coercing American citizens from pursuing their happiness as they saw fit. Thomas Paine's *The Rights of Man* (1791) captured the essence of his vision more fully than any other book of the age, depicting as it did a radical transformation of society once the last vestiges of feudalism were destroyed, and the emergence of a utopian world in which the essential discipline of government was internalized within the citizenry. The only legitimate form of government, in the end, was self-government.[36]

Shortly after his return to the United States in 1790, Jefferson began to harbor the foreboding sense that the American Revolution, as he understood it, had been captured by alien forces. As we have seen, the chief villain and core counterrevolutionary character in the Jeffersonian drama was Alexander Hamilton, and the most worrisome feature on the political landscape was Hamilton's financial scheme, with its presumption of a consolidated federal government possessing many of the powers over the states that Parliament had exercised over the colonies. Under Hamilton's diabolical leadership, the United States seemed to be re-creating the very political and economic institutions—the national bank became the most visible symbol of the accumulating corruption—that the Revolution had been designed to destroy. Jefferson developed a full-blooded conspiracy theory in which bankers, speculators, federal officeholders, and a small but powerful congregation of closet Tories permanently alienated from the agrarian majority ("They all live in cities," he wrote) had captured the meaning of the Revolution and were now proceeding to strangle it to death behind the closed doors of investment houses and within the faraway corridors of the Federalist government in New York and Philadelphia.[37]

Exactly where Washington fit in this horrific picture is difficult to determine. After all, he presumably knew something about the meaning and purpose of the Revolution, having done more than any man to assure its success. (As Jefferson's critics were quick to observe, the man ensconced at Monticello had never fired a shot in anger throughout the war.) Initially, Jefferson simply refused to assign Washington any culpability for the Federalist conspiracy, somehow suggesting that the person at the very center of the government was wholly oblivious to the schemes swirling around him. At some unspoken level of understanding Jefferson recognized that Washington was the American untouchable, and that any effort to include him in the indictment immediately placed his entire case against the Federalists on the permanent defensive.

Jefferson's posture toward Washington shifted perceptibly in 1794. The catalyst for the change was the Whiskey Rebellion, a popular insurgency in four counties of western Pennsylvania protesting an excise tax on whiskey. Washington viewed the uprising as a direct threat to the authority of the federal government and called out the militia, a massive thirteen-thousand-man army, to squelch the uprising. Jefferson regarded the entire affair as a shameful repetition of the

Shays's Rebellion fiasco nearly a decade earlier, in which a healthy and essentially harmless expression of popular discontent by American farmers, so he thought, had prompted an excessive and unnecessary military response. While his first instinct was to blame Hamilton for the whole sorry mess, Washington's speech justifying the action could not be so easily dismissed.[38]

Jefferson denounced Washington's speech as "shreds of stuff from Aesop's fables and Tom Thumb." In Jefferson's new version of the Federalist conspiracy, Washington was an unknowing and somewhat pathetic accomplice, like an overaged "captain in his cabin" who was sound asleep while "a rogue of a pilot [presumably Hamilton] has run them into an enemy's port." Washington was certainly the grand old man of the American Revolution, but his grandeur had now been eclipsed by his age, providing the Hamiltonians with "the sanction of a name which has done too much good not to be sufficient to cover harm also." Washington simply did not have control of the government and was inadvertently lending credibility to the treacheries being hatched all around him. Washington, in effect, was senile.[39]

While hardly true, this explanation had the demonstrable advantage of permitting Jefferson's vision of a Federalist conspiracy to congeal in a plausible pattern that formed around Washington without touching him directly. Jefferson was also careful never to utter any of his criticisms of Washington in public. But in his private correspondence with trusted Republicans, he developed the image of an old soldier past his prime, reading speeches he did not write and could not comprehend, lingering precariously in the misty edges of incompetence, a hollow hulk of his former greatness. The most famous letter in this mode— famous because it eventually found its way into the newspapers against Jefferson's will—was prompted by the passage of Jay's Treaty. "It would give you a fever," Jefferson wrote to his Italian friend Phillip Mazzei, "were I to name to you the apostates who have gone over to these heresies, men who were Samsons in the field and Solomons in the council, but who have had their heads shorn by the harlot of England." Since there was only one person who could possibly merit the mantle of America's Samson and Solomon, Jefferson's customary sense of discretion allowed him to make his point without mentioning the name. But everybody knew.[40]

One final and all-important piece of the Jeffersonian vision transcended the troubling particularities of domestic politics altogether. As Jefferson saw it, the American Revolution had been merely the opening shot in a global struggle against tyranny that was destined to sweep over the world. "This ball of liberty, I believe most piously," he predicted, "is now so well in motion that it will roll around the globe." Whereas Washington regarded the national interest as a discrete product of political and economic circumstances shaping the policies of each nation-state at a specific moment in history, Jefferson envisioned a much larger global pattern of ideological conflict in which all nations were aligned for or against the principles that America had announced to the world in 1776. The same moralistic dichotomy that Jefferson saw inside the United States between discernible heroes and villains, he also projected into the international arena. For Jefferson, all specific decisions about American foreign policy occurred within the context of this overarching, indeed almost cosmic, pattern.[41]

Therefore, while Jefferson could talk with genuine conviction about American neutrality and the need to remain free of European entanglements, thereby sounding much like Washington, his version of American neutrality was decidedly different. He did not view the clash between England and France for supremacy in Europe as a distant struggle far removed from America's long-term national interest. Instead, he saw the French Revolution as the European continuation of the spirit of '76. He acknowledged that the random violence and careening course of the French Revolution were lamentable developments, but he insisted they were merely a passing chapter in the larger story of triumphant global revolution. "I am convinced they [the French] will triumph completely," he wrote in 1794, "& the consequent disgrace of the invading tyrants is destined, in the order of events, to kindle the wrath of the people of Europe against those who have dared to embroil them in such wickedness, and to bring at length, kings, nobles & priests to the scaffolds which they have been so long deluging with blood." In one moment of revolutionary euphoria, he dismissed all critics of mass executions in France as blind to the historic issues at stake: "The liberty of the whole earth was depending on the issue of that contest," he observed in 1793, "and was ever such a prize won with so little blood? My own affections have been deeply wounded by some of the martyrs to this cause, but rather than it should have failed I would rather have seen half the earth desolated. Were there but an Adam and Eve left in every country, and left free, it would be better than it is now."[42]

If France was the revolutionary hero in this international drama, England was the counterrevolutionary villain. Jefferson's highly moralistic language castigating George III and the English government in the Declaration of Independence was not just propaganda, at least for Jefferson. It reflected his genuine conviction that England was an inherently corrupt society, the bastion of monarchical power, aristocratic privilege, and courtly intrigue. Since Washington had spent eight years sending American soldiers to their death in battle against Great Britain, one might expect that he harbored even more hostile opinions toward his former adversary. But he did not. Jefferson's Anglophobia was more virulent in part because it was more theoretical, a moral conclusion that followed naturally from the moralistic categories he carried around in his head. (If he wanted to stigmatize a political opponent, the worst name he could call him was "Angloman.") For Jefferson, France represented the brightest future prospects; England represented "the dead hand of the past." At the nub of his opposition to Jay's Treaty, then, was his utter certainty that it threw the weight of the United States onto the wrong side of history. "The Anglomen have in the end got their treaty through," he observed from his mountaintop in 1796, "and so far have triumphed over the cause of republicanism." But their victory, painful as it was to witness, had also exposed their vulnerability. For it was now quite obvious "that nothing can support them but the Colossus of the President's merits with the people, and the moment he retires, that his successor, if a Monocrat, will be overborne by the republican sense. . . . In the meantime, patience."[43]

Just a few weeks before he wrote these words, Jefferson had felt the urge to assure Washington that, contrary to the gossip circulating in the corridors and byways of Philadelphia, he was not responsible for the various rumors describing the president as a quasi-senile front man for the Federalist conspiracy against the vast majority of the American people. The historical record makes it perfectly clear, to be sure, that Jefferson *was* orchestrating the campaign of vilification, which had its chief base of operations in Virginia and its headquarters at Monticello. But Jefferson was the kind of man who could have passed a lie-detector test confirming his integrity, believing as he did that the supreme significance of his larger cause rendered conventional distinctions between truth and falsehood superfluous.

Washington's response was designed to let Jefferson know that his professed innocence itself sounded like the defensive comments of a guilty man, and that Washington already knew a good deal more than Jefferson realized about who was whispering what behind his back. "If I had entertained any suspicious before," wrote Washington, "the assurances you have given me of the contrary would have removed them; but the truth is, I harboured none." (Translation: Your protests confirm my suspicions.) Then Washington parted the curtain covering his soul just enough to show Jefferson a glimpse of what he truly felt: "As you have mentioned the subject yourself, it would not be frank, candid or friendly to conceal that your conduct has been represented as derogatory from the opinion I had conceived you entertained to me." (Translation: I am onto your game.) "That to your particular friends and connexions you have described, and they have described me, as a person under a dangerous influence." (Translation: My sources are impeccable.) "My answer has invariably been that I had never discovered any thing in the conduct of Mr. Jefferson to raise suspicions in my mind of his insincerity." (Translation: I have not done unto others what they have been doing unto me.)

Washington concluded with an impassioned defense of his support for Jay's Treaty: "I was using my utmost exertions to establish a national character of our own, independent, as far as our obligations and justice would permit, of every nation of the earth." But somehow he had "been accused of being the enemy of one Nation [France], and subject to the influence of another [England]; and to prove it, that every act of my administration should be tortured, and the most insidious misrepresentations of them be made (by giving one side only of a subject, and that too in such exaggerated and indecent terms as could scarcely be applied to a Nero, a notorious defaulter; or even to a common pickpocket.) But enough of this; I have already gone farther in the expression of my feelings than I intended." (Translation: Even this mere glimpse into my soul is more than you deserve, my former friend.)

For the next year, Jefferson attempted to sustain at least the veneer of a friendship with Washington by writing him letters in the Virginia gentleman mode, avoiding politics and foreign policy altogether, focusing instead on his crop-rotation scheme at Monticello, the vagaries of the weather, his vetch and wheat crop, and—a rather potent metaphor—the best way to spread manure. Washington responded in kind—that is, until the newspapers printed Jefferson's old letter to Phillip Mazzei (the one about America's degenerate Samson and Solomon). Then all communication from Mount Vernon to Monticello ceased forever.[44]

Beyond the purely personal dimensions of their estrangement, beyond Washington's sense of betrayal and Jefferson's artful minuet with duplicity, this episode provides an invaluable clue to the larger and more impersonal political concerns that were on Washington's mind when he sat down to compose the Farewell Address. They went far past the loss of Jefferson's friendship, important though it was, because Jefferson's behavior was symptomatic of more than a betrayal of trust; it accurately reflected a fundamental division within the revolutionary generation over the meaning of the Revolution and the different versions of America's abiding national interest that followed naturally from that disagreement. The words that were used at the time, or the words employed by historians later to capture the essence of the argument, are mere labels: Federalists versus Republicans; pro-English versus pro-French versions of American neutrality. Underlying the debate that surfaced in full-blown fashion over Jay's Treaty lurked a classic confrontation between those who wished America's revolutionary energies to be harnessed to the larger purposes of nation-building and those who interpreted that very process as a betrayal of the Revolution itself.

From Washington's perspective, the republic established by the Constitution created a government of laws that must be obeyed once the duly elected representatives had reached a decision. That was why he had acted so decisively to put down the Whiskey Rebellion and why he expected compliance with Jay's Treaty once its terms were approved by the Congress. From Jefferson's perspective, on the other hand, all laws and treaties that reined in the liberating impulses of the Revolution were illegitimate. That was why he regarded the suppression of the Whiskey Rebellion as reprehensible. Were not these Pennsylvania farmers protesting taxes to which they did not consent? As for Jay's Treaty, who in his right mind would countenance the acceptance of neocolonial status within the hated British Empire? Not obeying, but rather violating such unjust laws and treaties was the obligation of every citizen. Was this not the higher law that Americans should follow, arm in arm again with their trusted French brethren? In this formulation, political behavior that was, strictly speaking, traitorous and treasonable was, in fact, the only course that enjoyed the sanction of America's most hallowed revolutionary principles.

Perhaps the most extreme example of this Republican mentality in action was James Monroe, a zealous Jefferson protégé currently serving as the minister to France. Though not in Jefferson's league as a thinker or political strategist, Monroe more than made up for these deficiencies by embracing the core articles of the Republican faith with near-total abandon. He assured his French hosts that Jay's Treaty would never be approved by the Congress, that the vast majority of the American people were eager to join France in war with England, that the U.S. government stood ready to advance France a $5 million loan to subsidize its military expenses and that, when none of these wild predictions materialized, the French government should patiently but firmly disregard all messages from the American president, since he obviously spoke for the aristocratic Anglomen and would soon be hurled from office by the people. In the meantime, the French should feel perfectly free to retaliate against American ships on the high seas. When they began to do so in the spring of 1796 and the first prize confiscated was a ship named the *Mount Vernon,* Monroe thought it was a providential version of poetic justice. And by the way, he hoped that Benjamin Franklin Bache at the *Aurora* would see fit to publish, under a pseudonym of course, some of his confidential communiqués from Paris protesting the most outrageous provisions of Jay's Treaty. All this from America's official emissary to the French government.[45]

A slightly less extreme but infinitely more befuddled example of the same mentality had surfaced inside Washington's cabinet at the very moment he was making the decision to send Jay's Treaty to the Senate in August of 1795. The successor to Jefferson as secretary of state was Edmund Randolph, like Monroe a second-tier member of the Virginia dynasty, whose principal recommendation for the job was an unblinking loyalty to Washington, but whose chief political habit was to blink incessantly at any decision that demanded clear convictions of his own. Poor Randolph, an otherwise-decent man who was clearly in over his head, had granted an interview with the outgoing French minister to the United States, Joseph Fauchet, who had then transcribed the high points of the conversation in a dispatch that was subsequently intercepted at sea by a British cruiser. The British were only too willing to forward the dispatch to the American government. The day after Washington read it out loud to the full cabinet, Randolph submitted his resignation.[46]

What the Fauchet dispatch claimed and what we know on the basis of subsequent scholarship are not synonymous. According to Fauchet, Randolph requested a bribe as part of some mysterious scheme in support of the Whiskey Rebellion. Although Randolph was almost certainly innocent of this charge, the whole tenor and tone of Fauchet's account revealed Randolph confiding his personal opposition to the entire domestic and foreign policy of the Washington administration, lamenting the ascendance of a "financiering class" that aimed at the restitution of monarchy, decrying the enslavement of American trade to "the audacity of England," depicting Randolph himself as the sole voice of "the patriotic party" within the government and the last hope for bringing a sadly dazed and thoroughly confused President Washington to his senses. Randolph's unfortunate utterances were not truly treasonable, as he spent the remainder of his life trying vainly and in his foggy style to explain. In truth, he had simply allowed himself to get caught engaging in the same talk that Jefferson was conveying to friends and Monroe was sputtering out loud to anyone in Paris who would listen. The notion that a diabolical conspiracy of moneymen and monarchists had seized control of the federal government under Washington's very nose was so widespread within Virginia's political elite that they had lost all perspective on how conspiratorial their own words sounded to those denied the vision.[47]

And so when Washington sat down to draft his Farewell Address, three salient features rose up out of the immediate political terrain to command his attention: First, he needed to demonstrate that, while poised for retirement, he was still very much in charge, that those rumors of creeping senility and routinized ineptitude were demonstrably wrong; second, he wanted to carve out a middle course, and do so in a moderate tone, that together pushed his most ardent critics to the fringes of the ongoing debate, where their shrill accusations, loaded language, and throbbing moral certainty could languish in the obscurity they deserved; third, the all-time master of exits wanted to make his final departure from the public stage the occasion for explaining his own version of what the American Revolution meant. Above all, it meant hanging together as a united people, much as the Continental Army had hung together once before, so that those who were making foreign policy into a divisive device in domestic politics, all in the name of America's revolutionary principles, were themselves inadvertently subverting the very cause they claimed to champion. He was stepping forward into the battle one final time, planting his standard squarely in the center of the field, inviting the troops to rally around him rather than wander off in romantic cavalry charges at the periphery, assuring them by his example that, if they could only hold the position he defined, they would again prevail.

THE MANNER in which the Farewell Address was actually composed, as it turned out, served as a nearly perfect illustration of its central message—the need to subordinate narrow interests to the larger cause. Much ink has been spilled by several generations of scholars in an effort to determine who wrote the bulk of the words that eventually found their way into print and then into the history books. Like a false scent, the authorship question has propelled historians down labyrinthine trails of evidence in quest of the real and true author. Meanwhile, the object of the hunt sits squarely in the middle of the evidentiary trail, so obvious that it is ignored. Namely, the creation of the Farewell Address was an inherently collaborative process. Some of the words were Madison's; most of the words were Hamilton's; all the ideas were Washington's. The drafting and editing of the Farewell Address in effect became a metaphor for the kind of collective effort Washington was urging on the American people as a whole.[48]

The story had its start four years earlier, in May of 1792, when Washington approached Madison to help him compose a valedictory address. At the time fully convinced that he would step down after one term, Washington had chosen Madison because his two most trusted cabinet members, Hamilton and Jefferson, were too closely associated with the party disputes he wanted to condemn. Madison made extensive notes on the basis of three conversations with Washington, then drafted a document that employed the president's own language for many key passages: "a spirit of party in the Government was becoming a fresh source of difficulty"; "we are all Children of the same Country"; the nation's "essential interests are the same . . . its diversities arising from climate and from soil will naturally form a mutual relation of parts" and serve as the formulation for "an affectionate and permanent Union." It was Madison who first proposed that the Farewell Address not be delivered as a speech to Congress, but that it be printed in the newspapers as "a direct address to the people who are your only constituents." After Washington listened to the unanimous advice of all his cabinet officers and reluctantly agreed to serve a second term, he tucked away Madison's draft for another day.[49]

That day arrived exactly four years later. On May 15, 1796, Washington sent Hamilton the "first draft" of a retirement address—no amount of persuasion could change his mind this time—that would announce his departure from public life. The first section of this document reproduced Madison's draft of 1792, which was highly ironic, because Madison had become the primary leader of the Republican opposition to Washington's policies in the Congress and was therefore a rather dramatic example of the party spirit that his former words had warned against. (The Federalists referred to Madison as "the general" of the opposition, calling Jefferson, his mentor secluded at Monticello, "the generalissimo.") Washington included the earlier Madison draft for two reasons: First, it expressed in clear and forceful language a major point he still wanted to make about subordinating sectional and ideological differences to larger national purposes, all the more resonant because drafted by someone who seemed to have forgotten the lesson; and second, its inclusion publicized the fact that he had wanted to retire four years ago, so his current decision was really the culmination of a long-standing preference.[50]

This latter point was extremely important to Washington. His most virulent critics were currently claiming that his support for the unpopular Jay's Treaty made him unelectable in 1796, so his decision to retire was not truly a voluntary act, but a forced recognition of the political realities. Hamilton tried to reassure him that his sensitivities on this score were excessive, that if he did choose to run for a third term, he would win in a walk. (And Hamilton was surely correct.) But Washington wanted not a shred of doubt to remain that his decision to step aside was wholly voluntary. This was both a matter of personal pride and a crucial political precedent. By including the Madison draft of 1792, he advertised his reluctance to serve even his second term, thereby enhancing the credibility of his voluntary rejection of a third. As Washington put it, "it may contribute to blunt, if it does not turn aside, some of the shafts . . . among which—conviction of fallen popularity, and despair of being re-elected, [which] will be levelled at me with dexterity & keenness."[51]

The second section of this first draft that Washington sent to Hamilton focused on the foreign policy issues that had dominated his second term. He was fully aware that Hamilton had supported Jay's Treaty. (He had even recommended that Hamilton consult Jay before putting pen to paper.) But he also wanted Hamilton to know that none of his or Jay's pro-English prejudices should seep into his draft of the document; it should emphasize American neutrality and "promote the true and permanent interests of the country." Washington's views, not Hamilton's, must prevail. Hamilton would be the draftsman, but Washington must be the author. "I am anxious, always, to compare the opinions of those in whom I confide with one another," Washington explained, "and these again (without being bound by them) with my own, that I may extract all the good I can." Hamilton required no elaborate instructions on the procedure. It was the same process Washington had developed with his staff as commander in chief of the Continental Army, then implemented with his cabinet as president. Hamilton had played the same role in both contexts. All major decisions were collective occasions, in which advisers, like spokes on a wheel, made contributions, usually in written form. But in the end the final decision, to include the final choice of words, came together at the center, which was always Washington.[52]

Hamilton also realized that he was being asked to write for posterity as much as the present. "It has been my object to render this act importantly and lastingly useful," he confided to Washington, "and avoid all just cause of present exception, to embrace such reflections and sentiments as will wear well, progress in approbation with time & redound to future reputation." He devoted a full two months to revising Washington's draft, amplifying Madison's earlier account of the need to rise above party differences and rally behind the elected representatives of the national government.[53]

On July 30, he sent the fruits of his labors to Washington, who found the Hamilton draft "exceedingly just, & just such as ought to be inculcated." His only reservation related to length: "All the columns of a large Gazette would scarcely, I conceive, contain the present draft," Washington noted, adding at the end, "I may be mistaken." (He was.) Hamilton was less sure he had done the best job possible and immediately began work on a wholly new draft, which he submitted to Washington two weeks later. But Washington liked the earlier draft better.[54]

Over the next month, edited versions of that draft passed back and forth several times, with Washington pressing Hamilton for clarifications, deleting certain passages, adding others: "I shall expunge all that is marked in the paper as unimportant," he wrote on August 25, "and as you perceive some marginal notes, written with a pencil, I pray you to give the sentiments mature consideration." If Hamilton saw fit to make additional revisions on his own, he should "let them be so clearly interlined-erased-or referred to in the margins that no mistake may happen." Washington wanted no last-minute changes smuggled in without his approval. Even when the final draft was ready for the printer in September, he made changes in 174 out of 1,086 lines in his own hand and reviewed the punctuation throughout—a final scan, so the printer observed firsthand, "in which he was very minute." It seems fair to conclude that what we call "Washington's Farewell Address" is not misnamed.[55]

What was Hamilton's contribution? Chiefly to assure that the elaboration of Washington's ideas occurred within a rhetorical framework that maintained a stately and dignified tone throughout, and to sustain a palpable cogency and sense of proportion in developing Washington's argument, which itself embodied the self-assurance so central to his major theme about the nation itself. Hamilton had nearly perfect pitch for Washington's language, having begun his public career drafting letters and memoranda for Washington's signature as a staff officer during the war. He was therefore well practiced in subordinating his own inclinations and style to Washington's larger purposes. In the Farewell Address, the result is nearly seamless. When combined with the collaborative character of the drafting process, it becomes virtually impossible to tell where one voice ends and another begins.

But Hamilton was also such a virtuoso performer in his own right, unmatched within the revolutionary generation for his capacity to deliver powerful prose on a tight deadline, that there are moments in the Farewell Address when his own distinctive voice breaks through.

For example, while Washington agreed with Hamilton's version of what the constitutional settlement of 1787–1788 meant, only Hamilton could have put it this way:

> This government, the offspring of our own choice uninfluenced and unawed, adopted upon full investigation and mature deliberation, completely free in its principles, in the distribution of its powers, uniting security with energy, and containing within itself a provision for its own amendment, has a just claim to your confidence and support. . . . The very idea of the power and right of the People to establish Government presupposes the duty of every Individual to obey the established Government.[56]

Or on the question of America's national interest and the foreign policy it dictated, again the idea is pure Washington, but expressed in language that flowed in Hamiltonian cadences:

> The Great role of conduct for us, in regard to foreign nations is in extending our commercial relations to have with them as little political connection as possible. . . . Europe has a set of primary interests, which to us have none, or a very remote relation. Hence she must be engaged in frequent controversies, the causes of which are essentially foreign to our concerns. . . . 'Tis our true policy to steer clear of permanent Alliances, with any portion of the foreign world. . . . 'Tis folly for one Nation to look for disinterested favors from another. . . . There can be no greater error than to expect, or calculate upon real favours from Nation to Nation. 'Tis an illusion which experience must cure, which a just pride ought to discard.[57]

When Hamilton showed a late draft of this passage to John Jay for his commentary, Jay expressed admiration for the style but slight discomfort with the argument. "It occurs to me," he wrote to Washington, "that it may not be perfectly prudent to say that we can never expect Favors from a nation, for that assertion seems to imply that nations always are, or always ought to be moved only by interested motives." Jay's suggestion came too late—the Farewell Address was already in the hands of the printer—but would have made no difference. Washington meant exactly what Hamilton had said. Jay's views of prospective

English beneficence, like Jefferson's views of French solidarity with America, were only seductive pieces of sentimentality, juvenile illusions in the real world of international relations.[58]

Beyond the tight cogency and felicitous cadences, Hamilton's major contribution was to save Washington from his own personal sentiments. In his May draft, Washington had included the following paragraph near the start:

> I did not seek the office with which you have honored me . . . [and now possess] the grey hairs of a man who has, excepting the interval between the close of the Revolutionary War, and the organization of the new government—either in a civil, or military character, spent five and forty years—All the prime of his life—in serving his country; [may he] be suffered to pass quietly to the grave—and that his errors, however numerous; if they are not criminal, may be consigned to the Tomb of oblivion, as he himself will soon be to the Mansion of Retirement.[59]

Hamilton eliminated the references to "grey hairs," "prime of his life," and "errors, however numerous"; he also altered the wounded tone of the passage by placing it at the end rather than at the beginning of the Farewell Address, where it seemed less like a somewhat pathetic *cri de coeur* than a dignified personal testimonial. Washington recognized the improvement, congratulating Hamilton for rendering him "with less egotism," meaning the Hamilton draft covered the wounds, or at least prevented the president from displaying them too conspicuously.[60]

HAMILTON'S exquisite sense of affinity for Washington's mentality failed him only once, though the failure, and therefore what is in effect the missing section of the Farewell Address, opens a more expansive window into the national vision that Washington was trying to project. During the drafting process in the summer of 1796, Washington kept urging Hamilton to insert a separate section on the creation of a national university in the capital city now being constructed on the Potomac. Hamilton resisted the recommendation, arguing quite plausibly that such a specific proposal was inappropriate for an address designed to operate at a higher altitude. It was, he suggested, the kind of proposal better made in the final message to Congress in the fall. But Washington kept insisting that he wanted the idea to be a featured element in the Farewell Address: "But to be candid," he explained, "I much question whether a recommendation of this measure to the Legislature will have a better effect now than formerly—It may skew indeed my sense of its importance, and that it is a sufficient inducement with me to bring the matter before the public in some shape or another, at the closing Scenes of my political exit . . . to set the People ruminating on the importance of the measure."[61]

Hamilton eventually relented, though only grudgingly. At the last moment, he inserted a brief two-sentence paragraph rather awkwardly near the middle of the Farewell Address, calling for "Institutions for the general diffusion of knowledge" and urging quite harmlessly that "public opinion should be enlightened." Washington was not satisfied with the result but decided to let the matter drop. In so doing, however, he let Hamilton know that something was being lost, that his hopes for a national university linked up to something larger: "In the general Juvenal period of life, when friendships are formed, & habits established that will stick by one," he explained, "the Youth, or young men from different parts of the United States would be assembled together, & would by degrees discover that there was not just cause for those jealousies & prejudices which one part of the Union had imbibed against another part. . . . What, but the mixing of people from different parts of the United States during the War rubbed off these impressions? A Century in the ordinary intercourse, would not have accomplished what the Seven years association in Arms did."[62]

Here was a characteristically Washingtonian insight—rooted in his experience during the war years; simultaneously simple but essential; projecting developments into the future on the basis of patterns that were still congealing and that only now, in retrospect, seem so obvious. Like his misguided obsession with those Potomac canals, his campaign for a national university in the capital city never bore fruit. But both failed projects were also visionary projections linked to larger expectations. In the case of the national university, it was the recognition that the United States was still very much a nation in the making because its population was still a people in the making. Time, indeed a considerable stretch of time, would be required to allow the bonding together of this large, widely dispersed, and diverse population. But institutions devoted to focusing the national purposes, again like the Continental Army during the war, could accelerate time and move America past that vulnerable and problematic phase of its development when fragmentation, perhaps civil war, was still a distinct possibility.

Throughout the Farewell Address Washington had been exhorting Americans to think of themselves as a collective unit with a common destiny. To our ears, it sounds so obvious because we occupy the future location that Washington envisioned. But his exhortations toward national unity were less descriptions than anticipations, less reminders of the way we were than predictions of what we could become. Indeed, the act of exhorting was designed to enhance the prospect by talking about it as if it were a foregone conclusion, which Washington most assuredly knew it was not. In the end, the Farewell Address was primarily a great prophecy, accompanied by advice about how to make it come true.

It was also, at least implicitly, a justification for the strong executive leadership Washington had provided in the 1790s and that his critics had stigmatized as a monarchy. Without a republican king at the start, he was saying, the new quasi nation called the United States would never have enjoyed the opportunity to achieve its long-run destiny; it would have expired in the short run. In a sense, Washington was defending his presidency as an essential exception to full-blooded republican principles. Down the road, when the common experience of conquering the continent and the sheer passage of time had bound the American people together into a more cohesive whole, the more voluntaristic habits at the core of republican mentality could express themselves fully. For now, however, the center needed to hold. That meant a vigorous federal government with sufficient powers to coerce the citizenry to pay taxes and obey the laws. Veterans of the Continental Army, like Hamilton and John Marshall, fully understood this essential point. Intriguingly, the two chieftains of the Republican opposition, Jefferson and Madison, had never served in the army. They obviously did not understand.

How could this emerging nation manage its way through this first post-Washington phase of its development? In the Farewell Address Washington offered his general answer: Think of yourself as a single nation; subordinate your regional and political differences to your common identity as Americans; regard the federal government that represents your collective interest as an ally rather than an enemy (as "us," if you will, rather than "them"). In his eighth and final message to Congress, delivered the following December, Washington provided a more specific directive. His Republican critics had described Jay's Treaty as a pact with the devil that was certain to produce domestic and diplomatic catastrophe. Upon scanning the horizon for the last time, however, Washington saw serenity setting in: Treaties with the hostile Indian tribes on the southern and western frontiers were being negotiated; the British were removing their troops from posts in the West in accord with Jay's Treaty; thanks primarily to the resumption of trade with Great Britain, the American economy was humming along quite nicely, with revenues from the increased trade reducing the national debt faster than had been anticipated. The only dark spot on the political horizon was France, whose cruisers were intercepting American shipping in the West Indies. Washington counseled patience with what would soon be called this "quasi war" with the French Republic, predicting (correctly, as it turned out) that "a spirit of justice, candour and friendship . . . will eventually insure success." Confidence, he seemed to be saying, is a self-fulfilling prophecy, all the more so when the confidence was justified.[63]

Even more specifically, Washington suggested that his departure from the national scene would require the enlargement, not the diminution, of the powers of the federal government in order to compensate for his absence. He recommended that Congress undertake a whole new wave of federal initiatives: a new program to encourage domestic manufactures; a similar program to subsidize agricultural improvements; the creation of a national university (his old hobbyhorse) and a national military academy; an expanded navy to protect American shipping in the Mediterranean and the Caribbean; increased compensation for federal officials in order to ensure that public service was not dependent on private wealth. It was the most expansive presidential program for enlarged federal power until John Quincy Adams proposed a similar vision in his inaugural address of 1825. It was the tradition that the Whig party of Henry Clay and the Republican party of Abraham Lincoln sustained in the nineteenth century and that the Democratic party of Andrew Jackson rejected. In the more immediate context of 1796, Washington seemed to be saying that the departure of

America's only republican king necessitated the creation of centering forces institutionalized at the federal level to maintain the focusing functions he had performed personally.[64]

Finally, who were these American people being bonded together? If Washington wished the national government to be regarded as "us" rather than "them," how did he define the "us"? He addressed his remarks in the Farewell Address to his "Friends, and Fellow Citizens." While he undoubtedly thought this description cast a wide and inclusive net that pulled in residents from all the regions or sections of the United States, it did not include all inhabitants. The core of the audience he saw in his mind's eye consisted of those adult white males who owned sufficient property to qualify for the vote. Strictly speaking, such men were the only citizens. He told Hamilton that his Farewell Address was aimed especially at "the Yeomanry of the country," which meant ordinary farmers working small plots of land and living in households. This brought women and children into the picture, not as full-blooded citizens, to be sure, but as part of the American people whose political identity was subsumed within the family and conveyed by the male heads of household. They were secondary citizens, but unquestionably Americans. Landless rural residents and impoverished city dwellers lay outside the picture, though they—more likely, their descendants—could work their way into the American citizenry over time. If only potentially and prospectively, they were included.[65]

The largest unmentioned and presumably excluded constituency was the black population, about 90 percent of which was enslaved. Washington said nothing whatsoever about slavery in his Farewell Address, sustaining the silence that the Congress had adopted as its official posture early in his presidency. Silence, of course, can speak volumes, and in Washington's case, the unspoken message was that a moratorium had been declared on this most controversial topic, which more than any other issue possessed the potential to destroy the fragile union that he saw as his life's work and chief political legacy. Since the primary purpose of the Farewell Address was to affirm that legacy and foster the promotion of his national vision, the last thing Washington wanted to mention was the one subject that presented the most palpable threat to the entire enterprise. Like Madison in 1790, he wanted slavery off the American political agenda. Unlike Madison, however, and unlike most of his fellow Virginians, there is a reason to believe that he thought the moratorium on slavery as a political problem should lapse in 1808, when the Constitution permitted the slave trade to end.

His silence on the slavery question was strategic, believing as he did that slavery was a cancer on the body politic of America that could not at present be removed without killing the patient. The intriguing question is whether Washington could project an American future after slavery that included the African-American population as prospective members of the American citizenry. For almost all the leading members of the Virginia dynasty, the answer was clear and negative. Even those, like Jefferson and Madison, who looked forward to the eventual end of slavery, also presumed that all freed blacks must be transported elsewhere. Washington never endorsed that conclusion. Nor did he ever embrace the racial arguments for black inferiority that Jefferson advanced in *Notes on the State of Virginia.* He tended to regard the condition of the black population as a product of nurture rather than nature—that is, he saw slavery as the culprit, preventing the development of diligence and responsibility that would emerge gradually and naturally after emancipation.[66]

By 1796, he had begun to draft his last will and testament, in which he eventually made elaborate provisions to assure that all his slaves would be freed upon the death of his wife. He also made even more elaborate provisions to guarantee that Mount Vernon would be sold off in pieces, part of the proceeds used to support his freed slaves and their children for several decades into the future. His action on this score, as usual, spoke louder than his words, for they suggested an obligation beyond the grave to assist his former slaves in the transition to freedom within the borders of the United States. Whether he could conjure up a vision of blacks and whites living together in harmony at some unspecified time in the future remains unclear. But he was truly rare within the political elite of Virginia in leaving this question open.

He could and did imagine the inclusion of Native Americans. Late in August of 1796, at the same time he was making final revisions on his Farewell Address, Washington wrote his "Address to the Cherokee Nation." From a strictly legal point of view, each of the various Indian tribes east of the Mississippi was already a nation, or an indigenous quasi-nation within the expanding borders of the United States. Therein, of course, lay the chief problem and the makings for an apparently inevitable tragedy. For in Washington's projection, the westward flow of the American population would prove relentless and unstoppable: "I also have thought much on this subject," Washington declared to the Cherokees, "and anxiously wished that the various Indian tribes, as well as their neighbours, the White people, might enjoy in abundance all the good things which make life comfortable and happy. I have considered how this could be done; and have discovered but one path that would lead them to that desirable solution. In this path I wish all the Indian nations to walk."[67]

The "one path" Washington identified required the Indians to recognize that contesting the expansion of the white population was suicidal. The only realistic solution required the Indians to accept the inevitable, abandon their hunter-gatherer economies, which required huge tracts of land to work effectively, embrace farming as their preferred mode of life, and gradually over several generations allow themselves to be assimilated into the larger American nation. Washington acknowledged that he was asking a lot, that "this path may seem a little difficult to enter" because it meant subduing their understandable urge to resist and sacrificing many of their most distinctive and cherished tribal values. As he prepared for his own retirement, in effect he was encouraging the Indian tribes to retire from their way of life as Indians: "What I have recommended to you," he wrote somewhat plaintively, "I am myself going to do. After a few moons are passed I shall leave the great town and retire to my farm. There I shall attend to the means of increasing my cattle, sheep and other useful animals." If the Indians would follow his example, the peaceful coexistence of Indians and whites could follow naturally, and their gradual merger into a single American people would occur within the arc of the next century. Whatever moral deficiencies and cultural condescensions a modern-day American audience might find in Washington's advice, two salient points are clear: First, it was in keeping with his relentless realism about the limited choices that history offered; and second, it projected Indians into the mix of peoples called Americans.[68]

REACTIONS TO the Farewell Address fell into the familiar grooves. The overwhelming public response was tearfully exuberant, regretting the departure of America's political centerpiece for the last quarter century, but embracing his message, as one member of the cabinet put it, "as a transcript of the general expression of the people of the United States." Meanwhile, the Republican press denounced his warnings against political divisions at home and diplomatic involvement abroad as "the loathings of a sick mind." In the *Aurora,* Benjamin Franklin Bache reprinted the old charge that Washington had been a traitor who conspired with the English government during the war. "This man has a celebrity in a certain way," Washington remarked concerning Bache, "for his calumnies are to be exceeded only by his impudence, and both stand unrivaled." One of his last acts as president was to place on file in the State Department his rejoinder to Bache's accusations, which historians have long since discovered were based on forged English documents. He left office in March of 1797 with the resounding cheers of his huge army of supporters and the howls of that much smaller pack of critics echoing in his ears.[69]

Passing through Alexandria on his way to Mount Vernon, he stopped to deliver a speech in which he reiterated his allegiance to the principles articulated in the Farewell Address. "Clouds may and doubtless often will in the vicissitudes of events, hover over our political concerns," he announced, "but a steady adherence to these principles will not only dispel but render our prospects the brighter by such temporary obscurities." He remained supremely confident that he was right to the very end, though the "temporary obscurities" being spewed out by the Republican press—France was America's international ally and the national government its domestic enemy—produced fits of private despair and periodic flare-ups of the famous Washington temper. (Even ensconced under his "vine and fig tree" in retirement, he continued to subscribe to ten newspapers.) More than any great leader in American history before or since, he was accustomed to getting his way, and equally accustomed to having history prove him right. But his final two and a half years at Mount Vernon were beclouded by the incessant apprehension that his final advice to the country would be ignored, and his legacy, and with it his own place in history, abandoned.[70]

Part of his problem was a function of location. Mount Vernon, of course, lay within the borders of Virginia, and Virginia had become the homeland of the Republican opposition, which was dedicated to overturning the foreign policy and the entire edifice of national sovereignty that Washington stood for. In effect, Mount Vernon became an enclave within enemy territory, surrounded by neighbors committed to a Virginia-writ-large version of the American republic. Washington, once the supreme Virginian, had in their eyes gone over to the other side. Once the all-purpose solution, Washington was now the still-potent problem, a kind of Trojan horse planted squarely in the Virginia fortress. The fact that he devoted so much of his remaining time and energy to overseeing the construction of the new capital city on the Potomac—it was a foregone conclusion that it would be named after him—only confirmed their worst fears. For that city, and the name it was destined to carry, symbolized the conspiracy that threatened, so Jefferson and his followers thought, all that Virginia stood for. Washington, for his part, obliged his Virginia critics by urging his step-grandson to attend Harvard in order to escape the provincial versions of learning currently ascendant in the Old Dominion. Increasingly, he seemed to think of his home state in the same vein as the Indian tribes in his letter to the Cherokees. The destiny of the American nation was pointing one way, and if the tribal chieftains of Virginia chose to oppose that direction, so be it; but they were aligning themselves on the wrong side of history.[71]

The end came on December 14, 1799. The previous day, when it became clear that the combination of pneumonia and the bleeding and blistering remedies of his physicians could produce but one conclusion, Washington ordered the doctors to cease their barbarisms and permit him to die in peace: "I am just going," he apprised those around his bed. "Have me decently buried, and do not let my body be put into the vault in less than three days after I am dead. . . . Do you understand me?" Though he had no illusions of his own immortality, he apparently feared being buried alive, perhaps believing that was really what had happened with Jesus. His last words were " 'Tis well." Self-sufficient as always, his last act was to feel his own pulse at the moment he expired.[72]

CHAPTER FIVE

The Collaborators

AS A RESULT of Washington's Olympian status, the infant American republic had managed to avoid a contested presidential election prior to 1796. Exactly how such an event should proceed without tearing the country apart was still very much a matter of speculation and improvisation. Although some semblance of the routinized mechanisms for political parties had begun to congeal during the debate over Jay's Treaty, nothing remotely resembling the organized campaign structure of modern political parties yet existed. The method of choosing electors to that odd inspiration called the electoral college varied from state to state. And the very notion that a candidate should openly solicit votes violated the principled presumption that such behavior itself represented a confession of unworthiness for national office.

While a clear political distinction between Federalists and Republicans had emerged during Washington's second term, and fervent editorialists were blazing away as partisans from both sides in the popular press, party labels and issue-oriented platforms were less important than a prospective candidate's revolutionary credentials. Memories of the spirit of '76 were still warm twenty years later, and the chief qualification for the presidency remained a matter of one's historic role in the creation of American independence between 1776 and 1789. Only those leaders who had stepped forward at the national level to promote the great cause when its success was still perilous and problematic were eligible.

An exhaustive list of prospects would have included between twenty and thirty names, with Samuel Adams, Alexander Hamilton, Patrick Henry, and James Madison enjoying spirited support. But the four names topping everyone's list would have been almost unanimous: George Washington, Benjamin Franklin, John Adams, and Thomas Jefferson. By 1796, of course, Washington had done his duty. Franklin was dead and gone. That left Adams and Jefferson as the obvious options. And by the spring of 1796 it had become a foregone conclusion that the choice was between them.

They were an incongruous pair, but everyone seemed to argue that history had made them into a pair. The incongruities leapt out for all to see: Adams, the short, stout, candid-to-a-fault New Englander; Jefferson, the tall, slender, elegantly elusive Virginian; Adams, the highly combustible, ever combative, mile-a-minute talker, whose favorite form of conversation was an argument; Jefferson, the always cool and self-contained enigma, who regarded debate and argument as violations of the natural harmonies he heard inside his own head. The list could go on—the Yankee and the Cavalier, the orator and the writer, the bulldog and the greyhound. They were the odd couple of the American Revolution.[1]

And it was the Revolution that had brought them together. They had worked side by side in the Continental Congress, first as staunch opponents of reconciliation with England, then as members of the committee to draft the Declaration of Independence. In 1784 they were reunited in Paris, where Jefferson became an unofficial member of the Adams family and, as Abigail Adams put it, "the only person with whom my companion could associate with perfect freedom and reserve." The following year Jefferson visited Adams for several weeks in London, where, as America's two chief ministers in Europe, they endured the humiliation together when George III ostentatiously turned his back on them during a formal ceremony at court. Adams never forgot this scene; nor did he forget the friend who was standing beside him when it happened.[2]

There were, to be sure, important political and ideological differences between the two men, differences that became the basis for the opposing sides they took in the party wars of the 1790s. But as soulmates who had lived together through some of the most formative events of the revolutionary era and of their own lives, Adams and Jefferson bonded at a personal and emotional level that defied their merely philosophical differences. They were charter members of the "band of brothers" who had shared the agonies and ecstasies of 1776 as colleagues. No subsequent disagreement could shake this elemental affinity. They knew, trusted, even loved each other for reasons that required no explanation.

The two major contestants for the presidency in 1796, then, not only possessed impeccable revolutionary credentials; they had also earned their fame as a team. Within the revolutionary generation, several competing examples of fortuitous cooperation and collaboration had helped to make history happen: Washington and Hamilton during the war, and then again during Washington's second term; Hamilton and Madison on *The Federalist Papers;* Madison and Jefferson in orchestrating the Republican opposition to Hamilton's financial program and then Jay's Treaty. But in part because it seemed so seminal and symbolic of sectional cooperation, the Adams-Jefferson tandem stood out as the greatest collaboration of them all. Choosing between them seemed like choosing between the head and the heart of the American Revolution.

IF REVOLUTIONARY credentials were the major criteria, Adams was virtually unbeatable. His career, indeed his entire life, was made by the American Revolution; and he, in turn, had made American independence his life's project. Perhaps Franklin and Hamilton could claim to have come from further back in the pack, but Adams was another one of those American characters who would have languished in obscurity if born in England or Europe.

Instead, he was born in Braintree, twelve miles south of Boston, in 1735, the son of a farmer and shoemaker, who sent Adams to Harvard in the hope he might become a minister. For a decade after graduating from college he probed his soul for signs of a divine calling while earning his keep as a country schoolteacher and then apprentice lawyer. In the mid-1760s two crucial events determined his fate: First, in 1764 he married Abigail Smith and created with her a partnership of remarkable equity and intimacy; second, in 1765, he stepped forward to help lead the opposition against the Stamp Act and eventually against every aspect of British policy toward the American colonies. American independence became his ministerial calling, a mission he pursued with all the compressed energy of a latter-day Puritan pastor whose congregation was the American people.

Bedeviled by doubts about himself but never about his cause, Adams and his cousin Samuel had become the most conspicuous opponents of British authority in New England by the time the Continental Congress convened in 1774. In the debates within the Continental Congress, John Adams gained fame as "the Atlas of independence" for renouncing any reconciliation with England, and for his pamphlet, *Thoughts on Government,* which became the guidebook for several state constitutions. While other delegates in the Congress kept searching for ways to avoid a break with England, Adams insisted the Revolution had already begun. He successfully lobbied for Washington to head the Continental Army and personally selected Jefferson to draft the Declaration of Independence, two strategic decisions designed to assure Virginia's support for the cause. For over a year he served as chair of the Board of War and Ordinance, playing the role of secretary of war during the most tense and uncertain phase of the fighting.

In 1777 the Congress chose him to join Franklin in Paris to negotiate the alliance with France. He returned home for a few months in 1779, just long enough to draft almost single-handedly the Massachusetts Constitution. Then it was back to Paris to work on the peace treaty ending the war, an experience that generated his lifelong enmity toward Franklin, who found him insufferably austere and obsessively diligent. (Adams thought Franklin naïve about French motives, which were anti-English but not pro-American, and besotted with his own inflated reputation as the ultimate American in Paris.) Until 1788, he remained in Europe, first working with Jefferson for legal recognition of the new American nation as well as for loans from Dutch bankers in Amsterdam, then as America's first minister to the Court of St. James in London, where he confirmed his everlasting conviction that England "cares no more for us than for the Seminole Indians." His absence from the Constitutional Convention was regretted by all—along with Madison he was regarded as America's most sophisticated student of government. He used his spare time in London to toss off three volumes of political philosophy, entitled *Defence of the Constitution of the United States,* which emphasized the advantages of a strong executive, a bicameral legislature, and the principle of checks and balances. He returned to America in time to be elected the first vice president of the United States, which most observers, including Adams himself, interpreted as a popular mandate on his historical contribution to independence. In the American pantheon, with Franklin on his deathbed, he ranked second only to Washington himself.[3]

His reputation then fell victim to two nearly calamitous setbacks, one beyond his control and the other the product of his personal flair for perversity. On the former score, Adams had the misfortune to become the first occupant of what he described as "the most insignificant office that ever the Invention of Man contrived or his Imagination conceived." Subsequent occupants of the vice presidential office have lengthened the list of semihumorous complaints about inhabiting a prestigious political prison (for example, "not worth a bucketful of spit"), but Adams originated the jokes because he was the first prominent American statesman to experience the paradox of being a proverbial heartbeat away from maximum power while languishing in the political version of a *cul-de-sac*.[4]

According to the Constitution the vice president had two duties: to remain available if the president died, fell ill, or was removed from office; and to serve as president pro tem of the Senate, casting a vote only to break a tie. During his eight years in office Adams cast more tie-breaking votes—at least thirty-one and perhaps as many as thirty-eight—than any subsequent vice president in American history, in part because the small size of the Senate made ties more frequent. But after Adams's initial fling at participating in the debates, the members of the Senate decided that the vice president was not permitted to speak. "It is to be sure a punishment to hear other men talk five hours every day," Adams wrote to Abigail, "and not be at liberty to talk at all myself, especially as more than half I hear appears to me very young, inconsiderate, and inexperienced." It was a monumental irony: The man famous as the indefatigable orator of independence in the Continental Congress was obliged to remain silent in the legislative councils of the new government. "My office," Adams complained, "is too great a restraint upon such a Son of Liberty." The great volcano of American political debate was required to confine himself to purely private eruptions.[5]

These occurred sporadically in his personal correspondence with Abigail, who remained ensconced at home in Quincy, Massachusetts, and with old revolutionary comrades like Benjamin Rush. Adams deeply resented being marooned and muted in the Senate, like an old warhorse with several charges left in him, now put out to pasture while crucial battles about the direction of the republic raged around him. And, Adams being Adams, his bitterness found colorful and painfully self-defeating expression in his tirades about the injustice of it all: "The History of our Revolution will be one continued lye from one end to the other," he wrote Rush in 1790. "The essence of the whole will be that *Dr. Franklin's electric rod smote the Earth and out sprang General Washington. That Franklin electrified him with his rod and thence forward these two conducted all the Policy, Negotiations, Legislatures and War.*" As Adams saw it, he had been prepared, by both experience and training, to perform a central role in the unfolding drama of winning and securing the American Revolution. Instead, he was relegated to the sidelines as a marginal player while Johnny-come-latelies like Hamilton and Madison occupied center stage.[6]

To make matters worse, his duties in the Senate removed him from the deliberations of the cabinet. Washington seldom consulted him on policy questions, apparently believing that the vice presidency was a legislative office based in the Senate; therefore, to include Adams in executive decisions violated the constitutional doctrine of separation of powers. When asked by friends about his isolation from the presidential councils, Adams halfheartedly endorsed the same constitutional explanation. "The executive authority is so wholly out of my sphere," he observed, "and it is so delicate a thing for me to meddle in that, I avoid it as much as possible." He desperately wanted to be consulted, but he was too proud to push himself forward. He steadfastly supported all the major initiatives of the Washington administration, including Hamilton's financial plan, the suppression of the Whiskey Rebellion, the Proclamation of Neutrality, and Jay's Treaty, though he had almost no influence on their formulation and some private reservations about Hamilton's ties with bankers and speculators. It was difficult to think of the ever-combative, highly combustible champion of the American Revolution as extraneous and invisible, but that is what the vice presidency had made him.[7]

Adams deserved an assist for making himself into a marginal figure because of remarks he made during the first session of the Senate, before it was decided that the vice president could not participate in debates. The issue concerned a minor matter of etiquette: How should the president be addressed by members of Congress? While hardly an earthshaking question, it had symbolic significance because of the obsessive American suspicion of monarchy, which haunted all conversations about the powers of the presidency under the recently ratified Constitution. Anyone who favored a strong executive was vulnerable to the charge of being a quasi-monarchist, and therefore a traitor to the republican principles of the American Revolution.

Adams was so confident in his own revolutionary credentials that he regarded himself as immune to such charges. But when he lectured the Senate on the need for elaborate trappings of authority and proposed that President Washington be addressed as "His Majesty" or "His Highness," his remarks became the butt of several barbed jokes, including the suggestion that he had been seized by "nobilimania" during his long sojourn in England and might prefer to be addressed as "His Rotundity" or the "Duke of Braintree." Jefferson threw up his hands at the sheer stupidity of Adams's proposals, calling them "the most superlatively ridiculous thing I ever heard of."[8]

Adams tried to laugh himself out of the monarchical morass, claiming that he simply wanted to assure that the executive branch of the government enjoyed a fighting chance against the awesome powers of the legislature. "The little fishes will eat up the great one," he joked, "unless the great one should devour all the little ones." If all formal titles were to be stigmatized, he wrote to Benjamin Rush, then perhaps Rush's children should start addressing their father as "Ben."[9]

Mostly, however, Adams stewed and simmered and tried to defend himself. Ever the political pugilist who felt obliged to answer every bell, Adams refused to back away from his belief that the new American government needed a strong executive presence. In a series of thirty-one essays printed in the *Gazette of the United States* and subsequently published as *Discourses on Davila,* he argued that all stable governments required what he called a "monarchical principle," meaning a singular figure empowered to embody the will of the nation and to protect the ordinary citizenry from the inevitable accumulation of power by the more wealthy and wellborn. In most European states, he went on to argue, it was probably necessary for the monarchy to remain hereditary for the foreseeable future, in order to permit a more gradual transition to full-blown republican principles.

Such statements seemed almost designed to invite misunderstanding, which is precisely what they did. For the rest of his life, Adams lived under a cloud of suspicion that he wished to restore hereditary monarchy in America and that, once installed in the presidency, he fully intended to declare himself king for life and his son John Quincy his successor. He could argue till doomsday that such claims were preposterous, which they were and which he did, but Adams had tied a tin can labeled "monarchist" to his own tail, which then rattled through ages and pages of the history books. Since Washington had no children of his own—the Father of His Country was almost certainly sterile—he was less vulnerable to charges of hereditary aspirations. (Intriguingly, of the first six presidents, only Adams had a male heir.) If Washington became the quasi-monarchical president who could be trusted, Adams became the closet monarchist who could not.[10]

The *Davila* essays, in fact, became the basis for the first serious rift in his friendship with Jefferson. The publisher of the American edition of Tom Paine's *The Rights of Man* printed what we would now call a blurb for the book, a quote from Jefferson, who had presumed that his remarks would be anonymous. Jefferson mentioned in passing "the political heresies" of *Davila,* which everyone knew to be written by Adams. Adams was outraged, claiming that Jefferson, of all people, should know that he had not converted to monarchy while in Europe. Jefferson expressed his regrets, explaining to Washington: "I am afraid the indiscretion of a printer has compromised me with a friend, Mr. Adams, for whom, as one of the most honest and disinterested men alive, I have a cordial esteem." A somewhat touchy correspondence then ensued, in which Jefferson attempted to remind Adams that their much-valued friendship did not depend on complete agreement about forms of government. Adams, clearly hurt, responded in his typically aggressive style: "I know not what your idea is of the best form of government. You and I never had a serious conversation together that I can recollect concerning the nature of government. The very transient hints that have passed between us have been jocular and superficial, without ever coming to any explanation." Having scored his points, Adams then retreated to safer ground: "The friendship that has subsisted for fifteen years between us without the slightest interruption, and until this occasion without the slightest suspicion, ever has been and still is very dear to my heart."[11]

It was still dear to Jefferson as well, so much so that he preferred to misrepresent his emerging conviction that Adams had allowed himself to be "taken up by the monarchical federalists" and was, albeit inadvertently, lending his enormous prestige to the growing conspiracy against the revolutionary principles that the Adams-Jefferson team had done so much to create. That, at least, was what he was saying and writing to others. To Adams, on the other hand, he claimed that his remarks on the *Davila* essays had been misconstrued, that he was actually "not referring to any writing that I might suppose to be yours." This was patently untrue, but a justifiable distortion in the Jeffersonian scheme of things because motivated by an authentic urge to sustain the friendship. The Adams style was to confront, shout, rant, and then to embrace. The Jefferson style was to evade, maintain pretenses, then convince himself that all was well.[12]

For a time, the meshing of these two diametrically different styles worked. Adams and Jefferson maintained cordial relations throughout most of Washington's first term, even though it was clear for all to see that they stood on opposite sides of the chasm that was opening up between Federalists and Republicans. It helped that Adams was muzzled and largely ignored in the vice presidency, and that Jefferson, though covertly advising Madison on how best to counter Hamilton's financial program, was simultaneously and officially a member of the Washington administration. In 1793 Jefferson accompanied Adams for his induction into the American Philosophical Society. Adams commented to Abigail, "we are still upon terms," meaning that the friendship endured, but just barely.[13]

Jefferson's enthusiasm for the French Revolution, despite its wild and bloody excesses, pushed Adams over the edge. The notion that the cascading events in France bore any relation to the American Revolution struck Adams as outright lunacy. ("Danton, Robespierre, Marat, etc. are furies," he wrote to John Quincy in 1793. "Dragons' teeth have been sown in France and will come up as monsters.") He began to describe Jefferson as a dangerous dreamer who, like many of his fellow Virginians, was so deeply in debt to British creditors that his judgment of European affairs was tinged with a virulent form of Anglophobia that rendered him incapable of a detached assessment of America's interests abroad. He needed to "get out from under his debts . . . and proportion his style and life to his Revenue." As it was, Jefferson had become a man "poisoned by ambition and his Temper embittered against the Constitution and the Administration."[14]

By the time Jefferson stepped down as secretary of state late in 1793, only faint traces of the famous friendship lingered like nostalgic reminiscences in the Adams memory: "I have so long been in the habit of thinking well of his abilities and general good dispositions," Adams confided to Abigail, "that I cannot but feel some regret at this event [Jefferson's retirement]. . . . But his want of candor, his obstinate prejudices against all forms of government power, his real partiality in spite of all his pretensions . . . have so nearly reconciled me to it that I will not weep. . . . His mind is now poisoned with passion, prejudice, and faction."[15]

As a veteran Jefferson watcher, Adams offered a skeptical assessment of his former friend's decision to leave public life: "Jefferson thinks by this step to get a reputation of an humble, modest, meek man, wholly without ambition or vanity," he explained to John Quincy. "He may even have deceived himself into this belief. But if a prospect opens, the world will see and he will feel that he is as ambitious as Oliver Cromwell, though no soldier." In a sense, Adams was saying that he understood the psychological forces driving Jefferson's escape to Monticello better than Jefferson himself. He already sensed, in a way that Jefferson's elaborate denial mechanisms did not permit into his own interior conversations, that Jefferson's retirement was temporary, and the two old colleagues would soon be vying for the presidency. The great collaboration was destined to become the great competition.[16]

THE MOST savvy Jefferson watcher of all time, at least over the full stretch of their respective careers, was James Madison. While in the Adams partnership Jefferson was the younger man, he was senior to Madison. While he tended to defer to Adams on the basis of age and political experience, Jefferson dominated his relationship with Madison for the same reasons. The collaboration had begun in Virginia during the Revolution and had then congealed during the 1780s, when Jefferson was in Paris and Madison became his most trusted source of information about political events back home, most especially the drafting and ratification of the Constitution, which turned out to be Madison's most singularly creative moment and the only occasion when he acted independently of Jefferson's influence.

Although the trust between them had grown close to unconditional by the 1790s, when they assumed joint leadership of the Republican opposition to Federalist domestic and foreign policies, their partnership lacked the dramatic character of the Adams-Jefferson collaboration, which seemed to symbolize the creative tension between New England and Virginia and the fusion of ideological and temperamental opposites in a common cause. Madison was temperamentally the opposite of Jefferson—less sweeping in his intellectual style, more careful and precise, the prose to Jefferson's poetry—but because he instinctively subordinated his agenda to Jefferson's will, there were never the revealing clashes that gave the Adams-Jefferson dialogue its dynamic dimension. If the seams in the Adams-Jefferson collaboration were the source of its magic, the Jefferson-Madison alliance was seamless, and therefore less magical than smoothly and silently effective.

Whereas Adams and Jefferson had come together as Americans, first in 1776 as early advocates of independence from Great Britain, then in the 1780s as America's two chief ministers in Europe, Jefferson and Madison had bonded as Virginians, dedicated to assuring the triumph of Virginia's interests within the national government. While perhaps a more provincial cause, it had all the advantages of a more concerted and tightly focused political agenda in which each man played a clearly defined role.

Jefferson was the grand strategist, Madison the agile tactician. "I shall always receive your commands with pleasure," Madison wrote to Jefferson in 1794, "and shall continue to drop you a line as occasions turn up." Jefferson had recently ensconced himself at Monticello, relishing his retirement, and Madison was returning to the political wars in Philadelphia. Madison's message signaled the resumption of what can be considered the most successful political partnership in American history. And though Jefferson did not know it, indeed made a point of denying it to himself, it also signaled the start of his campaign for the presidency.[17]

Jefferson's letters during this reclusive phase avoided politics altogether, emphasizing instead his designs for a refurbished Monticello, his crop-rotation system, a somewhat bizarre proposal to transport the

University of Geneva to Virginia, and the ideal process for making manure. His letters to Madison also featured the Monticellan Jefferson, the statesman-turned-farmer sequestered in "my remote canton." Politics on occasion crept into the dialogue, much like an exotic plant growing amid descriptions of vetch as the ideal rotation crop. Madison's letters, on the other hand, were full of political news from the capital—Hamilton's treacheries and alleged cooking of the books in the Treasury Department, Washington's ominous overreaction to the Whiskey Rebellion, the groundswell of opposition to Jay's Treaty— with many of the letters written in code to foil snoopers at the post office.[18]

Madison was quietly orchestrating the Republican campaign on behalf of Jefferson to succeed Washington. In October of 1795 Aaron Burr visited Monticello, presumably to discuss the delivery of New York's electoral votes, probably as a condition for his own place on the ticket as vice president. Other Republican operatives like John Beckley, the Speaker of the House, were focusing on the political factions in Pennsylvania, another key state. On the other side, Federalist editors and polemicists, encountering this mounting campaign on Jefferson's behalf, began to generate anti-Jefferson propaganda: He had suffered humiliation as governor of Virginia when he fled before British troops; he was an inveterate Francophile; he was an intellectual dreamer, "more fit to be a professor in a College, President of a Philosophical Society . . . but certainly not the first magistrate of a great nation." While all this was going on around him, Jefferson professed complete ignorance of his candidacy. He would have been perfectly capable of swearing on the Bible that none of these initiatives came from him.[19]

Madison managed the particulars silently and surreptitiously. He understood—indeed, it was a crucial aspect of the collaboration—that Jefferson's eventual reentry into the political arena depended upon sustaining the fiction in his mentor's own mind that it would never happen. Jefferson required what we would call "deniability," not just for public purposes but also for his own private serenity. In the Jefferson-Madison collaboration, Madison was not just responsible for handling the messy particulars; he was also accountable for shielding his chief from the political ambitions throbbing away in his own soul.

As late as the summer of 1796, when Washington's retirement was a foregone conclusion and Jefferson's candidacy for the presidency was common knowledge throughout the country, Jefferson claimed to be completely oblivious to the campaign on his behalf. Madison spent four months at Montpelier, only a few miles from Monticello, but never visited Jefferson, for fear of being forced into a conversation that might upset Jefferson's denial mechanisms. "I have not seen Jefferson," he wrote Monroe in code, "and have *thought it best to present him no opportunity of protesting* to his *friend against* being *embarked on this contest.*" Jefferson thus became perhaps the last person in America to recognize that he was running for the presidency against his old friend from Massachusetts.[20]

Meanwhile up in Quincy, that very friend was also dancing a minuet with his own political ambitions. Adams's partner in the dance was Abigail, whose political instincts rivaled Madison's legendary skills and whose knowledge of her husband's emotional makeup surpassed all competitors. She had always been his ultimate confidante, the person he could trust with his self-doubts, vanities, and overflowing opinions. Now, however, with Jefferson gone over to the other side and their former friendship reduced to polite and nervously evasive exchanges, Abigail became his chief and, in most respects, his sole collaborator. One reason Adams fled from Philadelphia for nine months each year, apart from the oppressive summer heat, the annual yellow fever epidemics, and the fact he despised his job, was that he needed to be with her.

Ironically, we can only know what they were saying to each other while together from the letters they wrote when apart. During the months Congress was in session they wrote each other two or three times every week. Much of the correspondence was playfully personal: "No man even if he is sixty years of age ought to have more than three months at a time from his family," Abigail complained soon after he departed for Philadelphia. "Oh that I had a bosom to lean my head upon," Adams replied. "But how dare you hint or lisp a word about 'sixty years of age.' If I were near I would soon convince you that I am not above forty."[21]

Just as often, however, Adams also used the correspondence to unburden himself of opinions that his muzzled status in the Senate prevented him from sharing publicly. The quality of oratory in the Senate, he complained, was far below the standards at the Continental Congress, though he was intrigued by the fluid, nonchalant style of

Aaron Burr, whom he described "as fat as a duck and as ruddy as a roost cock." He was lonely for his wife's company and political advice: "I want to sit and converse with you about our debates every evening. I sit here alone and brood over political probabilities and conjectures." Abigail heard him out about the doomed course of the French Revolution but was somewhat more sanguine: "I ruminate upon France as I lie awake many hours before light," she wrote. "My present thought is that their virtuous army will give them a government in time in spite of all their conventions but of what nature it will be, it is hard to say."22

Abigail responded harshly to Republican critics of Jay's Treaty, calling them "mindless Jacobins and party creatures." Adams concurred, though he also thought the affection for England that the "ultras," or High Federalists, seemed to harbor was just as misguided as the Republican love affair with France: "I wish that misfortune and adversity could soften the temper and humiliate the insolence of John Bull, but he is not yet sufficiently humble. If I mistake not, it is the destiny of America one day to beat down his pride. But the irksome task will not soon, I hope, be forced upon us." Like Washington, he saw Jay's Treaty as a shrewd if bittersweet bargain designed to postpone war with England for perhaps a generation. In the meantime, he hoped that England and France would bleed each other to death. As for George III, "the mad idiot will never recover," but as in the old revolutionary days, "his idiocy is our salvation."23

When Adams offered a harsh appraisal of Washington's lack of formal education and knowledge of the classics, Abigail chided him: Washington was the only man apart from her husband capable of detachment and ought not be carped at behind his back. If anyone else had corrected him so directly, Adams would have gone into his Vesuvial mode. Coming from Abigail, however, the political advice was welcomed. "Send more," Adams pleaded. "There is more good thoughts, fine strokes, and mother wit in them than I hear [in the Senate] in the whole week." Abigail dismissed such praise as pure flattery. "What a jumble are my letters—politics, domestic occurrences, farming anecdotes—pray light your segars [*sic*] with them." Instead, he savored and saved them all.24

Then there was the touchy question of the presidency. At some unspoken level, Adams knew, which meant that Abigail also knew, that he considered the office his revolutionary right. No one else, save perhaps Jefferson, could match his record of service to the cause of independence. Why else had he been willing to languish in the shadow of the vice presidency for those godforsaken years if not to use it as a stepping-stone to the prize itself? Like Jefferson—indeed, like any self-respecting statesman of the era, save perhaps Burr—Adams had no intention of campaigning for the office. (Burr did, and acted on it.) "I am determined to be a silent spectator of the silly and wicked game," Adams explained to Abigail, "and to enjoy it as a comedy, a farce, or as a gymnastic exhibition at Sadler's Wells." Then he added a candid afterthought: "Yet I don't know how I should live without it."[25]

That was the Adams pattern: first to deny his political ambitions, much like Jefferson; then to confront them, feel guilty about them, fidget over them; then grudgingly admit they were part of who he was. Washington's successor would inherit "a devilish load . . . and be very apt to stagger and stumble." Who in his right mind would want the job? Moreover, he was not cut out for all the ceremonial obligations: "I hate speeches, messages, addresses and answers, proclamations, and such affected, studied, contraband things," he wrote sulkily to Abigail. "I hate levees and drawing rooms. I hate to speak to a thousand people to whom I have nothing to say." Then again the revealing afterthought: "Yet all this I can do."[26]

Abigail aligned her responses to fit alongside her husband's own internal odyssey toward the inevitable. Yes, the presidency was a thankless job, "a most unpleasant seat, full of thorns, briars, thistles, murmuring, fault-finding, calumny, obloquy." But—her version of the Adams internal ricochet—"the Hand of Providence ought to be attended to, and what is designed, cheerfully submitted to." Did this mean she could live with his candidacy and would consent to live with him if he won the election? Abigail refused to answer that question until the late winter of 1796. "My Ambition leads me not to be first in Rome," she observed somewhat coyly. Her only political ambition was to "reign in the heart of my husband. That is my throne and there I aspire to be absolute." On the other hand, if he was elected to the presidency, it would be "a flattering and Glorious Reward" for his lifetime of public service, and he would obviously need "a wife to hover about you, to bind up your temples, to mix your bark and pour out your coffee." Adams was ecstatic: "Hi! Ho! Oh Dear. I am most tenderly your forever friend." With her at his side, he had no real need for a cabinet.[27]

Now that his personal demons were out in the open and Abigail was on board, the collaboration moved into high gear. In March and April of 1796, the Adams team began to assess electoral projections on a state-by-state basis. He worried that New England might not rally to his candidacy. She was confident it would go solidly for him. (She was right.) Reports from New York and Pennsylvania suggested a strong surge for Jefferson, who was clearly the main threat. Adams foresaw a very close electoral vote, perhaps even a tie with Jefferson, which would then throw the election into the House of Representatives. Or suppose Jefferson finished a close second and therefore became vice president? (Until passage of the Twelfth Amendment, electors voted for two candidates, not one ticket of two.) Might this not create "a dangerous crisis in public affairs" by placing the president and vice president "in opposite boxes"? Abigail thought such speculations were too hypothetical to worry about. (Here events proved her wrong.) Moreover, she still had a soft spot in her heart for Jefferson and believed him fully capable of joining the Adams team: "Though wrong in politics, though formerly an advocate of Tom Paine's *Rights of Man*, and though frequently mistaken in men and measures, I do not think him an insincere or corruptible man." And all this fretful conjuring about prospective mishaps and crises, she scolded, was unbecoming a man who would be first magistrate of the nation. In a recent dream, Abigail reported, she was riding in a coach when, suddenly, several large cannonballs were flying toward her. All burst in the air before reaching her coach, the pieces of metal falling harmlessly in the middle distance. This was a clear sign: Stop worrying. The voters and the gods were on their side.[28]

EVENTS PROVED Abigail half-right. The electoral vote split along sectional lines, Adams carrying New England and Jefferson the South. As the results trickled in from different states in December, Adams threw several tantrums that required Abigail to nurse him back to composure. The Federalist ticket featured Adams and Thomas Pinckney of South Carolina as a tandem. Behind-the-scenes maneuverings by Hamilton threatened to propel Pinckney past Adams, though Hamilton claimed that his chief goal was to knock Jefferson out altogether. For a while, when it appeared that Pinckney might actually win and Adams come in second, the Sage of Quincy exploded: Pinckney was a "nobody"; the humiliation of serving under him was more than he could bear; he would resign the vice presidency if he finished in second place. On December 30, however, when results from Virginia and South Carolina revealed that Adams had captured one electoral vote in each of these southern states, Adams ceased erupting and started celebrating. "John Adams never felt more serene in his life," he wrote Abigail. It was a razor-thin victory, but he had prevailed over Jefferson 71 to 68, with Pinckney a close third and Burr, Jefferson's running mate, far back in the pack.[29]

Jefferson's posture throughout the drawn-out counting of the electoral votes remained a combination of studied indifference and calculated obliviousness. Quite obviously, he realized he was a candidate. Madison was relaying state-by-state assessments to Monticello, which were also being reported in the local press. Although Jefferson claimed to be too busy with his renovations at Monticello and his crop-rotation scheme to notice such things, some hidden portion of his mind was surely paying close attention, since he predicted that Adams would win by three electoral votes—the precise result—two months before it became official.

On December 28 he wrote a congratulatory letter to Adams, regretting "the various little incidents [that] have happened or been contrived to separate us" and disavowing any desire to have been thrust into the presidential election in the first place: "I have no ambition to govern men," he explained. "It is a painful and thankless task." He also went out of his way to squelch rumors that he might resent serving under his old friend and more recent opponent: "I can particularly have no feelings which would revolt at a secondary position to Mr. Adams. I am his junior in life, was his junior in Congress, his junior in the diplomatic line, his junior lately in our civil government." Up in Quincy, Abigail reiterated her abiding sense that Jefferson could be trusted to recover his earlier intimacy with her husband. "You know," she confided to Adams, "my friendship for that gentleman has lived through his faults and errors—to which I have not been blind. I believe he remains our friend."[30]

Over the course of the next few weeks Adams and Jefferson developed two equally cogent but wholly incompatible political strategies in response to their somewhat awkward reunion as a political pair. Both strategies began with the realistic recognition that whoever succeeded Washington as president was likely to face massive problems, in part because of the deep political divisions over foreign policy that had haunted his second term, mostly because Washington was destiny's choice as the greatest American of the age and therefore inherently irreplaceable. From that common starting point, they then devised diametrically different courses of action.

The core feature of the Adams strategy was to bring Jefferson into his confidence and his councils—in effect, to create a bipartisan administration in which Jefferson enjoyed the kind of access and influence that Adams himself had been denied as vice president in the Washington administration. Adams began to leak his thoughts along these lines in private conversations that he knew would find their way back to Jefferson. And they did: "My friends inform me that Mr. A. speaks of me with great friendship," Jefferson observed, "and with satisfaction in the prospect of administering the government in concurrence with me." Adams was suggesting that the old collaboration of 1776 be recovered and revived. If no single leader could hope to fill the huge vacuum created by Washington's departure, perhaps the reconstituted team of Adams and Jefferson, which had performed so brilliantly in previous political assignments, might enjoy at least a fighting chance of sustaining the legacy of national leadership that Washington had established. Abigail supported the initiative; indeed, it might very well have been her idea in the first place, convinced as she was that the political split between Jefferson and her husband had not destroyed the mutual affection and trust that had built up over the previous twenty years of friendship.[31]

Trust was crucial. On almost all the disputes over domestic and foreign policy in the 1790s Adams and Jefferson had found themselves on different sides. And each man had made brutally harsh assessments of the other, rooted in their quite different convictions about the proper course the American Revolution should take. Adams was distinctive, however, for his tendency to regard even serious political and ideological differences as eminently negotiable once elemental bonds of personal trust and affection were established. In the Adams scheme, intimacy trumped ideology.

Several of Adams's closest friends—Samuel Adams, Elbridge Gerry, Benjamin Rush, Mercy Otis Warren—were ardent Republicans but still retained his confidence. He was especially predisposed to forgive or ignore political differences when the other person had been one of the "band of brothers" in 1776. He harbored, as Fisher Ames described it, "a strong revolutionary taint in his mind, [and] admires the character, principles and means which that revolutionary system . . . seems to legitimate, and . . . holds cheap any reputation that was not then founded and top'd off." By this standard, Jefferson was a more reliable colleague than staunch Federalists who had been reluctant or merely peripheral participants in the climactic phase of the revolutionary drama. "His [Jefferson's] talents I know very well," Adams wrote to Gerry in a letter he knew would find its way to Monticello, "and have ever believed in his honour, Integrity, his Love of Country, and his friends."[32]

Because nothing like the full-blooded machinery of a modern political party system existed, Adams conveyed his tentative scheme for a bipartisan initiative informally through letters and conversations sure to be picked up by the press. That was how Jefferson learned that Adams was contemplating a truly bold response to the most glaring problem facing his presidency—namely, to send a delegation to France analogous to Jay's mission to England, this time to negotiate a treaty designed to avert war with the other great European power. What's more, Adams let it be known that he was considering either Jefferson or Madison to head the delegation—in effect, including the leadership of the Republican party in the shaping of foreign policy. When Madison got wind of this rumor, he could not believe it: "It has got into the Newspapers that an Envoy Extraordinary was to go to France," he wrote Jefferson, "and that I was to be that person. I have no reason to suppose a shadow of truth in the former part of the story; and the latter is pure fiction."[33]

But the rumor was true. Abigail endorsed the initiative. Again, the idea might have originated with her, though the communication within the Adams marriage was so seamless and overlapping that primacy is impossible to fix. When the trial balloon floated past several dedicated Federalists, they could not believe it either, since it seemed to them like willfully dragging the Trojan horse into the Federalist fortress. Adams heard about the Federalist reaction and told Abigail that if it persisted, he would threaten to "resign the office and let Jefferson lead them to peace, wealth, and power if he will." He was sure, in any event, that a bipartisan effort maximized the prospects for a truly neutral American foreign policy, which was what Washington had attempted and the vast majority of Americans wanted: "We will have neither John Bull nor Louis Baboon," he joked to Abigail. His response to those partisans of both parties who disagreed was one defiant word: "Silence."[34]

Jefferson was the master of silence, especially when he disagreed. But the early letters and leaks out of Monticello indicated that he was in fact disposed to agree and consider a bipartisan political alliance grounded in the personal trust of the once-great collaboration. He reiterated his claim, simultaneously sincere and misleading, that he had been embarrassed to learn that he had become a candidate for the presidency. "I never in my life exchanged a word with any person on the subject," he noted, "till I found my name brought forward generally, in competition with that of Mr. Adams." In fact, he claimed to feel quite awkward being pitted against a man whom he regarded much like an older brother and one with a superior claim to the office based on seniority and experience: "Few will believe the true dispositions of my mind," he told his son-in-law. "It is not the less true, however, that I do sincerely wish to be second on the vote rather than first." When a dispute over the electoral vote in Vermont threatened to produce a tie in the final tally and throw the election into the House of Representatives, Jefferson let out the word that he would defer to Adams so as "to prevent the phaenomenon of a Pseudo-president at so early a day." His posture seemed the model of graciousness and elegant accommodation.[35]

This was not a mere facade, but it was only the top layer of Jefferson's thinking. A level below the surface, he, much like Adams, was preoccupied with the long shadow of George Washington. Mixing his metaphors in uncharacteristic fashion, he confided to Madison his deeper reasons for embracing the Adams victory: "The President [Washington] is fortunate to get off just as the bubble is bursting, leaving others to hold the bag. Yet, as his departure will mark the moment when the difficulties begin to work, you will see, that they will be ascribed to the new administration, and that he will have his usual good fortune of repaying credit from the good acts of others, and leaving to them that of others." He was certain that "no man will bring out of that office the reputation which carries him into it." While strolling around the grounds of Monticello with a French visitor, he expanded on his strategic sense of the intractable political realities: "In the present situation of the United States, divided as they are between two parties, which mutually accuse each other of perfidy and treason . . . this exalted station [the presidency] is surrounded with dangerous rocks, and the most eminent abilities will not be sufficient to steer clear of them all." Whereas Washington had been able to levitate above the partisan factions, "the next president of the United States will only be the president of a party." There was no safe middle ground, only a no-man's-land destined to be raked by the cross fire from both sides.[36]

From Jefferson's perspective, then, Adams was essentially proposing that the two men join forces and stand back-to-back in the killing zone. To his credit, Jefferson's first instinct was to accept the invitation. After congratulating Adams on his electoral triumph, assuring him that "I never one single moment expected a different issue," Jefferson warned him of the partisan bickering that his administration would have to negotiate. "Since the days on which you signed the treaty of Paris," Jefferson noted ominously, "our horizon was never so overcast." He would be pleased and honored, however, to play a constructive role in moving the nation past this difficult moment and to recover the old patriot spirit of '76, "when we were working for our independence." He closed with a vague promise to renew the old partnership.[37]

Adams would have been overjoyed to receive such a message—given the stilted language of their most recent and rather contrived correspondence, it seemed to meet him more than halfway—but the letter was never sent. Instead, Jefferson decided to pass it to Madison in order to assure its propriety. Madison produced six reasons why Jefferson's gesture of support might create unacceptable political risks. The last and most significant was the clincher: "Considering the probability that Mr. A's course of administration may force an opposition to it from the Republican quarter, and the general uncertainty of the posture our affairs may take, there may be real embarrassments from giving written possession to him, of the degree of compliment and confidence which your personal delicacy and friendship have suggested." In short, Jefferson must choose between his affection for Adams, which was palpable and widely known, and his leadership of the Republican party. If registering a nostalgic sentiment of affinity was Jefferson's main intention, Madison suggested that could be done by leaking part of the message to mutual friends. (In fact, Madison had already handled that piece of diplomacy by sending such words to Benjamin Rush, who would presumably pass them along to Adams, and did.) But Jefferson must not permit himself to be drawn into the policy-making process of the Adams administration, lest it compromise his role as leader of the Republican opposition.[38]

When Madison offered tactical advice of this sort, Jefferson almost always listened. Nevertheless, he wanted Madison to know that it came at a price: "Mr. A. and myself were cordial friends from the beginning of the revolution," he explained. "The deviation from that line of politics on which we had been united has not made me less sensible of the rectitude of his heart: and I wished him to know this." That said and duly recorded on one portion of his soul, Jefferson concurred that a diplomatic leak of that message satisfied his conscience. "As to my participating in the administration," Jefferson then observed, "if by that he meant the executive cabinet, both duty and inclination will shut that door to me." By "duty," Jefferson meant his obligation to orchestrate the opposition to Adams's presidency. By "inclination," he meant his personal aversion to the kind of controversy and policy debate inside the cabinet that Adams seemed to be proposing. "I cannot have a wish," Jefferson concluded, "to descend daily into the arena like a gladiator to suffer martyrdom in every conflict." Instead of acknowledging that he was choosing loyalty to party over loyalty to Adams— for Jefferson, ideology was trumping intimacy—he preferred to cast his decision in personal terms. He simply did not have the stomach or the stamina to argue the Republican agenda from inside the tent. Though psychologically incapable of seeing himself as a party leader, in truth that was what he had become.[39]

It was a personally poignant and politically fateful decision. Adams did not know about it for several weeks. The reports he was receiving from mutual friends emphasized Jefferson's generosity of spirit in defeat. This sounded hopeful. Abigail remained confident that Jefferson could be trusted, that the bipartisan direction was the proper course, and the inclusion of a prominent Republican on the peace delegation to France, probably Madison, was a shrewd move. On the other hand, the Federalists whom Adams chose for his cabinet—he retained

Washington's advisers, his biggest blunder—had threatened to resign en masse if Adams tried to implement his bipartisan strategy. (In retrospect, this would have been the best thing that could have happened to Adams.) How the incoming president would have resolved this impasse if Jefferson had agreed to resume the collaboration is impossible to know.

As it was, events played out in a rather dramatic face-to-face encounter. On March 6, 1797, Adams and Jefferson dined with Washington at the presidential mansion in Philadelphia. Adams learned that Jefferson was unwilling to join the cabinet and that neither Jefferson nor Madison was willing to be part of the peace delegation to France. Jefferson learned that Adams had been battling his Federalist advisers, who opposed a vigorous Jeffersonian presence in the administration. They left the dinner together and walked down Market Street to Fifth, two blocks from the very spot where Jefferson had drafted the words of the Declaration of Independence that Adams had so forcefully defended before the Continental Congress almost twenty-one years earlier. As Jefferson remembered it later, "we took leave, and he never after that said one word to me on the subject or ever consulted me as to any measure of the government." But of course Jefferson himself had already decided that he preferred the anomalous role of opposing the administration in which he officially served.[40]

A few days later at his swearing-in ceremony as vice president, Jefferson joked about his rusty recall of parliamentary procedure, a clear sign that he intended to spend his time in the harmless business of monitoring debates in the Senate. After Adams was sworn in as president on March 13, he reported to Abigail that Washington had murmured under his breath: "Ay! I am fairly out and you fairly in! See which of us will be happiest." Predictably, the sight of Washington leaving office attracted the bulk of the commentary in the press. Adams informed Abigail that it was like "the sun setting full-orbit, and another rising (though less splendidly)." Observers with a keener historic sense noticed that the first transfer of power at the executive level had gone smoothly, almost routinely. Jefferson was on the road back to Monticello immediately after the inaugural ceremony, setting up the Republican government in exile, waiting for the inevitable catastrophes to befall the presidency of his old friend. As for Adams himself, without Jefferson as a colleague, with a Federalist cabinet filled with men loyal to Hamilton, he was left alone with Abigail, the only collaborator he could truly trust. His call to her mixed abiding love with a sense of desperation: "I never wanted your advice and assistance more in my life," he pleaded. "The times are critical and dangerous and I must have you here to assist me. . . . You must leave the farm to the mercy of the winds. I can do nothing without you."[41]

LOOKING BACK over the full sweep of American history, one would be hard-pressed to discover a presidency more dominated by a single foreign policy problem and simultaneously more divided domestically over how to solve it. The Adams presidency, in fact, might be the classic example of the historical truism that inherited circumstances define the parameters within which presidential leadership takes shape, that history shapes presidents, rather than vice versa. With all the advantages of hindsight, Jefferson's strategic assessment of 1796 appears more and more prescient: Whoever followed Washington was probably doomed to failure.

Beyond the daunting task of following the greatest hero in American history, Adams faced a double dilemma. On the one hand, the country was already waging an undeclared war against French privateers in the Atlantic and Caribbean. The salient policy question was clear: Should the United States declare war on France or seek a diplomatic solution? Adams chose the latter course; like Washington, he was committed to American neutrality at almost any cost. He coupled this commitment with a buildup of the navy, which would enable the United States to fight a defensive war if negotiations with France broke down.

In retrospect, this was the proper and indeed the only realistic policy. But successful negotiations required a French government sufficiently stable and adequately impressed with American power to bargain seriously. Neither of these conditions was present during Adams's term as president. Until the emergence of Napoleon as dictator, the French government, eventually called the Directory, was a misnamed coalition of ever-shifting political factions inherently incapable of either coherence or direction. What's more, from the French perspective—and the same could be said about the English perspective, as well—the infant American republic was at most a minor distraction, more often an utter irrelevancy, within the larger Anglo-French competition for primacy on the Continent. In short, at the international level, the fundamental conditions essential for resolving the central problem of the Adams presidency did not exist. The problem was inherently insoluble.[42]

On the other hand, and to make a bad situation even worse, the ongoing debate between Federalists and Republicans had degenerated into ideological warfare. Each side sincerely saw the other as traitors to the core principles of the American Revolution. The political consensus that had held together during Washington's first term, and had then begun to fragment into Federalist and Republican camps over the Whiskey Rebellion and Jay's Treaty, broke down completely in 1797. Jefferson spoke for many of the participants caught up in this intensely partisan and nearly scatological political culture when he described it as a fundamental loss of trust between former friends. "Men who have been intimate all their lives," he observed, "cross the street to avoid meeting, and turn their heads another way, lest they should be obliged to touch hats." He first used the phrase "a wall of separation," which would later become famous as his description of the proper relation between church and state; here, however, describing the political and ideological division between Federalists and Republicans: "Politics and party hatreds destroy the happiness of every being here," he reported to his daughter. "They seem, like salamanders, to consider fire as their element."[43]

Jefferson's interpretation of the escalating party warfare was richly ironic, since he had contributed to the breakdown of personal trust and the complete disavowal of bipartisan cooperation by rejecting Adams's offer to renew the old partnership. But Jefferson was fairly typical in this regard, lamenting the chasm between long-standing colleagues while building up the barricades from his side of the divide. Federalists and Republicans alike accused their opponents of narrow-minded partisanship, never conceding or apparently even realizing that their own behavior also fit the party label they affixed to their enemies.

The very idea of a legitimate opposition did not yet exist in the political culture of the 1790s, and the evolution of political parties was proceeding in an environment that continued to regard the word *party* as an epithet. In effect, the leadership of the revolutionary generation lacked a vocabulary adequate to describe the politics they were inventing. And the language they inherited framed the genuine political differences and divisions in terms that only exacerbated their nonnegotiable character. Much like Jefferson, Adams regarded the impasse as a breakdown of mutual trust: "You can witness for me," he wrote to John Quincy concerning Jefferson's opposition, "how loath I have been to give him up. It is with much reluctance that I am obliged to look upon him as a man whose mind is warped by prejudice. . . . However wise and scientific as a philosopher, as a politician he is a child and the dupe of the party."[44]

At the domestic level, then, Adams inherited a supercharged political atmosphere every bit as ominous and intractable as the tangle on the international scene. It was a truly unprecedented situation in several senses: His vice president was in fact the leader of the opposition party; his cabinet was loyal to the memory of Washington, which several members regarded as embodied now in the person of Alexander Hamilton, who was officially retired from the government altogether; political parties were congealing into doctrinaire ideological camps, but neither side possessed the verbal or mental capacity to regard the other as anything but treasonable; and finally, the core conviction of the entire experiment in republican government—namely, that all domestic and foreign policies derived their authority from public opinion—conferred a novel level of influence to the press, which had yet to develop any established rules of conduct or standards for distinguishing rumors from reliable reporting. It was a recipe for political chaos that even the indomitable Washington would have been hardpressed to control. No one else, including Adams, stood much of a chance at all.

If hindsight permits this realistic rendering of the historical conditions, which in turn defined the limited parameters within which the policies of the Adams presidency took shape, it also requires us to notice that none of the major players possessed the kind of clairvoyance required to comprehend what history had in store for them. (They believed they were making history, not the other way around.) In effect, the political institutions and the very authority of the federal government were too new and ill-formed to cope effectively with the foreign and domestic challenges facing the new nation.

What happened as a result was highly improvisational and deeply personal. Adams virtually ignored his cabinet, most of whom were more loyal to Hamilton anyway, and fell back to his family for advice, which in practice made Abigail his unofficial one-woman staff. Jefferson resumed his partnership with Madison, the roles now reversed, with Jefferson assuming active command of the Republican opposition from the seat of government in Philadelphia and Madison dispensing his political wisdom from retirement at Montpelier. While the official center of the government remained in the executive and congressional offices at Philadelphia, the truly effective centers of power were located in two political partnerships based on personal trust. Having failed to revive the great collaboration of the revolutionary era, Adams and Jefferson went their separate ways with different intimates.

THERE WAS an almost tribal character to the Adams collaboration. Adams himself, while vastly experienced as a statesman and diplomat, had no experience whatsoever as an executive. He had never served as a governor, as Jefferson had, or as a military commander, as Washington had. And he regarded the role of party leader of the Federalists as not just unbecoming but utterly incompatible with his responsibilities as president, which were to transcend party squabbles in the Washington mode and reach decisions like a "patriot king" whose sole concern was the long-term public interest. As a result, the notion that he was supposed to manage the political factions in the Congress or in his cabinet never even occurred to him. Instead, he would rely on his own judgment and on the advice of his family and trusted friends.

This explains two of his earliest and most controversial decisions. First, he insisted on including Elbridge Gerry in the peace delegations to France. Gerry was a kind of New England version of Benjamin Rush, a lovable gadfly with close personal ties to the Adams family but with ideological convictions that floated in unpredictable patterns over the entire political landscape. The most recent breezes had carried him into the Republican camp as a staunch defender of the French Revolution, which was the chief reason Abigail thought that Gerry "had a kink in his head." Adams himself warned Gerry not to confuse what was happening in France with the American Revolution. "The French are no more capable of a republican government," he insisted, "than a snowball can exist a whole week in the streets of Philadelphia under a burning sun." Despite Abigail's reservations, Adams wanted Gerry on the peace delegation to demonstrate his bipartisan principles and also to assure that he would receive candid reports from a trusted friend.[45]

Second, he appointed John Quincy as American minister to Prussia. His son objected, protesting that the appointment would surely be criticized as an act of nepotism and would fuel charges that Adams was grooming an heir for the presidency: "Your reasons will not bear examination," Adams retorted. "It is the worst founded opinion I ever knew you to conceive." This was vintage Adams bravado, shouting his denial at political advice he knew to be sound, refusing to listen because it was patently political and merely self-protective. Mostly, he wanted John Quincy located in one of the diplomatic capitals of Europe as his own personal listening post. "I wish you to continue your practice of writing freely to me," he wrote, then added, "and more cautiously to the office of state." He would be his own secretary of state and trust his son's quite impressive knowledge of European affairs more than official reports.[46]

Both of these decisions paid dividends the following year, when the prospects for an outright declaration of war against France looked virtually certain. The ever agile and forever unscrupulous Talleyrand, foreign minister of France, had refused to receive the American peace delegation and had then sent three of his operatives to demand a bribe of fifty thousand pounds sterling as the prerequisite for any further negotiations. When Adams received word of this outrageous ultimatum, he ordered the delegation to return home, but he also withheld the official dispatches describing the bribery scheme from the Congress and the public. Abigail described this decision as "a very painful thing" because "the President could not play his strongest card." But Adams knew that popular reaction to what became known as the XYZ Affair (after the three French operatives) would be virulently patriotic and intensely belligerent. By delaying publication of the dispatches, he bought time. And during that time, Gerry, always the maverick, had opted to remain in Paris to confer unofficially with French diplomats about averting the looming war. His reports home counseled patience, based on the growing recognition within the Directory that the bribery demand had been a terrible miscalculation. John Quincy's network of European sources also urged enlightened procrastination. Despite considerable pressure from the Federalists in Congress and mounting war fever in the wake of the XYZ revelations, Adams held out hope for reconciliation based primarily on these reports.[47]

Abigail was his chief domestic minister without portfolio. In a very real sense Adams did not have a domestic policy, indeed believed that paying any attention to the shifting currents of popular opinion and the raging party battles in the press violated his proper posture as president, which was to remain oblivious to such swings in the national mood. Abigail tended to reinforce this belief in executive independence. Jefferson, she explained, was like a willow who bent with every political breeze. Her husband, on the other hand, was like an oak: "He may be torn up by the roots. He may break. But he will never bend."[48]

Nevertheless, she followed the highly partisan exchanges in the Republican newspapers and provided her husband with regular reports on the machinations and accusations of the opposition. When an editorial in the *Aurora* described Adams as "old, guerelous [*sic*], bald, blind, and crippled," she joked that she alone possessed the intimate knowledge to testify about his physical condition. Popular reaction to the XYZ Affair generated a surge of hostility toward French supporters in America, and Abigail noted with pleasure the appearance of William Cobbett's anti-Jefferson editorials in *Porcupine's Gazette,* where Jefferson was described as head of "the frenchified faction in this country" and a leading member of "the American Directory." She relished reporting the Fourth of July Toast: "John Adams. May he, like *Samson,* slay thousands of Frenchmen with the *jawbone* of Jefferson." She passed along gossip circulating in the streets of Philadelphia about plans to mount pro-French demonstrations, allegedly orchestrated by "the grandest of all grand Villains, that traitor to his country—the infernal Scoundrel Jefferson." She predicted that the Republican leaders "will . . . take ultimately a station in the public's estimation like that of the Tories in our Revolution."[49]

Although we can never know for sure, there is considerable evidence that Abigail played a decisive role in persuading Adams to support passage of those four pieces of legislation known collectively as the Alien and Sedition Acts. These infamous statutes, unquestionably the biggest blunder of his presidency, were designed to deport or disenfranchise foreign-born residents, mostly Frenchmen, who were disposed to support the Republican party, and to make it a crime to publish "any false, scandalous, and malicious writing or writings against the Government of the United States." Adams went to his grave claiming that these laws never enjoyed his support, that their chief sponsors were Federalist extremists in the Congress, and that he had signed them grudgingly and reluctantly.[50]

All this was true enough, but sign them he did, despite his own reservations and against the advice of moderate Federalists like John Marshall. (Even Hamilton, who eventually went along, too, was at best lukewarm and fearful of the precedent set by the Sedition Act.) Abigail, on the other hand, felt no compunctions: "Nothing will have an effect until Congress passes a sedition bill," she wrote her sister in the spring of 1798, which would then permit "the wrath of the public to fall upon their [the Republican editors'] devoted heads. . . . In any other country Bache and all his papers would have been seized long ago." Her love for her husband, and her protective sense as chief guardian of his presidency, pushed her beyond any doubts. She even urged that the Alien Act be used to remove Albert Gallatin, the Swiss-born leader of the Republican party in the House of Representatives. Gallatin, she observed, "that specious, subtle, spare Cassius, that imported foreigner," was guilty of treasonable behavior by delivering speeches or introducing amendments "that obstruct their cause and prevent their reaching their goals." Gallatin, along with all the henchmen in the Jefferson camp, should be regarded "as traitors to their country."[51]

Ultimately, of course, Adams himself must bear the responsibility for signing into law the blatantly partisan legislation that has subsequently haunted his historic reputation. But if, as he forever insisted, the Alien and Sedition Acts never enjoyed his enthusiastic support, Abigail's unequivocal endorsement of the legislation almost surely tilted the decision toward the affirmative. To put it somewhat differently, if she had been opposed, it is difficult to imagine Adams taking the action he did. It is the one instance when the commingling of their convictions and the very intimacy of their partnership led him astray.

Ironically, the most significant—and in the long run most successful—decision of the Adams presidency occurred when Abigail was recovering from a bout with rheumatic fever back in Quincy, and the Federalists who opposed the policy attributed it to her absence. This was Adams's apparently impulsive decision, announced on February 18, 1799, to send another peace delegation to France. Theodore

Sedgwick, a Federalist leader in the Congress, claimed to be "thunder-struck" and summed up the reaction of his Federalist colleagues: "Had the foulest heart and the ablest head in the world, been permitted to select the most ruinous measure, perhaps it would have been precisely the one which had been adopted." Timothy Pickering, the disloyal secretary of state, whom Adams had come to despise, also described himself as "thunderstruck" and offered a perceptive reading of Adams's motives: "it was done without any *consultation with any member of the government* and for a reason *truly remarkable—because he knew we should all be opposed to the measure.*" Abigail herself reported that all the bedrock Federalist enclaves of New England were taken by surprise: "the whole community were like a flock of frightened pigions; nobody had their story ready."[52]

The stories circulating in the Philadelphia press suggested that Adams had acted impulsively because his politically savvy wife had not been available to talk him out of it. For the preceding two months he had in fact complained in public and private that he was no good as a "solitudionarian" and he "wanted my talkative wife." Abigail had noted an editorial in *Porcupine's Gazette* regretting her absence: "I suppose," she wrote her husband, "they will want somebody to keep you warm." The announcement of the new peace initiative then gave added credibility to the charge that, without Abigail, Adams had lost either his balance or his mind. Adams joked about these stories: "They ought to gratify your vanity," he wrote Abigail, "enough to cure you and bring you here." For her part, Abigail returned the joke, but with a clear signal of support: "This was pretty saucy, but the old woman can tell them they are mistaken, for she considers the measure a master stroke of policy."[53]

This has pretty much been the verdict of history, for the delegation Adams appointed eventually negotiated a diplomatic end to the "quasi-war" with France; Adams's decision became the first substantive implementation of Washington's message in the Farewell Address, as well as a precedent for American isolation from European wars—one that would influence American foreign policy for over a century. In the immediate context of the party wars then raging, however, Adams's unilateral action was politically suicidal: "He has sustained the whole force of an unpopular measure," Abigail observed, "which he knew would . . . shower down upon his head a torrent of invective. As he expected, he has been abused and calumniated by his enemies, that was to be looked for—but in the *house of his friends,* they have joined loudest in the clamor." What Abigail meant was that Adams had chosen to alienate himself from the mainstream of the Federalist party, which regarded his policy as pro-French, indeed just the kind of decision one might have expected from Jefferson and the Republicans. The editorials in *Porcupine's Gazette* turned against him. Federalist gossip suggested that their erstwhile leader was mentally unbalanced. (Adams, feeling his oats, wrote Abigail that he might now use the Sedition Act to shut down the Federalist press.) He was the archetypal illustration of the president without a party.[54]

Why did he do it? Three overlapping reasons appear to have converged in Adams's mind and provided decisive direction to a foreign policy that, until then, had been vacillating between the incompatible agendas of the Federalists and the Republicans.

First, his lingering suspicions of Hamilton developed into unbridled distrust and then outright personal hatred. For two years, Hamilton had been issuing directives to Adams's cabinet behind the scenes. Though Adams was vaguely aware of these machinations, he gave them little attention; after all, he never paid much heed to his cabinet anyway. In the summer of 1798, however, Hamilton persuaded his Federalist colleagues in the Congress to authorize the creation of a vastly expanded Provisional Army (subsequently called the New Army) of between ten thousand and thirty thousand soldiers in preparation for the looming outbreak of war with France. Adams had always supported military preparations more as a diplomatic maneuver to impress the French government of American resolve. And he had strongly preferred a naval force, what he called "Floating batteries and wooden walls." Standing armies struck him as inherently dangerous and expensive items. "Regiments are costly articles everywhere," he explained to his secretary of war, "and more so in this country than any other under the sun." What possible rationale could exist for a large American land force, since the conflict with France was occurring on the high seas? "At present," he observed, "there is no more prospect of seeing a French army here than there is in Heaven."[55]

Then the whole horrid picture came into focus for Adams. Hamilton intended to make the New Army his personal instrument of power. It was a foregone conclusion that Washington would be called out of retirement to head the force, but equally predictable that the aging general would delegate actual command to his former aide-de-camp. Adams suspected that Hamilton, whom he had formerly distrusted and now utterly loathed, saw himself as an American Napoleon, poised to declare martial law and present himself as the available savior. Abigail seconded the assessment, calling Hamilton "a second Buonaparty" whose imperialistic designs could only be guessed at. (If they had been able to read Hamilton's private correspondence, they would have discovered that his plans were quite grandiose: He hoped to march his conquering army through Virginia, where recalcitrant Republicans would be treated like the Whiskey Rebels, then down through the Louisiana Territory and into Mexico and Peru, liberating all the inhabitants from French and Spanish domination and offering membership in the expanded American republic.) Although Adams had gone along with the Alien and Sedition Acts, the prospect of a Hamilton-led army marching heaven knows where conjured up the demise of republican government altogether in the classical last act—a military dictatorship. No one recognized this historical pattern more clearly than Adams. No one, not even Jefferson, hated Hamilton more than Adams. Abigail described the decision to resume negotiations with France as "a master stroke of policy" because it averted a French war and removed the rationale for Hamilton's army at one fell swoop.[56]

Second, the reports Adams was receiving from John Quincy in Prussia, based on his network of contacts in Paris and Amsterdam, provided fresh evidence that Talleyrand was now eager for peace with the United States. In January of 1799 Adams's second son, Thomas Boylston, returned from Europe with additional dispatches from John Quincy, indicating that Talleyrand would not only receive an American peace delegation but would also be open to a consideration of compensation for American shipping losses over the past three years. However impulsive Adams's February decision might have appeared to outsiders, it was really the culmination of considerable deliberation, based on diplomatic advice from his most trusted and strategically located confidant, who also happened to be his son.

Third, and finally, Adams derived deep personal satisfaction from singular acts of principle that defied the agendas of both political parties. The fact that the decision to send the delegation rendered him unpopular, that it struck most observers as an act of political suicide, only confirmed for him that it must be right. The office of the presidency, as he saw it, was designed to levitate above the party squabbles and transcend partisan versions of the national interest. Even more palpably, the fullest expression of his best energies always occurred when the long-term public interest, as he understood it, clashed with the political imperatives of the moment.

The trademark Adams style might be described as "enlightened perversity," which actually sought out occasions to display, often in conspicuous fashion, his capacity for self-sacrifice. He had defended the British troops accused of the Boston Massacre, insisted upon American independence in the Continental Congress a full year before it was fashionable, argued for a more exalted conception of the presidency despite charges of monarchical tendencies. It was all part of the Adams pattern, an iconoclastic and contrarian temperament that relished alienation. (John Quincy and then great-grandson Henry Adams exhibited the same pattern over the next century, suggesting that the predilections resided in the bloodstream.) The political conditions confronting the presidency in 1798 were tailor-made to call forth his excessive version of virtue. Though Abigail was with him all the way, for Adams himself it was the supreme collaboration with his own private demons and doubts, his personal declaration of independence.

ALL THE DOMESTIC and international challenges facing the Adams presidency looked entirely different to Jefferson and Madison. Once they decided to reject Adams's overture and set themselves up as the leaders of the Republican opposition, they closed ranks around their own heartfelt convictions and interpreted the several crises confronting him as opportunities to undermine the Federalist party, which they sincerely regarded as an organized conspiracy against the true meaning of the American Revolution. "As to do nothing, and to gain time, is everything with us," Jefferson wrote to Madison, the very intractability of the French question and "the sharp divisions within the Federalist camp" between the Hamiltonians and what Jefferson called "the Adamites" worked to their political advantage. In order for the Republican agenda to win, the Federalist agenda needed to fail. Although Adams never fit comfortably into either party category, and eventually acted decisively to alienate himself from both sides, as the elected leader of the Federalists he became the unavoidable target of the organized Republican opposition.[57]

Madison had never shared Jefferson's personal affection for Adams, so it was easier for him to take the lead in stigmatizing Adams's motives and character:

> There never was perhaps a greater contrast between two characters than between those of the present President and of his predecessor. . . . The one cold considerate and cautious, the other headlong and kindled into flame by every spark that lights on his passions. The one ever scrutinizing into the public opinion, and ready to follow where he could not lead it; the other insulting it by the most adverse sentiments and pursuits. W. a hero in the field, yet overweighing every danger in the Cabinet. A. without a single pretension to the character of a soldier, a perfect Quixote as a statesman. The former chief magistrate pursuing peace every where with sincerity, tho' mistaking the means; the latter taking as much pains to get into war, as the former took to keep out of it.

The latter point became an article of faith within the Jefferson-Madison collaboration—namely, that Adams actually wanted war with France. He was, declared Madison, "the only obstacle to accommodation, and the real cause of war, if war takes place."[58]

Jefferson and Madison even managed to persuade themselves that Adams had concocted the entire XYZ Affair to mobilize popular support for a declaration of war. Talleyrand, they told each other, was neither so stupid nor so dishonorable to attempt bribery of the American peace delegation. Adams had orchestrated "a libel on the French government" as part of his "swindling experiment." Instead of regarding Adams's decision to delay release of the dispatches exposing the bribery demands as a prudent and statesmanlike effort to avoid a public outcry for war, Madison insisted it was timed to produce maximum damage. "The credit given to Mr. Adams for a spirit of conciliation towards France is wonderful," Madison observed caustically, meaning that it was wholly undeserved. When Jefferson halfheartedly suggested that his old friend had once been a man of revolutionary principles, Madison retorted, "Every answer he gives to his addresses unmasks more and more his true principles. . . . The abolition of Royalty was it seems not one of his Revolutionary principles. Whether he always made this profession is best known to those, who knew him in the year 1776." Jefferson, in effect, needed to liberate himself from nostalgic memories. Adams was a traitor.[59]

Although he certainly knew better, Jefferson went along. He reported gossip in the corridors of Congress to the effect that Adams had been heard to declare "that such was his want of confidence in the faith of France, that were they ever to agree to a treaty ever so favorable, he should think it his duty to reject it." (Adams was in fact, at that very moment, listening to Gerry's pleadings for a renewal of the peace effort.) Another rumor circulating in the streets of Philadelphia caught Jefferson's ear: Washington had leaked the news that he opposed Adams's foreign policy. (The exact opposite was true. Washington was endorsing the Adams initiative as the effective implementation of his own long-standing commitment to American neutrality.) Yet another rumor had it that Adams was working behind the scenes to scuttle the plans for moving the capital to the Potomac (also untrue). And then, when the president announced his unexpected decision to send a new American peace delegation to France in February of 1799, Jefferson apprised Madison that this "event of events" had been forced upon Adams. Jefferson had reliable evidence that Talleyrand had threatened to leak news of his previous peace initiative, thereby requiring Adams to reciprocate. "Mark that I state this as conjecture," Jefferson told Madison, "but founded on workings and indications which have been under our eyes" (all contrived).[60]

If the primary function of the collaboration within the Adams family was to insulate and eventually isolate Adams from the ideological warfare raging between both political parties, the primary function of the collaboration between Jefferson and Madison was to generate mutual reinforcement for their uncompromising assault on the presidency, frequently at the expense of even the most rudimentary version of factual accuracy. In their minds, the political stakes were enormous, the threat posed by the Federalists put the entire republican experiment at risk, the battle was to the death, and taking prisoners was not permitted. They convinced themselves that Adams was the enemy, and then all the evidence fell in place around that rock-ribbed, if highly questionable, conviction.

Jefferson's nearly Herculean powers of self-denial also helped keep the cause pure, at least in the privacy of his own mind. In 1798, he commissioned James Callender, a notorious scandalmonger who had recently broken the story on Hamilton's adulterous affair with Maria Reynolds, to write a libelous attack on Adams. In *The Prospect Before Us,* Callender delivered the goods, describing Adams as "a hoary headed incendiary" who was equally determined on war with France and on declaring himself president for life, with John Quincy lurking in the background as his successor. When confronted with the charge that, despite his position as vice president, he had paid Callender to write diatribes against the president, Jefferson claimed to know nothing about it. Callender subsequently published Jefferson's incriminating letters, proving his complicity, and Jefferson seemed genuinely surprised at the revelation, suggesting that for him the deepest secrets were not the ones he kept from his enemies but the ones he kept from himself.[61]

When Congress began the debates over the Sedition Act in the spring of 1798, Jefferson's first fear was that it was aimed pointedly at him. He complained to James Monroe that "my name is running through all the city as detected in criminal correspondence with the French directory." Editorials in Federalist newspapers accused him of passing information to the French government through pro-French agents in America and meeting routinely with Benjamin Franklin Bache, editor of the *Aurora,* the chief vehicle for the opposition. Jefferson privately acknowledged to Madison that these accusations were essentially true. Even though he was the second-ranking member of the Adams administration, he was, as the Federalist leadership in the House described him, "the very life and soul of the opposition." Jefferson defended himself by claiming that his consultations with Bache were not clandestine meetings; he had met with Bache many times, true enough, but he was not, as the Federalists charged, "closeted" with him. More basically, Jefferson simply did not regard his behavior as seditious or treasonable. Indeed, it was the Federalist government, though duly elected, that was guilty of treason.[62]

Here was the core of the problem. Jefferson genuinely believed, and Madison reinforced the belief, that the Federalists had captured the government from the American people. Despite its electoral mandate, the programs and policies the Federalists were implementing at the national level—an expansive agenda for the federal government, a version of neutrality that aligned the United States more with England than France—represented a repudiation of the spirit of '76. The passage of the Alien and Sedition Acts, then the creation of the New Army, only confirmed that the Federalist agenda violated the central tenets of the American Revolution, conjuring up memories of Parliament's restrictions on the colonial press and British troops quartered in the major colonial cities. How could opposition to such measures be treasonable now when they had been legitimate expressions of American dissent back then?

The legal guidelines that might permit a clear answer to that question had not yet congealed. By modern standards Jefferson's active role in promoting anti-Adams propaganda and his complicity in leaking information to pro-French enthusiasts like Bache were impeachable offenses that verged on treason. But then Hamilton had been guilty of similar indiscretions with pro-English advocates during the Jay's Treaty negotiations. And his conduct in providing clandestine instructions to Adams's cabinet undermined the constitutional authority of the executive branch in ways that would have landed him in jail in modern times. Only ten years after the passage and ratification of the Constitution, however, what were treasonable or seditious acts remained blurry and more problematic judgments without the historical sanction that only experience could provide. Lacking a consensus on what the American Revolution had intended and what the Constitution had settled, Federalists and Republicans alike were afloat in a sea of mutual accusations and partisan interpretations. The center could not hold because it did not exist.

The capstone of the Jefferson-Madison collaboration occurred at this volatile political moment—namely, their joint authorship of the Kentucky and Virginia Resolutions. Jefferson visited Madison at Montpelier on July 2–3 to discuss their response to the Sedition Act, which passed the Senate the following day. (The Federalists, ironically, thought it was the perfect way to celebrate the Fourth of July.) They agreed to launch a pamphlet campaign against what Jefferson called "the reign of witches." Working alone at Monticello, Jefferson composed what became known as the Kentucky Resolutions in August and September. His core argument was that the Sedition Act was unconstitutional because it violated the natural rights of the citizens of each state to control their own domestic affairs. Moreover, each state "has a natural right in cases not within the compact"—that is, in all cases not specified as under federal jurisdiction in the Constitution—"to nullify of their own authority all assumptions of power by others within their limits." Here was the classic states' rights position, topped off by the sweeping claim that federal laws could be nullified by the states, which then had a legitimate right to secede, what Jefferson called "scission," if the federal Congress or courts defied their decision. If the Sedition Act was a serious threat to civil liberties, Jefferson's response was an equally serious threat to the sovereignty of the national government and the survival of the union.[63]

Fortunately for Jefferson, the leadership of the Kentucky legislature decided to delete the sections of his draft endorsing nullification, presumably because such open defiance of federal law seemed excessive and unnecessarily risky. Madison's more judicious arguments, published as the Virginia Resolutions, were circulating in the national press and achieving the same goal—condemning the Sedition Act—but without recourse to nullification. In fact, the Virginia Resolutions described the Alien and Sedition Acts as "alarming infractions" of the Constitution that violated the free speech guarantees of the First Amendment. Instead of challenging the authority of the federal government, Madison invoked the protections afforded by that very government, implicitly suggesting that the federal courts and not the individual states were the ultimate arbiters of the Constitution. Whereas Jefferson's line of thought led logically to the compact theory of the Constitution eventually embraced by the Confederacy in 1861, Madison's arguments led toward the modern doctrine of judicial review and constitutional guarantees for free speech and freedom of the press.[64]

When Madison wrote or spoke on constitutional questions, Jefferson always deferred. To Republican confidants in Virginia, he reiterated his conviction that "the true principles of our federal compact" left the states sovereign over all domestic policy; if Congress failed to rescind the Sedition Act, "we should sever ourselves from that union we so much value, rather than give up the rights of self government which we have reserved." After a personal visit from Madison in September of 1799, however, Jefferson agreed to soften his stance on secession, "not only in deference to his judgment," as he put it, "but because we should never think of separation but for respected and enormous violations"—or, as he had previously written in the Declaration of Independence, after "a long train of abuses." Madison's prudent and silent intervention rescued Jefferson from the secessionist implications of his revolutionary principles and artfully concealed the huge discrepancy between their respective views of the Constitution. The imperatives of their collaboration, plus the need to present a united front against the Federalists, took precedence over their incompatible notions of where sovereignty resided in the American republic.[65]

THERE ARE only a few universal laws of political life, but one of them guided the Republicans during the last year of the Adams presidency—namely, never interfere when your enemies are busily engaged in flagrant acts of self-destruction. As soon as the Federalists launched their prosecutions of Republican editors and writers under the Sedition Act—a total of eighteen indictments were filed—it became clear that the prosecutions were generally regarded as persecutions. Most of the defendants became local heroes and public martyrs. Madison quickly concluded that "our public malady may work its own cure," meaning that the spectacle of Federalist lawyers descending upon the Republican opposition with such blatantly partisan accusations only served to create converts to the cause they were attempting to silence. The threatened prosecution of aliens also backfired on the Federalists, when Irish immigrants in New York and Germans in Pennsylvania, formerly staunch supporters of the Adams administration, went over to the Republicans in droves.[66]

What Jefferson had described as "the reign of witches" even began to assume the shape of a political comedy in which the joke was on the Federalists. In New Jersey, for example, when a drunken Republican editor was charged with making a ribald reference to the president's posterior, the jury returned a not guilty verdict on the grounds that truth was a legitimate defense. There was even room for irony. It was while James Callender was serving his sentence for libel in a Richmond jail that he first heard rumors of Jefferson's sexual liaison with a mulatto slave named Sally Hemings. He subsequently published the story after deciding that Jefferson had failed to pay him adequately for his hatchet job on Adams.[67]

But this delectable morsel of scandal, which was only confirmed as correct beyond any reasonable doubt by DNA studies done in 1998, did not arrive in time to help Adams in the presidential election of 1800. Indeed, Adams's string of bad luck or poor timing, call it what you will, persisted to the end. The peace delegation he dispatched to France so single-handedly negotiated a treaty ending the "quasi-war," but the good news arrived too late to influence the election. Moreover, the New Army, which Adams had opposed and then rendered superfluous, had strained the federal budget to a point that demanded new sources of revenue. Even as the army was being disbanded, much to Adams's credit and relief, the cost of raising it landed on the voting public. Adams had somehow managed to miss the political rewards due him and catch the criticism that properly belonged to others.

Abigail's earlier characterization of the Adams-Jefferson competition— the oak versus the willow—proved prophetic. Perhaps the supreme example of Jefferson's greater flexibility occurred on the foreign policy front. Throughout the Adams presidency, Jefferson and his Republican followers had been insisting that the French Revolution was the American Revolution on European soil and that France was therefore America's major international ally. But when Napoleon overturned the French Republic and declared himself omnipotent military dictator, again just as Adams had predicted would happen, Jefferson quickly shifted his position to accommodate the new reality. "It is very material for the . . . [American people] to be made sensible that their own character and situation are materially different from the French," he observed in 1800, "and that whatever may be the fate of republicanism there, we are able to preserve it inviolate here." This was precisely the neutral foreign policy that both Washington and Adams had been urging for a decade and that Jefferson had condemned as a betrayal of the spirit of '76. Jefferson's conversion occurred with such breathtaking speed that hardly anyone noticed how deftly he was discarding the chief weapon the Republicans had wielded against two Federalist administrations. That weapon was unnecessary now, as both Jefferson and Madison understood, because the superior organization of the Republicans at the state level virtually assured their victory in the looming presidential election.[68]

Given this formidable array of bad luck, poor timing, and the highly focused political strategy of his Republican enemies, Adams actually did surprisingly well when all the votes were counted. He ran ahead of the Federalist candidates for Congress, who were swept from office in a Republican landslide. Outside of New York, he even won more electoral votes than he had in 1796. But thanks in great part to the deft political maneuverings of Aaron Burr, all twelve of New York's electoral votes went to Jefferson. As early as May of 1800, Abigail, the designated vote counter on the Adams team, had predicted that "New York will be the balance in the scaile, skaill, scaill (is it right now? it does not look so.)" Though she did not know how to spell *scale,* she knew where the election would be decided. In the final tally, her husband lost to the tandem of Jefferson and Burr, 73 to 65.[69]

Though it probably occurred too late to have much, if any, bearing on the results, the most dramatic event of the campaign was provided by Hamilton. In October he wrote and privately printed a fifty-four-page pamphlet assailing the character of Adams, describing him as an inherently unstable creature, a man driven by vanity and his own perverse version of independence, a pathetic bundle of twitches and tantrums who was "unfit for the office of chief Magistrate." Adams responded with uncharacteristic calmness to this personal vendetta. "I am confident," he observed, "that it will do him more harm than me." He was right. Coming too late to affect many voters, Hamilton's diatribe exposed the deep rift within the Federalist camp for all to see and suggested to most readers that Hamilton himself was out of his mind. In political terms, the Hamilton pamphlet was fully as fatal, and perhaps suicidal, as his subsequent decision to face Aaron Burr on the plains of Weehawken. His reputation never recovered.[70]

The same could be said for the Federalist party. The Jefferson-Madison collaboration was not just committed to capturing the federal government for the Republicans. As Jefferson put it so graphically, their larger goal was "to sink federalism into an abyss from which there shall be no resurrection of it." When Madison declared that the Republican cause was now "completely triumphant," he not only meant that they had won control of the presidency and the Congress but also that the Federalist party was in complete disarray. Though pockets of Federalist power remained alive in New England for over a decade, as a national movement with the capacity to dominate the debate about America's proper course, it was a spent force. Jefferson had not yet invented the expression "the revolution of 1800" to describe the Republican ascendancy. Nor had historians translated that term to mean the emergence of a more authentically democratic brand of politics, a translation that Jefferson would have understood dimly, if at all. (Jefferson actually thought that his victory represented a recovery rather than a discovery, a renewal of the principles of '76 and a repudiation of the constitutional settlement of 1787 as the Federalists had attempted to define it.) But the more historically correct reality was that no one quite knew what the Republican triumph meant in positive terms for the national government. What was clear, however, was that a particular version of politics and political leadership embodied in the Washington and Adams administrations had been successfully opposed and decisively defeated. The Jefferson-Madison collaboration was the politics of the future. The Adams collaboration was the politics of the past.[71]

What died was the presumption, so central to Adams's sense of politics and of himself, that there was a long-term collective interest for the republic that could be divorced from partisanship, indeed rendered immune to politics altogether; and that the duty of an American statesman was to divine that public interest while studiously ignoring, indeed remaining blissfully oblivious to, the partisan pleadings of particular constituencies. After 1800, what Adams had called "the monarchical principle" was dead in American political culture, along with the kind of towering defiance that both Washington and Adams had harbored toward what might be called the "morality of partisanship." That defiance had always depended upon revolutionary credentials— those present at the creation of the republic could be trusted to act responsibly—and as the memory of the Revolution faded, so did the trust it conferred. Of course Jefferson could, and decidedly did, claim membership in "the band of brothers," but his election marked the end of an era. The "people" had replaced the "public" as the sovereign source of political wisdom. No leader could credibly claim to be above the fray. As Jefferson had understood from the moment Washington stepped down, the American president must forever after be the head of a political party.

Neither member of the Adams team could ever comprehend this historical transition as anything other than an ominous symptom of moral degeneration. "Jefferson had a party," Adams observed caustically, "Hamilton had a party, but the commonwealth had none." If the very idea of virtue was no longer an ideal in American politics, then there was no place for him in public life. If the Adams brand of states-manship was now an anachronism—and it was—then the Adams presidency would serve as a fitting monument to its passing. In February of 1800, Adams signed the Treaty of Mortefontaine, officially ending hostilities with France. He could leave office in the knowledge that his discredited policies and singular style had worked. As he put it, he had "steered the vessel . . . into a peaceable and safe port."[72]

Rather ironically, the last major duty of the Adams collaboration was to supervise the transition of the federal government to its permanent location on the Potomac. Though the entire archive of the executive branch required only seven packing cases, Abigail resented the physical burdens imposed by this final chore, as well as the cold, cavernous, and still-unfinished rooms of the presidential mansion. For several weeks it was not at all clear whether Jefferson would become the next abiding occupant, because the final tally of the electoral vote had produced a tie between him and Burr. Rumors circulated that Adams intended to step down from office in order to permit Jefferson, still his vice president, to succeed him, in an effort to forestall a constitutional crisis. Adams let out the word that Jefferson was clearly the voters' choice and the superior man, that Burr was "like a balloon, filled with inflammable air." In the end, the crisis passed when, on the thirty-sixth ballot, the House voted Jefferson into office.[73]

Despite all the accumulated bitterness of the past eight years, and despite the political wounds Jefferson had inflicted over the past four years on the Adams presidency, Abigail insisted that her husband invite their "former friend" for cake and tea before she departed for Quincy a few weeks before the inauguration ceremony. No record of the conversation exists, though Jefferson had already apprised Madison that he knew the Adamses well enough to expect "dispositions liberal and accommodating." On the actual day of the inauguration, however, Jefferson did not have Adams by his side as he rode down a stump-infested Pennsylvania Avenue to the yet-unfinished capitol. Rather than lend his presence to the occasion, Adams had taken the four o'clock stage out of town that morning in order to rejoin Abigail. He did not exchange another word with Jefferson for twelve years.[74]

CHAPTER SIX

The Friendship

ADAMS CORRECTLY regarded the five-hundred-mile trek back to Quincy as his final exit from the public stage. Upon arriving home he noted that his barnyard was full of seaweed, which then prompted a characteristically indiscreet observation: He had made "a good exchange . . . honors and virtues for manure." When a violent storm struck on the day of his return, he took it as a providential sign that trouble was following him into retirement, as he put it, "substituting fermentations in the elements for revolutions in the moral, intellectual and political world." As one who had helped to make those political revolutions happen, he claimed to be completely comfortable in stormy weather. But now, at the advanced age of sixty-six, was it not natural to expect some semblance of serenity? "Far removed from all the intrigues, and now out of reach of all the great and little passions that agitate the world," he explained, "I hope to enjoy more tranquillity than has ever before been my lot."[1]

The trouble with Adams was not that storms seemed to follow him, but rather that he carried them inside his soul wherever he went. Abigail spied him in the field that July of 1801, working alongside the hired hands, swinging his sickle and murmuring obscenities at his political opponents. From his letters we know that Hamilton topped his enemies list; he called him that "bastard brat of a Scotch pedlar," who was "as ambitious as Bonaparte, though less courageous, and, save for me, would have involved us in a foreign war with France & a Civil war with ourselves."[2]

Not far behind Hamilton came his former friend and successor to the presidency. Though the hate for Jefferson was far less, the hurt was more. They had done so much together, struggled together against the odds in 1776, represented America in Europe during the 1780s, risen above their political differences during Washington's administration. But during his own presidency Adams believed that Jefferson had betrayed him and their friendship. And it was all done so indirectly, so craftily, like a burglar who left no fingerprints. Jefferson was "a shadow man," Adams now believed, a man whose character was "like the great rivers, whose bottoms we cannot see and make no noise." When commenting on his other enemies, Adams displayed considerable flair. Tom Paine, for example, came off as "the Satyr of the Age . . . a mongrel between Pig and Puppy, begotten by a wild Boar on a Butch Wolf." With Jefferson, however, the colorful epithets and irreverent images did not come so easily. It was difficult to be specific when the core of a man's character was elusiveness.[3]

The character of Adams's own complicated feelings toward Jefferson eventually revealed itself through Abigail. The occasion was poignant. In 1804 Jefferson's younger daughter, Maria Jefferson Eppes, died from complications during childbirth. Abigail decided to write a letter of consolation, explaining that "reasons of various kinds witheld my pen, until the powerful feelings of my heart, have burst through the restraint." She recalled caring for Maria as a nine-year-old girl just arrived in London. "It has been some time that I conceived of any event in this Life, which would call forth, feelings of mutual sympathy," Abigail confided to Jefferson, but the loss of a child overcame all her rational reservations. She wanted Jefferson to know that her heart was with him.[4]

Jefferson normally had perfect pitch when interpreting the tone of a letter, but in this instance, he missed Abigail's clear warning signals and read her words as an invitation to resume the friendship with the Adams family. He seized the opportunity to review the long political partnership he had enjoyed with her husband. Their mutual affection "accompanied us thro' long and important scenes," he wrote, and "the different conclusions we had drawn from our political reading and reflections were not permitted to lessen mutual esteem." Though they had twice run against each other for the presidency, he insisted that "we never stood in one another's way." The political rivalry had never eroded the personal respect between them.

There was only one occasion, Jefferson confided, when a decision by Adams struck him as "personally unkind." That was his appointment of Federalists to several vacant judgeships during his last weeks as president. These appointments, somewhat misleadingly described as "the midnight judges," had occurred after the presidential election, and therefore denied Jefferson the right to choose his own men. (The major offense was the appointment of John Marshall as chief justice of the Supreme Court, arguably Adams's most enduring anti-Jeffersonian legacy, in part because of Marshall's magisterial career on the bench and in part because Jefferson and Marshall utterly despised each other.) But this one offense, as Jefferson put it, "left something for friendship to forgive," so that "after brooding it over for some little time . . . I forgave it cordially, and returned to the same state of esteem and respect for him [Adams] which had so long subsisted."[5]

Jefferson's letter sent Abigail into a controlled rage. "You have been pleased to enter upon some subjects which call for a reply," she began ominously. The very notion that Jefferson should feel himself the injured party with the moral leverage to forgive her husband was a preposterous presumption. Now that Jefferson had raised the issue of political betrayal, he would have to "excuse the freedom of this discussion . . . which has taken off the Shackles I should otherwise found myself embarrassed with." The pent-up anger poured out: "And now Sir, I freely disclose to you what has severed the bonds of former Friendship, and placed you in a light very different from what I had once viewed you in."

After delivering a spirited defense of her husband's right to make judicial appointments before he left office, Abigail launched a frontal attack on Jefferson's character. Throughout Adams's presidency, she claimed, Jefferson had used his position as vice president to undermine the policies of the very man he had been elected to support. This was bad enough. But the worst offenses occurred during the election of 1800. Jefferson was guilty of "the blackest calumny and foulest falsehoods" during that bitter campaign. While affecting disinterest and detachment, he was secretly hiring scandalmongers like James Callender to libel Adams with outrageous charges: Adams was mentally deranged; Adams intended to have himself crowned as an American monarch; Adams planned to appoint John Quincy his successor to the presidency. "This, Sir, I considered as a personal injury," Abigail observed, "the Sword that cut the Gordion knot." It was richly ironic and wholly deserving that the infamous Callender had then turned on Jefferson and accused him of a sexual liaison with Sally Hemings, his household slave. "The serpent you cherished and warmed," she noted with satisfaction, "bit the hand that nourished him." And so, if there was any forgiving to be done, it would all happen on the Adams side. In the meantime, Jefferson was the one who needed to do some soul searching. She concluded with one last verbal slap: "Faithful are the wounds of a Friend."[6]

Throughout his extraordinarily vast correspondence, Jefferson never received another letter like this one. He had his detractors, to be sure, but Federalist critics tended to attack him in the public press, which he could and did dismiss as partisan propaganda. Abigail's accusations, on the other hand, were private and personal, came from someone whom he respected as an intimate friend, and went beyond mere matters of political partisanship to questions of honor and trust. His first instinct was to claim that both sides, Republicans and Federalists alike, had engaged in lies and distortions during the election of 1800, and that he had suffered equivalent "calumnies and falsehoods" along with Adams. (This was completely true.) He then went on to disclaim that "any person who knew either of us could possibly believe that either meddled in that dirty work." In effect, he had no role whatsoever in promoting Callender's libels against Adams. (This was a lie.) "What those who wish to think amiss of me," Jefferson pleaded, "I have learnt to be perfectly indifferent." But with those like Abigail, "where I know a mind to be ingenious, and need only truth to set it to rights, I cannot be as passive."[7]

Abigail was having none of it. As she saw it, Jefferson's denials only offered further evidence of his duplicity. His complicity in behind-the-scenes political plotting was common knowledge. Abigail had initially resisted the obvious because, as she put it, "the Heart is long, very long in receiving the convictions that is forced upon it by reason." Even now, she acknowledged, "affection still lingers in the Bosom, even after esteem has taken its flight." But there was no denying that Jefferson had mortgaged his honor to win an election. His Federalist critics had always accused him of being a man of party rather than principle. "Pardon me, Sir, if I say," Abigail concluded, "that I fear you are."[8]

We can be reasonably sure that Abigail was speaking for her husband as well as herself in this brief volley of letters. The Adams team, then, was charging Jefferson with two serious offenses against the unwritten code of political honor purportedly binding on the leadership class of the revolutionary generation. The first offense, which has a quaint and wholly anachronistic sound to our modern ears, was that Jefferson was personally involved in his own campaign for the presidency and that he conducted that campaign with only one goal in mind—namely, winning the election. This was the essence of the charge that he was a "party man." Such behavior became an accepted, even expected, feature of the political landscape during the middle third of the nineteenth century and has remained so ever since. Within the context of the revolutionary generation, however, giving one's allegiance to a political party remained illegitimate. It violated the core of virtue and disinterestedness presumed essential for anyone properly equipped to oversee public affairs. Neither Washington nor Adams had ever played a direct role in their own campaigns for office. And even Jefferson, who was the first president to break with that tradition, felt obliged to do so surreptitiously, then issue blanket denials when confronted by Abigail. Jefferson, in fact, was on record as making one of the strongest statements of the era against the influence of political parties. He described party allegiance as "the last degradation of a free and moral agent" and claimed that "if I could not go to heaven but with a party, I would not go there at all."[9]

Jefferson's position on political parties, like his stance on slavery, seemed to straddle a rather massive contradiction. In both instances his posture of public probity—slavery should be ended and political parties were evil agents that corrupted republican values—was at odds with his personal behavior and political interest. And in both instances, Jefferson managed to convince himself that these apparent contradictions were, well, merely apparent. In the case of his active role behind the scenes during the presidential campaign of 1800, Jefferson sincerely believed that a Federalist victory meant the demise of the spirit of '76. Anything that avoided that horrible outcome ought to be justifiable.

He then issued so many denials of his direct involvement in the campaign that he probably came to believe his own lies. That is why Abigail's relentless refusal to accept his personal testimonials on this score struck a nerve. He was not accustomed to having his word questioned and his excuses exposed, not even by himself.

His second offense was more personal. Namely, he had vilified a man whom he claimed was a long-standing friend. He had sponsored Callender's polemics against the Adams administration even though he knew them to be gross misrepresentations. Adams had no monarchical ambitions, though he did believe in a strong executive. He did not want war with France, though he did think that American neutrality should take precedence over the Franco-American alliance. Both positions were in accord with Washington's preferred policy. Unlike Washington, however, Adams had political vulnerabilities, which Jefferson exploited for his own political advantage. If the gross distortions had been orchestrated by Madison or any number of lesser political operatives, it would have been bad enough. But for Jefferson himself to have sanctioned the defamation was the essence of betrayal. It was akin to Hamilton's behind-the-scenes slandering of Burr, except in the case of Adams, the slander was more contemptible because essentially untrue. If Adams had been a believer in the *code duello,* which he was not (nor, for that matter, was Jefferson), this defamation of the Adams character would have presented a prime opportunity for a resolution with pistols on the field of honor. For at the highest level of political life in the early republic, relationships remained resolutely personal, dependent on mutual trust, and therefore vulnerable to betrayals whenever the public and private overlapped.

Although Jefferson probably presumed that Abigail was sharing their correspondence with her husband, Adams himself never saw the letters until several months later. After reading over the exchange, he made this written comment for the record: "The whole of this correspondence was begun and conducted without my Knowledge or Suspicion, and this morning at the desire of Mrs. Adams I read the whole. I have no remarks to make upon it at this time and in this place." A steely silence thereupon settled over the dialogue between Quincy and Monticello for the following eight years.[10]

.   .   .

DURING THAT time Jefferson was too busy to indulge in retrospective fretting over the loss of a friend. His first term as president would go down as one of the most brilliantly successful in American history, capped off by the Louisiana Purchase (1803), which effectively doubled the size of the national domain. His second term, on the other hand, proved to be a series of domestic tribulations and foreign policy failures, capped off by the infamous Embargo Act (1807), which devastated the economy while failing to avert the looming war with England. Adams's assessment of Jefferson's presidency mixed fairminded criticism of his policies with prejudicial comments on his character:

> Mr. Jefferson has reason to reflect upon himself. How he will get rid of his remorse in retirement, I know not. He must know that he leaves the government infinitely worse than he found it, and that from his own error or ignorance. I wish his telescopes and mathematical instruments, however, may secure his felicity. But if I have not mismeasured his ambition . . . the sword will cut away the scabbard. . . . I have no resentment against him, although he has honored and salaried almost every villain he could find who had been an enemy to me.[11]

Despite his brave posturings of nonchalance and indifference, Adams was, in fact, obsessed with Jefferson's growing reputation as one of the major figures of the age. As Adams remembered it, Jefferson had played a decidedly minor role in the Continental Congress. While he, John Adams, was delivering the fiery speeches that eventually moved their reluctant colleagues to make the decisive break with England, Jefferson lingered in the background like a shy schoolboy, so subdued that "during the whole Time I sat with him in Congress, I never heard him utter three sentences together." Now, however, because of the annual celebrations on July 4, the symbolic significance of the Declaration of Independence was looming larger in the public memory, blotting out the messier but more historically correct version of the story, transforming Jefferson from a secondary character to a star player in the drama. "Was there ever a Coup de Theatre," Adams complained, "that had so great an effect as Jefferson's Penmanship of the Declaration of Independence." Jefferson was an elegant stylist, to be sure, which was one of the main reasons that he, John Adams, had selected him to draft the famous document in the first place. But he was not a mover-and-shaker, only a draftsman; the words he wrote were merely the lyrical expression of ideas that had been bandied about in the Congress and the various colonial legislatures for years. Adams had actually led the debate in the Congress that produced its passage, as Jefferson sat silently and sullenly while the delegates revised his language. What was really just "a theatrical side show" was now being enshrined in memory as the defining moment in the revolutionary drama. "Jefferson ran away with the stage effect," Adams lamented, "and all the glory of it."[12]

Adams was not the kind of man to suffer in silence. His jealousy of Jefferson was palpable, and his throbbing vanity became patently obvious as he relived the contested moments from the past in the privacy of his own memory, then reported on his admittedly self-serving findings to trusted confidants like Benjamin Rush. For the simple truth was that the aging Sage of Quincy had nothing else to do. Jefferson had the all-consuming duties of the presidency, then two major retirement projects—the completion of his architectural renovations of Monticello and the creation of the University of Virginia. But the sole project for Adams lay within himself. His focus, indeed his obsession, was the interior architecture of his own remembrances, the construction of an Adams version of American history, a spacious room of his own within the American pantheon.

He was doing what we would now call therapy: thrashing about inside himself in endless debate with his internal demons while seated by the fireside in what he self-mockingly called "my throne"; twitching in and out of control as he attempted to compose his autobiography, which turned into a series of salvos at his political enemies (Hamilton, no surprise, was the chief target) and ended, literally in midsentence, when he realized that it was all catharsis and no coherence; outraging his old friend Mercy Otis Warren with embarrassing tantrums because her three-volume *History of the American Revolution* (1805) failed to make him the major player in the story. Warren responded in kind: "I am so much at a loss for the meaning of your paragraphs, and the rambling manner in which your angry and undigested letters are written," she explained, "that I scarcely know where to begin my remarks." Warren concluded with a scathing diagnosis of the Adams correspondence with her as a scattered series of verbal impulses and "the most captious, malignant, irrelevant compositions that have ever been seen."

Undeterred, he launched another round of his memoirs in the *Boston Patriot,* designed to "set the record straight," an act that quickly gave rise to another cascade of emotional eruptions. "Let the jackasses bray or laugh at this," he declared defiantly: "I am in a fair way to give my criticks and enemies food enough to glut their appetites. . . . I take no notice of their billingsgate." While drafting the nearly interminable essays for the *Patriot,* he compared himself to a wild animal who had "grabbed the end of a cord with his teeth, and was drawn slowly up by pulleys, through a storm of squills, crackers, and rockets, flashing and blazing around him every moment," and although the "scorching flames made him groan, and mourn, and roar, he would not let go." He was, to put it bluntly, driving himself half-crazy in frantic but futile attempts at self-vindication. Every effort to redeem his reputation only confirmed what Hamilton had claimed in his infamous pamphlet during the presidential campaign of 1800—namely, that Adams was an inherently erratic character who often lacked control over his own emotional impulses.[13]

In 1805 Adams resumed a correspondence with Benjamin Rush, in which he actually seemed to embrace that very conclusion: "There have been many times in my life when I have been so agitated in my own mind," Adams confessed, "as to have no consideration at all of the light in which my words, actions, and even writings would be considered by others. . . . The few traces that remain of me must, I believe, go down to posterity in much confusion and distraction, as my life has been passed." The correspondence with Rush, which lasted for eight years, permitted Adams to confront his personal demons and exorcise them in a series of remarkable exchanges that, taken together, are the most colorful, playful, and revealing letters he ever wrote. Rush set the terms for what became a high-stakes game of honesty by proposing that they dispense with the usual topics and report to each other on their respective dreams.[14]

Adams leapt at the suggestion and declared himself prepared to match his old friend "dream for dream." Rush began with "a singular dream" set in 1790 and focusing on a crazed derelict who was promising a crowd that he could "produce rain and sunshine and cause the wind to blow from any quarter he pleased." Rush interpreted this eloquent lunatic as a symbolic figure representing all those political leaders in the infant nation who claimed they could shape public opinion. Adams subsequently countered: "I dreamed that I was mounted on a lofty scaffold in the center of a great plain in Versailles, surrounded by an innumerable congregation of five and twenty millions." But the crowd was not comprised of people. Instead, they were all "inhabitants of the royal menagerie," including lions, elephants, wildcats, rats, squirrels, whales, sharks—the litany went on for several paragraphs—who then proceeded to tear one another to pieces as he tried to lecture them on the advantages of "the unadulterated principles of liberty, equality and fraternity among all living creatures." At the end of the dream, he was forced to flee the scene with "my clothes torn from my back and my skin lacerated from head to foot."[15]

As befits a dialogue framed around reports from the subconscious regions, the Adams-Rush correspondence tended to emphasize the power of the irrational. Adams recalled a French barber in Boston who used the phrase "a little crack," meaning slightly crazy: "I have long thought the philosophers of the eighteenth century and almost all the men of science and letters 'crack' . . . and that the sun, moon, and stars send all their lunatics here for confinement." Then, ever playful with Rush, Adams signed off with the following self-deprecating joke: "I must tell you that my wife, who took a fancy to read this letter upon my table, bids me tell you that she 'thinks my head, too, a little crack,' and I am half of that mind myself."[16]

Adams had a lifelong tendency to view the world "out there" as a projection of the emotions he felt swirling inside himself. The overriding honesty and intimacy of the correspondence with Rush permitted this projection to express itself without restraint. The question he had posed to others, simultaneously poignant and pathetic, had the authentic ring of a *cri de coeur:* "How is it that I, poor ignorant I, must stand before Posterity as differing from all the other great Men of the Age?" In his monthly exchanges with Rush, Adams worked out his answer to that question. There is a Mad Hatter character to the Adams-Rush correspondence, as both men swapped stories and shared anecdotes in a kind of "Adams and Rush in Wonderland" mode. But there was a deadly serious insight buried within the comedy.[17]

The insight was precocious, anticipating as it did the distinction between history as experienced and history as remembered, most

famously depicted in Leo Tolstoy's *War and Peace*. (The core insight—
that all seamless historical narratives are latter-day constructions—lies
at the center of all postmodern critiques of traditional historical explanations.) Under Rush's prodding influence and in response to his
dreamy inspirations, Adams realized that the act of transforming the
American Revolution into history placed a premium on selecting
events and heroes that fit neatly into a dramatic formula, thereby dis-
torting the more tangled and incoherent experience that participants
actually making the history felt at the time. Jefferson's drafting of the
Declaration of Independence was a perfect example of such dramatic
distortions. The Revolution in this romantic rendering became one
magical moment of inspiration, leading inexorably to the foregone
conclusion of American independence.

As Adams remembered it, on the other hand, "all the great critical
questions about men and measures from 1774 to 1778" were desperately
contested and highly problematic occasions, usually "decided by the
vote of a single state, and that vote was often decided by a single individual." Nothing was clear, inevitable, or even comprehensible to the
soldiers in the field at Saratoga or the statesmen in the corridors
at Philadelphia: "It was patched and piebald policy then, as it is now,
ever was, and ever will be, world without end." The real drama of
the American Revolution, which was perfectly in accord with Adams's
memory as well as with the turbulent conditions of his own soul,
was its inherent messiness. This meant recovering the exciting but ter-
rifying sense that all the major players had at the time—namely, that
they were making it up as they went along, improvising on the edge of
catastrophe.[18]

Adams derived his authority for a deconstructed version of the
American Revolution from his incontestable claim to have been "present at the creation." He had been a participant during most, if not all,
of the crucial moments from the Stamp Act crisis in 1765 to his own
retirement from the presidency in 1801. And he knew all the major
players personally. This conferred instant credibility upon his preferred
role as designated truth teller, poised to expose the chaotic reality
beneath all uplifting accounts of the Revolution. Support for American
independence, for example, was always fragile and shifted with each
victory or defeat in the field, which was often a matter of pure luck. Or
the decision to locate the national capital on the Potomac was a back-

room deal involving so many secret bargains and bribes that no one would ever unravel the full story.[19]

In the same vein, all the heroic portraits of the great men were romanticized distortions. Franklin, for example, was a superb scientist and masterful prose stylist, to be sure, but also a vacuous political thinker and diplomatic fraud, who spent the bulk of his time in Paris flirting with younger women of the salon set. Washington was an indisputable American patriarch, but more an actor than a leader, brilliant at striking poses "in a strain of Shakespearean . . . excellence at dramatic exhibitions." He was also poorly read, seldom wrote his own speeches, and, according to one member of his cabinet, "could not write a sentence without misspelling some word." In general, the Virginians were the chief beneficiaries of all the highly stylized histories, though, as Adams observed, "not a lad upon the Highlands is more clannish than every Virginian I have ever known." Virginians were also the most adept at employing what Adams called "puffers," what we would call "spinners" or public-relations experts. "These puffers, Rush, are the only killers of scandal," Adams noted. "You and I have never employed them, and therefore scandal has prevailed against us." When Rush somewhat mischievously suggested that Adams himself enjoyed the support of Federalist "puffers," specifically mentioning William Cobbett, Adams pleaded total ignorance: "Now I assure you upon my honor and the faith of the friendship between us that I never saw the face of Cobbett; and that I should not know him if I met him in my porridge dish."[20]

This last remark, while vintage Adams-Rush banter, also exposed the painfully egotistical motives lurking beneath the entire Adams campaign for a more realistic, nonmythologized version of the American Revolution. While his insistence on a deconstructed history was certainly a precocious intellectual insight, there is also no question that the Adams urge to discredit the dramatic renderings of the revolutionary era was driven by his own wounded vanity. To put it squarely, such versions of the story failed to provide *him* with a starring role in the drama. At its nub, his critique of the historical fictions circulating as seductive truths was much like a campaign to smash all the statues, because the sculptor had failed to render a satisfactory likeness of yours truly.

On the other hand, Adams possessed a congenital affinity for deconstructed interpretations of history, of his own life, indeed of practically everything. It was the way he saw the world. By temperament, he was inherently impulsive, highly combustible, instinctively irreverent. All his major published works on political philosophy, including his *Defence of the Constitution of the United States of America* and *Discourses on Davila,* along with his unpublished autobiography, lacked coherent form. They were less books than notebooks, filled with rambling transcriptions of his own internal conversations that ricocheted off one another at unpredictable angles. While his most devoted enemies, chiefly Franklin and Hamilton, claimed that his erratic habits of mind were symptomatic of mental illness, some recent scholarship has suggested the problem was physical, that he might well have been afflicted with hyperthyroidism, or Graves' disease. For our purposes, however, the ultimate cause of the condition is less important than its systemic manifestation, which was a congenital inability to separate his thoughts from his feelings about them. This caused him to mistrust all purely rational descriptions of human behavior as incompatible with the more passionate stirrings he felt within his own personality. As he told Rush, "Deceive not thyself. There is not an old friar in France, not in Europe, who looks on a blooming young virgin with *sang-froid.*" These same internal stirrings also predisposed him to regard all perfectly symmetrical narratives or stories preaching an obvious moral message and populated by larger-than-life heroes as utter fabrications. Like straight lines in nature, such things did not exist for him.[21]

They did, however, for his former friend at Monticello, who had spent the bulk of his adult life keeping his head and his heart in separate chambers of his personality. Starting in 1807, Jefferson's name began to come up sporadically in Adams's letters to Rush. Prior to that time, Jefferson had remained a forbidden subject. When asked to comment on his renowned partnership with Jefferson during the early days of the American Revolution, Adams developed a standard statement of denial: "You are much mistaken when you say that no man living have so much knowledge of Mr. Jefferson's transactions as myself," Adams insisted. "I know but little concerning him." With Rush, however, Adams began to slip Jefferson into their conversation as an example of the kind of enigmatic temperament destined to flourish in the history books.[22]

He recalled Jefferson's retirement from the Washington administration in 1793, quite obviously a shrewd tactical retreat designed to position Jefferson for his ascent "toward the summit of the pyramid"—that is, the presidency—but which was described by the Republican press "as unambitious, unavaricious, and perfectly disinterested." Somehow, Jefferson was even able to persuade himself that he was beyond temptation and happily ensconced on his mountaintop for the duration. "When a man has one of the two greatest parties in a nation interested in representing him to be disinterested," Adams observed with amazement, "even those who believe it to be a lie will repeat it so often to one another that at last they will seem to believe it to be true."[23]

The same pattern materialized later in the 1790s, when Jefferson embraced two misguided propositions about European affairs. The first was that England was "tottering to her fall," that her economy was collapsing and "she must soon be a bankrupt and unable to maintain her naval superiority." The second misguided opinion, "still more erroneous and still more fatal," was that France was the wave of the future, that she "would establish a free republican government and even a leveling democracy, and that monarchy and nobility would forever be abolished in France," all of which would occur peacefully and bloodlessly. In both instances, events proved Jefferson wrong. In both instances Adams had disagreed with Jefferson and been proven right. But despite his underestimation of England and his overestimation of France, Jefferson's reputation and popularity soared. "I have reason to remember it," Adams recalled, "because my opinion of the French Revolution produced a coldness towards me in all my Revolutionary friends, and an inclination towards Mr. Jefferson, which broke out in violent invectives and false imputations upon me and in flattering panegyrics upon Mr. Jefferson."

Once again, Jefferson seemed uniquely equipped to become the chief beneficiary of romanticized versions of history, in part because his own capacity for self-deception permitted him to deny, and with utter sincerity, the vanities and ambitions lurking in his own soul, and in part because the moralistic categories that shaped all his political thinking fit perfectly the romantic formula that history writing seemed to require. The fact that these categories were blatant illusions (for example, the French Revolution was not a European version of the American Revolution) seemed to matter less than the fact that they confirmed a potent and seductive mythology that was more appealing than the messier reality. Through some complex combination of duplicity and disposition, Jefferson had come to embody the will to believe. He was not so much living a lie as living a fiction that he had come to believe himself.[24]

Adams had come to see himself as the mirror image of Jefferson: "Mausoleums, statues monuments will never be erected to me," he wrote with resignation to Rush. "Panegyrical romances will never be written, nor flattering orations spoken, to transmit me to posterity in brilliant colors. No, nor in true colors. All but the last I loathe." Facing that unattractive truth took time, a full decade of shouting and pouting, relieved by converting his despair into comedy with Rush, but it also came naturally to Adams, whose entire career had been spent preaching the unattractive truths to everybody else. If Jefferson seemed predestined to tell people what they wanted to hear, Adams now acknowledged that his own destiny was just the opposite: to tell them what they needed to know.[25]

This was Adams's resigned but bittersweet mood in 1809, when Rush reported his most amazing dream yet. He dreamed that Adams had written a short letter to Jefferson, congratulating him on his recent retirement from public life. Jefferson had then responded to this magnanimous gesture with equivalent graciousness. The two great patriarchs had then engaged in a correspondence over several years in which they candidly acknowledged their mutual mistakes, shared their profound reflections on the meaning of American independence, and recovered their famous friendship. Then the two philosopher-kings "sunk into the grave nearly at the same time, full of years and rich in the gratitude and praises of their country . . . and to their numerous merits and honors posterity has added that they were rival friends."[26]

Adams responded immediately: "A DREAM AGAIN! I have no other objection to your dream but that it is not history. It may be prophecy." Then he offered a satirical account of his relationship with Jefferson, claiming that "there has never been the smallest interruption of the personal friendship between Mr. Jefferson that I know of." This convenient lie was then followed by a humorous piece of bravado: "You should remember that Jefferson was but a boy to me. I was at least ten years older than him in age and more than twenty years older in politics. I am bold to say I was his preceptor in politics and taught him everything that was good and solid in his whole political conduct."

How could one hold a grudge against a disciple? On the other hand, given Jefferson's junior status, was it not more appropriate for him to initiate the reconciliation? "If I should receive a letter from him," Adams concluded tartly, "I should not fail to acknowledge and answer it." Jefferson, in short, would have to extend the hand first.[27]

That was not going to happen. Rush was simultaneously writing Jefferson, somewhat misleadingly suggesting that Adams had indicated he was now eager for a reconciliation and virtually on his deathbed: "I am sure an advance on your side will be a cordial to the heart of Mr. Adams," Rush explained. "Tottering over the grave, he now leans wholly upon the shoulders of his old Revolutionary friends." But Jefferson would not rise to the bait, convinced as he was after his earlier exchange with Abigail that he had already made a heroic effort that had been summarily rejected. It was now Adams's turn to attempt a bridging of the gap. That was how it stood for more than two ensuing years: the two sages circling each other, marking off their territory like old dogs, sniffing around the edges of a possible reconciliation, reluctant to close the distance.[28]

The distance was reduced in 1811 when Edward Coles, a Jefferson protégé who was attempting, in vain it turned out, to persuade his mentor to assume a more forthright position opposing slavery, visited Adams in Quincy. Adams let it be known that his political disagreements with Jefferson had never killed his affection for the man. "I always loved Jefferson," he told Coles, "and still love him." When word of this exchange reached Jefferson, as Adams knew it would, Jefferson declared his conversion. "This is enough for me," he wrote Rush, adding that he knew Adams to be "always an honest man, often a great one, but sometimes incorrect and precipitate in his judgments." This latter caveat rewidened the gap that the earlier statement had seemed to close. The gap became a chasm when Jefferson went on to explain that he had always valued Adams's judgment, "with the single exception as to his political opinions," a statement roughly equivalent to claiming that the Pope was otherwise infallible, except when he declared himself on matters of faith and morals.[29]

On Christmas Day of 1811, Adams apprised Rush that he was fully aware of the benevolent duplicities Rush was performing as intermediary: "I perceive plainly, Rush, that you have been teasing Jefferson to write me, as you did me to write him." Adams also knew full well that

Rush was sending edited versions of his letters to Jefferson, removing the potentially offensive passages. In the Christmas letter Adams reviewed the full range of political disagreements with Jefferson, mixing together serious controversies (for example, the Alien and Sedition Acts, the French Revolution, the American navy) with a lighthearted list of personal differences (for example, Adams held levees once a week as president, while Jefferson's entire presidency was a levee; Jefferson thought liberty favored straight hair, while Adams thought curled hair "just as republican as straight"). That was the tone Adams wanted to convey to Jefferson: still feisty and critical of Jefferson's principles and policies, but fully capable of controlling the dialogue with humor and diplomatic nonchalance; the fires still burned, but the great volcano of the revolutionary generation was at last in remission.[30]

In the end, it was Adams who made the decisive move. On January 1, 1812, a short but cordial note went out from Quincy to Monticello, relaying family news and referring to "two pieces of Homespun" coming along by separate packet. Rush was ecstatic, as well as fully convinced that he had orchestrated a reconciliation: "I rejoice in the correspondence which has taken place between you and your old friend Mr. Jefferson," he declared triumphantly to Adams. "I consider you and him as the North and South Poles of the American Revolution. Some talked, some wrote, and some fought to promote and establish it but you and Mr. Jefferson *thought* for us all." Adams went along with the celebratory mood, hiding his pride behind a mask of jokes and the rather fraudulent pretense that his famous friendship with Jefferson had never really been interrupted: "Your dream is out . . . your prophecy fulfilled! You have worked wonders! You have made peace between powers that were never at Enmity. . . . In short, the mighty defunct Potentates of Mount Wollaston and Monticello by your sorceries . . . are again in being." In the same self-consciously jocular style he soon began to refer to his Quincy estate as "Montezillo," which he claimed meant "very little mountain," in deference to Jefferson's Monticello, which meant "little mountain." He insisted that Rush was making more of the reunion with Jefferson than it deserved. Nothing momentous or historic was at stake. "It was only as if one sailor had met a brother sailor, after twenty-five years' absence," Adams joked, "and had accosted him, how fare you, Jack?"[31]

Nothing could have been further from the truth. Adams's ever-vibrating vanities were now, true enough, under some measure of control. But his dismissive posture toward the rupture in the friendship—what breech and what betrayal?—was obviously only a bravado pose. Even the start of the correspondence exposed the awkward tensions just below the surface. Jefferson presumed, quite plausibly, that the "two pieces of Homespun" Adams was sending along referred to domestically produced clothing, a nice symbol of the American economic response to the embargo and a fitting reminder of the good old days when Adams and Jefferson had first joined the movement for American independence. And so Jefferson responded with a lengthy treatise on the merits of domestic manufacturing and grand memories of the nonimportation movement in the 1760s, only to discover that Adams had intended the homespun reference as a metaphor. His gift turned out to be a copy of John Quincy's recent two-volume work, *Lectures on Rhetoric and Oratory.*

Why, then, did Adams take the fateful step, which led to a fourteen-year exchange of 158 letters, a correspondence that is generally regarded as the intellectual capstone to the achievements of the revolutionary generation and the most impressive correspondence between prominent statesmen in all of American history? The friendship and the mutual trust on which it rested had, in fact, not been recovered by 1812. It took the correspondence to recover the friendship, not the other way around. What, then, motivated Adams to extend his hand across the gap that existed between Quincy and Monticello, then write more than two letters for every one of Jefferson's?

Two overlapping but competing answers come to mind. First, there was a good deal of unfinished business between the two men, a clear recognition on both sides that they had come to fundamentally different conclusions about what the American Revolution meant. Adams believed that Jefferson's version of the story, while misguided, was destined to dominate the history books. The resumption of his correspondence with Jefferson afforded Adams the opportunity to challenge the Jeffersonian version and to do so in the form of a written record virtually certain to become a major historical document of its own. "You and I ought not to die," Adams rather poignantly put it in an early letter, "before We have explained ourselves to each other." But both men knew they were sending their letters to posterity as much as to each other.[32]

Second, the reconciliation and ensuing correspondence permitted Adams to join Jefferson as the costar of an artfully arranged final act in the revolutionary drama. Adams had spent most of his retirement years denouncing such contrivances as gross distortions of history. But he had also spent those same years marveling at the benefits that accrued to anyone willing to pose for posterity in the mythical mode. If he could only control himself, if he could speak the lines that history wanted to hear, if he could fit himself into the heroic mold like a kind of living statue, he might yet win his ticket to immortality.

BOTH ADAMS and Jefferson knew their roles by heart, especially in its Ciceronian version as a pair of retired patriarchs now beyond ambition and above controversy. The dialogue they sustained from 1812 to 1826 can be read at several levels, but the chief source of its modern appeal derives from its elegiac tone: the image of two American icons, looking back with seasoned serenity at the Revolution they have wrought, delivering eloquent soliloquies on all the timeless topics, speaking across their political differences to each other and across the ages to us. If we wished to conjure up a mental picture of this rendition of the dialogue, it would feature Jefferson standing tall and straight in his familiar statuesque posture, his arms folded across his chest, as was his custom, while the much shorter Adams paced back and forth around him, jabbing at the air in his nervous and animated style, periodically stopping to grab Jefferson by the lapels to make an irreverent point.

This, of course, is the constructed or posed version that ought to provoke our immediate skepticism. (In Adams's terms, this is not history, but romance.) For several reasons, however, this beguiling depiction cannot be summarily dismissed. First of all, the friendship *was,* in fact, recovered and the reconciliation realized during the course of the correspondence. The clinching evidence comes late, in 1823, when Jefferson responded to a series of letters that appeared in the newspapers. Adams had written them much earlier and had described Jefferson as a duplicitous political partisan. "Be assured, my dear Sir," Jefferson wrote Adams, "that I am incapable of receiving the slightest impression from the effort now made to plant thorns on the pillow of age, worth, and wisdom, and to sow tares between friends who have been such for nearly half a century. Beseeching you then not to suffer your mind to be disquieted by this wicked attempt to poison its peace, and praying you to throw it by." Adams was overjoyed. He insisted that Jefferson's letter be read aloud to his entire extended family at the breakfast table, calling it "the best letter that ever was written . . . just such a letter as I expected, only it was infinitely better expressed." He concluded with an Adams salvo against "the peevish and fretful effusions of politicians," then signed off as "J.A. In the 89 year of his age still too fat to last much longer." Clearly, this was no dramatic contrivance. The old trust had been fully recovered.[33]

Second, the improbably symmetrical ending to the dialogue casts an irresistibly dramatic spell over the entire story and the way to tell it. Rush had predicted that the two patriarchs would reconcile, then go to their graves "at nearly the same time." But their mutual exit was even more exquisitely timed than Rush had dreamed. (No serious novelist would ever dare to make this up.) They died within five hours of each other, on the fiftieth anniversary to the day and almost to the hour of the official announcement of American independence to the world in 1776. Call it a miracle, an accident, or a case of two powerful personalities willing themselves to expire on schedule and according to script. But it happened.

Third, the correspondence can be read as an extended conversation between two gods on Mount Olympus because both men were determined to project that impression: "But wither is senile garrulity leading me?" Jefferson asked rhetorically. "Into politics, of which I have taken final leave. . . . I have given up newspapers in exchange for Tacitus and Thucydides, for Newton and Euclid; and I find myself much happier." Adams then responded with his own display of classical learning and literary flair: "I have read Thucydides and Tacitus so often, and at such distant periods of my Life, that elegant, profound and enchanting is their Style, I am weary of them," then joked that "My Senectutal Loquacity has more than retaliated your 'Senile Garrulity.' "[34]

Many of the most memorable exchanges required no staging or self-conscious posing whatsoever, since there was a host of safe subjects the two sages could engage without risking conflict and that afforded occasions for conspicuous displays of their verbal prowess. They were, after all, two of the most accomplished letter writers of the era, men who had fashioned over long careers at the writing desk distinctive prose styles that expressed their different personalities perfectly. Thus, Jefferson waxed eloquent on the aging process and their mutual intimations of mortality: "But our machines have now been running for 70 or 80 years," he observed stoically, "and we must expect that, worn as they are, here a pivot, there a wheel, now a pinion, next a spring, will be giving way, and however we may tinker with them for awhile, all will at length surcease motion." Adams responded in kind but with a caveat: "I am sometimes afraid that my 'Machine' will not 'surcease motion' soon enough; for I dread nothing so much as 'dying at the top,' " meaning becoming senile and a burden to his family. He then went on to chide Jefferson for talking like an old man. Of all the original signers of the Declaration of Independence, "You are the youngest and the most energetic in mind and body," and therefore most likely to be the final survivor. Like the last person in the household to retire for the night, it would be Jefferson's responsibility to close up the fireplace and "rake the ashes over the coals."[35]

Most modern readers come to the correspondence fully aware of Jefferson's proficiency with a pen, and are therefore somewhat surprised to discover that Adams could more than hold his own in the verbal dueling, indeed delivered the most quotable lines. For example, after Jefferson produced a lengthy exegesis on the origins of the Native American population of North America, Adams dismissed all the current theories about the original occupants of the continent: "I should as soon suppose that the Prodigal Son, in a frolic with one of his Girls, made a trip to America in one of Mother Carey's Eggsels, and left the fruits of their amours here." Or when Jefferson embraced the development of an indigenous American language, arguing that everyday usage "is the workshop in which new ones [words] are elaborated," rather than the English dictionaries compiled by the likes of Samuel Johnson, Adams went into a colorful tirade. All English dictionaries, he declared, were vestiges of the same British tyranny that the American Revolution destroyed forever. "We are no more bound by Johnson's Dictionary," he pronounced, "than by the Cannon [sic] Law of England." By what right did Samuel Johnson deny him, John Adams, the freedom to fashion his own vocabulary? "I have as good a right to make a Word," he insisted, "as that Pedant Bigot Cynic and Monk."[36]

Speaking of words, the pungency of the Adams prose comes through so impressively in the correspondence in part because Adams invested himself in the exchange more than Jefferson. He composed more memorable passages because he wrote many more words. When the torrent from Quincy threatened to flood Monticello, he apologized for getting so far out ahead. Jefferson then apologized in return, claiming that he received over twelve hundred letters a year, all of which required responses, so it was difficult for him to match the Adams pace. Adams replied that he received only a fraction of that number but chose not to answer most of them, which allowed him to focus all his allegedly waning energies on Jefferson.

Beyond sheer verbal volume, the punch so evident in the Adams prose reflected his more aggressive and confrontational temperament. The Jefferson style was fluid, lyrical, cadenced, and melodious. Words for him were like calming breezes that floated across the pages. The Adams style was excited, jumpy, exclamatory, naughty. Words for him were like weapons designed to pierce the pages or explode above them in illuminating airbursts. While the Adams style generated a host of memorable epigrammatic flashes, it was the worst-possible vehicle for sustaining the diplomatic niceties. Jefferson was perfectly capable of remaining on script and in role as philosopher-king to the end. If it had been up to him, the demigod version of the Adams-Jefferson dialogue would have captured its essence and ultimate meaning as a staged performance for posterity. Adams, however, despite all his vows of Ciceronian serenity, was congenitally incapable of staying in character. For him, the only meaningful kind of conversation was an argument. And that, in the end, is what the dialogue with Jefferson became, and the best way to understand its historical significance.

ADAMS REMAINED on his best behavior for over a year. There were a few brief flurries, chiefly jabs at Jefferson's failure to prepare the nation for the War of 1812, especially his negligence in building up the American navy, which had always been an Adams hobbyhorse. Ever diplomatic, Jefferson never quite conceded that Adams had been right about a larger navy, but when the American fleet won some early battles in the war, Jefferson graciously noted that "the success of our little navy . . . must be more gratifying to you than to most men, as having been the early and constant advocate of wooden walls." The potentially explosive issues lay buried further back in the past. Both men recognized that touching them placed the newly established reconciliation at risk.[37]

The first Adams eruption occurred in June of 1813, followed immediately by a chain reaction of explosions over the ensuing six months. (Adams wrote thirty letters, Jefferson five.) The detonating device was publication of a letter Jefferson had written in 1801 to Joseph Priestley, the English scientist and renowned critic of Christianity. In that letter Jefferson had mentioned Adams in passing as a retrograde thinker opposed to all forms of progress, one of the "ancients" rather than "moderns." "The sentiment that you have attributed to me in your letter to Dr. Priestley I totally disclaim," Adams protested, "and I demand in the French sense of the word demand of you the proof." Sensing that Adams was in mid-explosion, Jefferson responded at length. The Priestley letter was "a confidential communication" that was "never meant to trouble the public mind." He then went on to remind Adams that the party wars were still raging back then, that both sides had been guilty of some rather extreme denunciations of the others, and that his real target had been the Federalists, who had defamed his own notions of government as dangerous innovations.[38]

Then came the crucial acknowledgment and quasi-apology. Adams had been targeted for criticism because he was the standard-bearer for the Federalist party. But Jefferson had always realized that Adams did not fit into the party grooves: "I happened to cite it from you, [though] the whole letter shows I had them only in view," Jefferson explained. "In truth, my dear Sir, we were far from considering you as the author of all the measures we blamed. They were placed under the protection of your name, but we were satisfied they wanted much of your approbation." (Notice the collective "we," an inadvertent acknowledgment of the coordinated campaign of the Republican party.) Adams, in effect, happened to be in the line of fire, which was really directed at the Hamiltonian wing of the Federalist party: "You would do me great injustice therefore," Jefferson concluded, "by taking to yourself what was intended for men who were your secret, as they are now your open enemies."[39]

Jefferson's explanation was ingenious. It shifted the blame for the rupture of the friendship onto the Hamiltonians, whom he knew

Adams utterly despised, then invited Adams to align himself, at least retrospectively, with the Republican side of the debate. The trouble with Adams, of course, was that he was unwilling to align himself with any political party; indeed, his trademark had always been to embody the virtuous ideal, the Washington quasi-monarchical model of executive leadership, and stand above party. The clear, if unspoken, message of Jefferson's letter was that this admirable posture was no longer possible in American politics. Adams had gotten himself caught in the cross fire created by the new conditions and the partisan imperatives they generated. Most important, from the point of view of the friendship, Jefferson admitted that his behind-the-scenes criticism of Adams had been a willful misrepresentation. While not really an apology—indeed, forces beyond his control had dictated his actions—this was at least a major concession.

Adams's immediate impulse was to fire off several illumination rounds designed to expose the inaccuracies in Jefferson's account of the Adams presidency, inaccuracies that Jefferson had already acknowledged: "I have no thought, in this correspondence, but to satisfy you and myself," Adams observed, adding, "My Reputation has been so much the Sport of the public for fifty years and will be with Posterity, that I hoped it a bubble a Gossameur, that idles in the wanton Summer Air." Jefferson had mentioned the Alien and Sedition Acts as a major source of partisan hatred. "As your name is subscribed to that law, as Vice President," Adams declared, "and mine as President, I know not why you are not as responsible for it as I am." Jefferson had used the phrase "the Terrorism of the day" to describe the supercharged atmosphere of the late 1790s. Adams launched into a frenzied recollection of the mobs gathered around his house, protesting his decision to send a peace delegation to France: "I have no doubt you was fast asleep in philosophical Tranquillity," Adams noted caustically, "when ten thousand People, and perhaps many more, were parading the Streets of Philadelphia. . . . What think you of Terrorism, Mr. Jefferson?" Jefferson had blamed the Federalists for the lion's share of the party mischief. Adams thought the blame was equally shared: "Both parties have excited artificial Terrors," he concluded, "and if I were summoned as a Witness to say upon Oath . . . I could not give a more sincere Answer, than in the vulgar Style. 'Put them in a bagg and shake them, and then see which comes out first.' " However anachronistic it might seem to Jefferson, he, John Adams, would go to his grave defying party politics.[40]

This was the defining moment in the correspondence. In the summer of 1813 the dialogue ceased being a still-life picture of posed patriarchs and became an argument between competing versions of the revolutionary legacy. All the unmentionable subjects were now on the table because a measure of mutual trust had been recovered. The best bellwether of the Adams psyche was always Abigail, and on July 15, 1813, she appended a note to her husband's letter, her first communication with Jefferson since the lacerating letters she had written him nine years earlier. "I have been looking for some time for a space in my good Husbands Letters to add the regards of an old Friend," she now wrote, "which are still cherished and preserved through all the changes and v[ic]issitudes which have taken place since we first became acquainted, and will I trust remain as long as, A Adams." Abigail's voice, as always, was the surest sign. Jefferson had been forgiven. The friendship, so long in storage, had never completely died. The recovered sense of common affection and trust now made it possible to act on Adams's classic pronouncement, that they ought not die before they had explained themselves to each other.[41]

Although Adams tended to set the intellectual agenda in the dialogue that ensued, Jefferson inadvertently provided the larger framework within which the debate played out. He was actually trying to make amends for his unfair characterization of Adams in the Priestley letter as one of the "ancients." He now wanted to go on record as agreeing with Adams that, while the progress of science was indisputable, certain political principles were eternal verities that the ancients understood as well as the moderns: "The same political parties which now agitate the U.S. have existed thro' all time," he observed. "And in fact the terms of whig and tory belong to natural as well as to civil history. They denote the temper and constitution and mind of different individuals." Was this Jefferson's roundabout way of suggesting that he and Adams had in effect been acting out a timeless political argument? As the lengthy letter proceeded, it became clear that Jefferson was, in fact, attempting to place his friendship and eventual rivalry with Adams within a broader context, to see it through the more detached lens of history.[42]

In the Jeffersonian version of the story, Adams and Jefferson fought shoulder-to-shoulder against the Tories, served together in Europe as a dynamic team, then returned to serve again in the new national government. And then the classic distinction appeared again:

> the line of division was again drawn, we broke into two parties, each wishing to give a different direction to the government; the one to strengthen the most popular branch, the other the more permanent branches, and to extend their performance. Here you and I separated for the first time: and as we had been longer than most in the public theatre, and our names were more familiar to our countrymen, the party which considered you as thinking with them placed your name at the head: the other for the same reason selected mine. . . . We suffered ourselves, as you so well expressed it, to be the passive subjects of public discussion. And these discussions, whether relating to men, measures, or opinions, were conducted by the parties with an animosity, a bitterness, and an indecency, which had never been exceeded. . . . To me then it appears that there have been differences of opinion, and party differences, from the first establishment of governments, to the present day; and on the same question which now divides our own country: that these will continue thro' all future time: that every one takes his side in favor of the many, or the few, according to his constitution, and the circumstances in which he is placed.[43]

Here was the classic Jeffersonian vision, and the beautiful simplicity of its narrative structure makes it even more clear why Adams was absolutely right to admire Jefferson's knack for fitting himself into a story line with immense appeal to future historians. Jefferson's mind consistently saw the world in terms of clashing dichotomies: Whigs versus Tories; moderns versus ancients; America versus Europe; rural conditions versus urban; whites versus blacks. The list could go on, but it always came down to the forces of light against the forces of darkness, with no room for anything in between. What Adams called a romance was actually a melodrama. And the specific version Jefferson was now offering Adams cast the Federalists in the role of latter-day Tories who had betrayed the expansive legacy of the American Revolution, the corrupt guardians of the privileged "few" aligned defiantly against the Jeffersonian "many."

But how could this be? Even Jefferson seemed to acknowledge that Adams did not quite fit into this rigid formula. "If your objects and opinions have been misunderstood," Jefferson noted, "if the measures and principles of others have been wrongly imputed to you, as I believe they have been, that you should leave an explanation of them, would be an act of justice to yourself." In effect, if Adams had a different story to tell, if he saw a different pattern in the historical swirl they had both lived through, he should write out his account and let posterity judge.[44]

Adams, of course, had been trying to do just that for over a decade. And, as we have seen, the result had been a bewildering jumble of tortured protestations, endless harangues, and futile displays of wounded pride, all leading to the rather disquieting conclusion that there was no pattern to be discovered, only one invented by fiction writers masquerading as historians. Glimmers of an un-Jeffersonian outline peeked through the cloud of words Adams had spewed out. The neat divisions between Whigs and Tories did not accord with the Adams sense of the political landscape during the 1770s. Between a third and a half of the American people, he guessed, had been indifferent and floated with the prevailing tide of the moment. The divisions of the 1790s did not match up with Jefferson's categories, either, since those supporting and those opposing a more powerful national government had all been good Whigs. Certainly neither he nor Washington had viewed themselves as traitors to the revolutionary cause. They had regarded their Federalist programs as a fulfillment, rather than a betrayal, of American independence. Nor did Jefferson's distinction between the "few" and the "many" work very well south of the Potomac, except in the ironic sense that only a few Virginians were willing to address the forbidden subject that shaped their lives, their fortunes, and that cast a long shadow over their sacred honor.

But glimmerings do not a story make. Jefferson had a story. In the absence of a coherent alternative with equivalently compelling appeal, his story was destined to dominate the history books. Adams sensed that it was not the true story, even doubted whether such a thing as a true story existed. But once Jefferson laid it out before him so elegantly in the summer of 1813, Adams at last possessed a target on which to focus his considerable firepower. He was utterly hopeless as a grand designer of narratives, and he knew it. The artifice required to shape a major work of history or philosophy was not in him. But he was a natural contrarian, a born critic, whose fullest energies manifested themselves in the act of doing intellectual isometric exercises against the fixed objects presented by someone else's ideas. Jefferson now became the fixed object against which he strained.

The conversational format of the correspondence with Jefferson also suited his temperament perfectly, since it permitted topics to pop up, recede, then appear again episodically, without any pretense of some overall design, the give-and-take rhythms of the dialogue matching nicely the episodic surgings of his own mind. As a result, no neatly arranged rendering of the running argument Adams had with Jefferson after 1813 can do justice to its dynamic character. All one can do is to identify the major points of contention, then impose a thematic order that draws out the deeper implications of the argument, all the while knowing that the coherence that results is itself a construction.

THE MAJOR argument running through the letters throughout 1813–1814 concerned their different definitions of social equality and the role of elites in leading and governing the American republic. Without ever saying so directly, they were talking about themselves and the other prominent members of the revolutionary generation. The argument was prompted by Jefferson's long letter on the "few" and the "many" and his accompanying assertion that the eternal political question had always been "Whether the power of the people, or that of the *aristoi* should prevail." Even the ever-combative Adams realized that this was heavily mined ground, so he began on an agreeable note. "Precisely," he told Jefferson, the distinction between "the few and the many . . . was as old as Aristotle," and the timeless clash between them was the major reason he believed that the ancients had much to teach the moderns about politics. Having established some common ground, Adams then veered off in a direction that had always gotten him into political trouble—namely, the inevitable role that elites play in making history happen. He recalled that it was Jefferson himself who had first encouraged him "to write something upon Aristocracy" when they were together in London thirty years earlier. "I soon began, and have been writing Upon that Subject ever since. I have been so unfortunate as never to make myself understood."[45]

"Your *aristoi*," he lectured to Jefferson, "are the most difficult Animals to manage, of anything in the Whole Theory and practice of Government." In his *Defence,* Adams had written three volumes of relentless and seemingly endless prose to show that political power invariably rested in the hands of a few prominent individuals and families. Whether it was the feudal barons of medieval France, the landed gentry of Elizabethan England, the merchant class of colonial New England, or the great planter families of the Chesapeake, history showed that the many always deferred to the few. Why? "I say it is the Ordonance of God Almighty, in the Constitution of human nature, and wrought into the Fabric of the Universe," Adams answered. "Philosophers and Politicians may nibble and quibble, but they will never get rid of it. Their only resource is to controul it." In the Adams formulation, aristocracies were to society as the passions were to the individual personality, permanent fixtures susceptible to disciplined containment and artful channeling, but never altogether removable. "You may think you can eliminate it," Adams warned, but "Aristocracy like Waterfowl dives for Ages and rises again with brighter Plumage." All the Jeffersonian chants about human equality were delusions that pandered to mankind's urge to believe an impossible dream. "Inequalities of Mind and Body are so established by God Almighty in the Constitution of Human Nature," Adams declared, "that no Art or policy can ever plain them down to a level."[46]

Jefferson's response took the form of two distinctions that together pointed in decidedly more optimistic directions. First, he agreed that there was "a natural aristocracy among men" based on "virtue and talents." Then there was an artificial or "pseudo-aristocracy founded on wealth and birth, without either virtue or talents." Was not the whole point of the republican experiment they had helped to launch in America to provide for the selection of the natural aristocrats and block the ascendance of the artificial pretenders, thereby separating "the wheat from the chaff"? And had that, in fact, not occurred during and after the American Revolution, with the "band of brothers" he and Adams had come to symbolize being the obvious beneficiaries of the republican selection process?[47]

Second, Jefferson suggested that Adams's description of aristocratic power was appropriate for Europe, where feudal privileges, family titles, and more limited economic opportunities created conditions that sustained class distinctions. In America, on the other hand, there were no feudal barons or family coats of arms, and "everyone may have land to labor for himself as he causes," so the endurance of artificial elites was impossible. Jefferson noted, somewhat gratuitously, that perhaps in New England vestiges of feudalism remained and thereby misled Adams. In Massachusetts and Connecticut there still lingered "a traditional reverence for certain families, which has rendered the offices of government nearly hereditary in those families." In Virginia, however, laws abolishing primogeniture and entail had been passed during the Revolution. "These laws, drawn by myself, laid the axe to the root of the Pseudo-aristocracy," Jefferson claimed, thereby clearing the ground for the growth of political institutions based on merit and an admittedly imperfect form of equality of opportunity. Jefferson concluded on a gracious note. "I have thus stated my opinion on a point on which we differ," he observed, "not with a view to controversy, for we are too old to change opinions which are the result of a long life in inquiry and reflection; but on the suggestion of a former letter of yours, that we ought not to die before we have explained ourselves to each other."[48]

Adams contested both of Jefferson's distinctions. Europe was, to be sure, burdened with aristocratic legacies and gross disparities in wealth that were not present to the same degree in America. But unless one believed that human nature underwent some magical metamorphosis in migrating from Europe to America, or unless one believed that the American Revolution had produced a fundamental transformation in the human personality, the competition for wealth and power would also yield unequal results in America: "After all," Adams observed, "as long as Property exists, it will accumulate in Individuals and Families. . . . I repeat it, so long as the Idea and Existence of PROPERTY is admitted and established in Society, Accumulations of it will be made, the SNOW ball will grow as it rolls." Jefferson's version of a classless American society was therefore a pipe dream, because the source of the problem was not European feudalism but human nature itself. As far as Jefferson's description of Virginia's allegedly egalitarian conditions were concerned, "No Romance would be more amusing." Here Adams confined himself to the still-dominant role played by the planter class in the Chesapeake region, not even mentioning the fact that 40 percent of the population was enslaved, a feudal remnant of awesome and ominous proportions.[49]

Finally, Adams apprised Jefferson: "Your distinction between natural and artificial Aristocracy does not appear to me well founded." One might be able to separate wealth from talent in theory, but in practice, and in all societies, they were inextricably connected: "The five Pillars of Aristocracy," he argued, "are Beauty, Wealth, Birth, Genius and Virtues. Any one of the three first, can at any time, over bear any one or both of the two last." But it would never come to that anyway, because the qualities Jefferson regarded as artificial and those he regarded as natural were all mixed together inside human nature, then mixed together again within society, in blended patterns that defied Jefferson's neat dissections.[50]

In a separate correspondence about the same time with John Taylor, another prominent Virginia planter and political thinker who had also questioned Adams's views on aristocracy, Adams called attention to the irony of the situation. The son of a New England farmer and shoemaker was being accused of aristocratic allegiances by an owner of slaves with vast estates, much of both inherited from his wife's side of the family. "If you complain that this is personal," Adams explained to Taylor, "I confess it, and intend it should be personal, that it might be more striking to you." Though precisely the same situation obtained for Jefferson, as well—he owned about two hundred slaves and ten thousand acres, a goodly portion inherited from his father-in-law—Adams never confronted him so directly. (The closest he came was his running joke about the difference between Monticello and Montezillo.) Adams was fully prepared to include Jefferson as a charter member of the natural aristocracy that made and then secured the American Revolution. Along with most of the Virginia dynasty, however, his ascent into the revolutionary elite was not the exclusive function of talent and virtue.[51]

What Adams could never quite fathom, and Jefferson understood intuitively, was that the very word "aristocracy" had become an epithet in the political culture of postrevolutionary America. Even though Adams was surely correct about the disproportionate power exercised by elites throughout history, and even though the revolutionary generation had succeeded in establishing a republican government in large part because a small group of talented statesmen had managed the enterprise throughout its earliest and most vulnerable phrases, a "republican aristocracy" seemed the same contradiction in terms as a "republican king." It violated the central premise of the revolutionary legacy—namely, that the people at large were the sovereign source of all political authority. Therefore, the only kind of political elite permissible was one that repudiated its elite status and claimed to speak for "the many" rather than "the few." The Republicans had been the first to grasp this elemental fact of American political culture in the 1790s. The Federalists, who were no more a social or economic elite than the Republicans, had come to ruin because they never grasped it. Adams could argue till doomsday that the American experiment in republicanism had succeeded because it had managed to harness the energies and talents of its best and brightest citizens, the very "band of brothers" he and Jefferson supposedly symbolized, but as long as he referred to them as an "aristocracy," whether natural or artificial, he seemed to be defying the republican legacy itself.

Another argumentative thread, which began in 1815 and then ran throughout the remainder of the correspondence, concerned the French Revolution. Adams loved to bring the subject up in his correspondence with others, especially Benjamin Rush, because events had tended to vindicate his early apprehensions, which had produced the first fissures in his relationship with Jefferson in the early 1790s and then became central ingredients in the Republican polemic against Adams in the presidential campaign of 1800. But it was Jefferson who first broached the subject in the correspondence, and he did so in a wholly conciliatory way: "Your prophecies . . . proved truer than mine; and yet fell short of the fact, for instead of a million, the destruction of 8 or 10 millions of human beings has probably been the effect of these convulsions. I did not, in 89, believe they would have lasted so long, nor have cost so much blood." Jefferson went on to acknowledge that Adams's critical perspective on the French Revolution had been a major source of his unpopularity. Now that Napoleon was finally defeated—word of Waterloo had just reached America—and the outcome was perfectly clear, Jefferson graciously observed that Adams was due an apology for "the breach of confidence of which you so justly complain, and of which no one has more frequent occasion of fellow-feeling than myself."[52]

Only someone thoroughly familiar with the political history of the 1790s could recognize what a major concession and personal confession of regret Jefferson was making. Adams caught the message immediately. "I know not what to say of your Letter," he wrote, "but that it is one of the most consolatory I have ever received." For Jefferson was not only admitting that his optimistic assessment of events in revolutionary France had been misguided; he was also conceding that the Republican party, to include himself, had played politics with the French Revolution in order to undermine the Adams presidency. Jefferson was making amends for what the Adams family had understandably regarded as "the singular act" of betrayal. He was saying, at last, that he was sorry.[53]

Adams suggested that Jefferson had misread the meaning of the French Revolution—sincerely misread it and *not* just manipulated it for political purposes—because of a faulty way of thinking conveniently conveyed by the new French word, "ideology." Napoleon had popularized the word, which had first been used by the French philosophe Destutt de Tracy, whom Jefferson had read and admired enormously. Adams claimed to be fascinated by the new word "upon the Common Principle of delight in every Thing We cannot understand." What was an "ideology"? he asked playfully: "Does it mean Idiotism? The Science of Non Compos Menticism. The Science of Lunacy? The Theory of Delerium?" As Adams explained it, the French philosophes had invented the word, which became a central part of their utopian style of thinking and a major tenet in their "school of folly." It referred to a set of ideals and hopes, like human perfection or social equality, that philosophers mistakenly believed could be implemented in the world because it existed in their heads. Jefferson himself thought in this French fashion, Adams claimed, confusing the seductive prospects envisioned in his imagination with the more limited possibilities history permitted. Critics of Jefferson's visionary projections, like Adams, were then accused of rejecting the ideals themselves, when in fact they were merely exposing their illusory character.[54]

"Ideology," then, had provided Jefferson with a politically attractive pro-French platform, which had turned out to have enormous rhetorical advantages no matter how wrong it proved in reality. Jefferson had thought that France was the wave of the future and England was a relic of the past. "I am charmed by the fluency and rapidity of your Reasoning," Adams observed, "but I doubt your Conclusion." England, not France, was destined to become the dominant European power of the nineteenth century, Adams correctly predicted, though he, like Jefferson, retained a deep suspicion of English designs on America, a permanent legacy of their mutual experience as American revolutionaries. "They have been taught from their Cradles to despise, scorn, insult and abuse Us," Adams wrote of the English, adding in his most relentlessly realistic mode that "Britain will never be our Friend, till we are her Master." Both Adams and Jefferson, it turned out, were too deeply shaped by the desperate struggle against England to foresee the Anglo-American alliance that flourished throughout the Victorian era and beyond.[55]

They both did anticipate, albeit from decidedly different perspectives, the looming sectional crisis between North and South that their own partnership stretched across. "I fear there will be greater difficulties to preserve our Union," Adams warned, "than You and I, our Fathers Brothers Disciples and Sons have had to form it." Jefferson concurred, though the subject touched the most explosive issue of all—namely, the unmentionable fact of slavery. Even the ever-candid Adams recognized that this was the forbidden topic, the one piece of ground declared off-limits by mutual consent. With one notable exception, the dialogue between Adams and Jefferson, so revealing in its engagement of the conflicting ideas and impulses that shaped the American Revolution, also symbolized the unofficial policy of silence within the revolutionary generation on the most glaring disagreement of all.[56]

The exception occurred in 1819, prompted by the debate then raging over passage of the Missouri Compromise. Prior to that time, Adams and Jefferson had not only avoided the subject in their correspondence; they had also independently declared the matter intractable: "More than fifty years has it attracted my thoughts and given me much anxiety," Adams confessed in 1817. "A Folio Volume would not contain my Lucubrations on this Subject. And at the End of it, I should leave my reader and myself at a loss, what to do with it, as at the beginning." For his part, Jefferson kept repeating the avoidance argument he had fashioned in 1805. "I have most carefully avoided every public act or manifestation on that subject," he announced, explaining that the abolition of slavery was a task for the next generation, "who can follow it up, and bear it through to its consummation."[57]

Even though the congressional debate over the Missouri question was essentially an argument about the extension of slavery into the territories, the code of silence governed the lengthy exchanges in the House of Representatives, which focused exclusively on the constitutional question of federal versus state jurisdiction rather than on the problem of slavery itself. Jefferson, for his part, was outraged that the issue was being discussed at all: "But the Missouri question is a breaker on which we lose the Missouri country by revolt, and what more God only knows," he complained to Adams. "From the battle of Bunker's hill to the treaty of Paris we never had so ominous a question." Jefferson understood full well that the constitutional argument over federal jurisdiction merely masked the deeper issue at stake, and he said so to Adams:

> The real question, as seen in the states afflicted with this unfortunate population, is Are our slaves to be presented with freedom and a dagger? For if Congress has a power to regulate the conditions of the inhabitants of states, within the states, it will be but another exercise of that power to declare that all shall be free. Are we then to . . . wage another Peloponessian War to settle the ascendancy between them. That question remains to be seen: but not I hope by you or me. Surely they will parlay awhile, and give us time to get out of the way.[58]

Adams, usually the more apocalyptic member of the team, in this instance adopted the more sanguine Jeffersonian posture. "I hope some good natured way or other will be found out to untie this very intricate knot," he counseled. With his other correspondents, though not with Jefferson, he was much more forthright. "Negro Slavery is an evil of Colossal magnitude," he wrote to William Tudor, "and I am utterly averse to the admission of Slavery into the Missouri Territory." What's more, he welcomed the very debate that Jefferson abhorred. "We must settle the question of slavery's extension now," he told his daughter-in-law, "otherwise it will stamp our National Character and lay a Foundation for calamities, if not disunion." As for the constitutional question, he regarded federal jurisdiction over the western territories as a clear precedent that had been established, irony of ironies, by Jefferson's executive action in the Louisiana Purchase.[59]

Over the course of the next four decades, the national debate over slavery and its expansion into the West was often framed as an argument over the intent of the founders. Here were two of the unequivocally original patriarchs, declaring that their respective understandings of the Revolution's legacy concerning slavery were fundamentally different. Jefferson's version led directly to the doctrine of "popular sovereignty" embraced by Stephen Douglas, to the states' rights position of John C. Calhoun and then the Confederacy. Adams's version led directly to the "house divided" position of Abraham Lincoln, the conviction that abolishing slavery was a moral imperative bequeathed by the revolutionary generation to their successors, and the doctrine of federal sovereignty established by the victory of the Union in the Civil War. When it came to slavery, it would seem, there was no singular vision, only contradictory original intentions.

The dominant legacy, of course, was avoidance and silence. Jefferson objected so strenuously to the debate over the Missouri question because it violated that legacy. "In the gloomiest moments of the Revolutionary War," he wrote in 1820, "I never had any apprehensions equal to what I feel from this source." In their last exchange on the topic, Adams suggested that he, too, would observe the unwritten code and carry his concerns to the grave: "Slavery in this Country I have seen hanging over it like a black cloud for half a Century. . . . I might probably say I had seen Armies of Negroes marching and counter-marching in the air, shining in Armour. I have been so terrified with this Phenomenon that I constantly said in former times to the Southern Gentlemen, I cannot comprehend this object; I must leave it to you. I will vote for forcing no measure against your judgments." Neither the Revolution nor the infant republic could have succeeded without the support of the southern states, so Adams had deferred to the Virginians to assume leadership of the antislavery movement. By 1820 it was abundantly clear that they had failed in this mission, with Jefferson himself the most visible symbol of the failure. But Adams chose to keep his vow of silence, at least with Jefferson, thereby honoring the etiquette of the friendship above his moral reservations, and simultaneously making the dialogue between Quincy and Monticello a final testament to the most problematic legacy of the revolutionary generation.[60]

THE CORRESPONDENCE lost its argumentative edge and shifted back to an elegiac, still-life pattern after 1820. One final flurry occurred in 1819, when a document appeared in the newspapers purportedly drafted by a group of citizens in Mecklenburg County, North Carolina, in May of 1775, and containing language eerily similar to Jefferson's later draft of the Declaration of Independence. Adams called Jefferson's attention to the discovery, noting that he wished he had known about it back then: "I would have made the Hall of Congress Echo and re-echo, with it fifteen Months before your Declaration of Independence." Nothing could have been better calculated to activate all of Jefferson's interior antennae, since his primacy as the author of the Declaration was his major claim to everlasting fame. He responded promptly, insisting that "this paper is a fabrication," urging Adams to remain skeptical "until positive and solemn proof of its authenticity shall be provided." Adams quickly reassured Jefferson that he now believed "that the Mecklenburg Resolutions are a fiction." Meanwhile, however, he was telling other correspondents quite the opposite. "I could as soon believe that the dozen flowers of the Hydrangia now before my Eyes were the work of chance," he joked, "as that the Mecklenburg Resolutions and Mr. Jefferson's declaration were not derived one from the other."[61]

Adams himself derived great satisfaction from the Mecklenburg incident, not so much because he believed Jefferson was a plagiarist, but because he thought the whole emphasis on one man, one moment, and one document distorted the true story of the American Revolution. Even though the Mecklenburg Declaration was subsequently exposed as a forgery, it accurately reflected the Adams sense that there were multiple venues or theaters where the drama of the movement for independence was playing out and multiple culminating moments besides July 4, 1776. In his own memoirs he had selected May 15, 1776, as the most decisive moment, because that was the day the Continental Congress passed a resolution calling for new constitutions in each of the states. (Not so coincidentally, Adams had drafted and moved the resolution.) In the Adams version, this decision was truly decisive because it created separate and independent American governments. It also meant that the Revolution was a responsible and positive commitment to new forms of political discipline rooted in the experience of the old colonial governments, not just a negative assertion of separation from England and a complete break with the past, as Jefferson's Declaration seemed to suggest. According to Adams, the Revolution succeeded because of its ties to the past, which meant that, in the Jeffersonian sense, it was not really a revolution at all.[62]

Though the brief exchange over the Mecklenburg Declaration touched on these significant differences of opinion, the diplomatic imperatives of the dialogue ruled out full disclosure. By 1820 even Adams had stopped firing off his illumination rounds and had adopted the Jeffersonian posture of benign duplicity, preferring to risk hypocrisy rather than the friendship. Though his prose remained pungent, the more dangerous bursts of candor had subsided, especially after Abigail passed away in October of 1818. (As she lay in bed dying, Adams remained composed but told the gathered relatives, "I wish I could lay down beside her and die too.") Jefferson had always claimed that each generation should not linger beyond its allotted time, that one had almost a moral obligation to clear the ground for the next generation by placing oneself beneath it. Now both patriarchs seemed to sense that they had outlived their time. Looking back on life, wrote Jefferson, was "like looking over a field of battle. All, all dead: and ourselves left alone amidst a new generation whom we know not, and who know not us."[63]

The vicissitudes of aging began to crowd out the more controversial topics. "Crippled wrists and fingers make writing slow and laborious," Jefferson complained. "But while writing to you, I lose the sense of these things, in the recollection of ancient times, when youth and health made happiness out of every thing. I forget for awhile the hoary winter of age when we can think of nothing but how to keep ourselves warm, and how to get rid of our heavy hours until the friendly hand of death shall rid us of all at once." Adams agreed that memories of the past were all that was left, and he too preferred to remember only the good ones: "I look back with rapture to those golden days when Virginia and Massachusetts lived and acted together like a band of brothers," he recalled, and though the end was near, "While I breath I shall be your friend."[64]

They referred to life in the hereafter, not as a chance to see God so much as an opportunity to converse with each other and the other "band of brothers." As Jefferson put it, "May we meet there again . . . with our antient Colleagues, and receive with them the seal of approbation." Adams concurred that the reunion in heaven would permit them to laugh at their human follies and foibles, though he would talk with Franklin only after the great man did proper penance for his sins. Neither man was completely convinced that heaven was anything more than a metaphor. Adams was on record as thinking that the belief in life everlasting was more important than the thing itself. "If it would be revealed or demonstrated that there is no future state," he apprised one friend, "my advice to every man, woman, and child would be, as our existence would be in our own power, to take opium." Or as he put it to Jefferson, "if we are disappointed, we shall never know it." Each man was hedging his bets on the hereafter by preparing his private papers for posterity, the one place where they knew their prospects of immortality were assured. And both men regarded the letters they were writing to each other as the capstone to that final project.[65]

There is no question that the emotional bond between the two patriarchs was restored and the friendship recovered toward the end. They no longer had to pose as partners; or what amounts to the same thing, the posing reflected a deeply felt sense of affinity. In part, the bonding occurred because the correspondence of their twilight years permitted both sages to confront and argue out their different notions of the history they had lived and made together. Jefferson had made his amends and some crucial concessions. Adams had expressed his feisty and passionate objections to the Jeffersonian constructions in one last catharsis. One would like to believe, and there is some basis for the belief, that each man came to recognize in the other the intellectual and temperamental qualities lacking in himself; that they, in effect, completed each other; that only when joined could the pieces of the story of the American Revolution come together to make a whole. But the more mundane truth is that they never faced and therefore never fully resolved all their political differences; they simply outlived them.

At the start of the correspondence Adams had felt deep resentment toward Jefferson for the libels he had sponsored during the Adams presidency. By 1823 the whole subject of scandal had become a nostalgic joke. Adams read in the newspapers that Jefferson had compiled "a Magazine of slips of newspapers, and pamphlets, vilifying, calumniating and defaming you." This was an inspired idea that Adams wished he had had first: "What a dunce I have been all my days, and what lubbers my Children, and Grand Children, were, that none of us have ever thought to make a similar collection. If we had I am confident I could have produced a more splendid Mass than yours." Jefferson regretted to inform Adams that the story was untrue; he had not compiled a collection of the libels against himself. If he had, however, "it would not indeed have been a single volume, but an Encyclopedia in bulk."[66]

They had become living relics. In 1824 the Marquis de Lafayette, the great French champion of American independence, paid a final visit to America. Monticello and Quincy were obligatory stops on his tour. In each location the reunion drew large crowds, in which witnesses claimed they saw two ghosts from a bygone era materializing one final time for the benefit of the present generation. The American sculptor John Henri Browere also visited both sages, who were asked to sit for "life masks" designed to produce reliable likenesses of their faces and heads—in effect, to make realistic icons of the icons. (Jefferson found the process, which required pouring successive coats of a hot plasterlike liquid over the head, so uncomfortable that he vowed to "bid adieu for ever to busts and portraits.") His final adieu to Adams conveyed the same strange sense of being regarded as living statues. He entrusted his last letter to his grandson, Thomas Jefferson Randolph, who was traveling to Boston and would make a stop in Quincy: "Like other young people, he wishes to be able, in the winter nights of old age, to recount to those around him what he has learnt of the Heroic age preceding his birth, and which of the Argonauts particularly he was in time to have seen." For most Americans coming of age in the 1820s, the American Revolution had long since been enshrined as a sacred moment in the distant past, when a gallery of heroes had been privileged to see God face-to-face. It was awkward to realize that a few of them were still alive.[67]

But they were. And as the fiftieth anniversary of Independence Day approached, requests poured into Monticello and Quincy from across the land, asking the patriarchs to share their wisdom and memories about the meaning of it all. Though seriously ill with an intestinal disorder that would eventually prove fatal, Jefferson summoned up the energy for one final spasm of eloquence. For several days, he worked over the draft of a letter to the committee responsible for the Independence Day ceremonies in Washington, crossing out and revising the language with as much attention to detail as he had given the original Declaration. He regretted that his deteriorating health prevented him from attending the ceremonies in person and joining "the small band, the remnant of that host of worthies who joined with us on that day." (Only three of the original signers survived: Adams, Jefferson, and Charles Carroll of Maryland.) Then he offered the Jeffersonian version of what the "host of worthies" had done:

> May it be to the world, what I believe it will be, (to some parts sooner, to others later, but finally to all,) the signal of arousing men to burst the chains under which monkish ignorance and superstition had persuaded them to bind themselves, and to assume the blessings and security of self-government. . . . All eyes are opened or opening to the rights of man. The general spread of the light of science has already laid open to every view the palpable truth, that the mass of mankind has not been born with saddles on their backs, nor a favored few, booted and spurred, ready to ride them legitimately, by the grace of God. These are grounds of hope for others; for ourselves, let the annual return of this day forever refresh our recollections of these rights, and an undiminished devotion to them.[68]

Here was the vintage Jeffersonian vision. It viewed the American Revolution as an explosion that dislodged America from England, from Europe, from the past itself, the opening shot in a global struggle for liberation from all forms of oppression that was destined to sweep around the world. In this formulation, all forms of authority not originating within the self were stigmatized and placed on the permanent defensive. The American Revolution had not just repudiated the tyranny of the English king and Parliament; it had defied all political institutions with coercive powers of any sort, including the kind of national government established by the Federalists in the 1790s.

The inspirational rhetoric of the statement was not original. The phrases "saddles on their backs" and "a favored few, booted and spurred" had been lifted from a famous speech delivered by Col. Richard Rumbold, a Puritan soldier convicted of treason in 1685, who spoke the words from the gallows. Jefferson owned several copies of English histories that reprinted the Rumbold speech. (Perhaps as a dying man, like Rumbold, Jefferson thought he had every right to claim a favorite piece of eloquence as his own.) But the borrowed rhetoric was only one small feature of a uniquely Jeffersonian message that was *inherently* rhetorical in character—that is, it framed the issues at a rarefied altitude, where all answers were self-evident and no real choices had to be made. And that was the ultimate source of its beguiling charm. The Jeffersonian vision floated. It functioned at inspirational levels above the bedeviling particularities, like a big bang theory of the American Revolution, now destined to expand throughout the world naturally and inevitably, no longer in doubt or in human hands.[69]

Adams also received many requests from federal and state committees charged with organizing the celebration of what was being called "the Jubilee of Independence." Irreverent to the end, for a time he resisted, insisting that the Fourth of July was not really the right date, indeed there was no one right date, and the passage of the Declaration of Independence was merely an ornamental occasion bereft of any larger historical significance. When a delegation from Quincy came out to visit him to request words for a toast at the local celebration, he was curt. "I will give you INDEPENDENCE FOREVER," he replied. When asked to enumerate or explain, he refused. "Not a word," he insisted.

Eventually, several family friends prodded a few amplifying rewards from the otherwise-loquacious patriarch. He conceded that the era of the American Revolution had been "a memorable epoch in the annals of the human race," but the jury was still out on its significance. He doubted whether the republican principles planted by the founding generation would grow in foreign soil. Neither Europe nor Latin America were ready for them. Even within the United States, the fate of those principles was still problematic. He warned that America was "destined in future history to form the brightest or blackest page, according to the use or the abuse of those political institutions by which they shall in time to come be shaped by the *human mind.*" Asked to pose for posterity, he chose to go out hurling it a challenge.[70]

The Adams formulation was precisely the opposite of Jefferson's. It lacked the lyrical eloquence and the floating optimism of the Jeffersonian version because it was grounded in the palpable sense of contingency Adams had internalized over his long career. For Adams, the

American Revolution was still an experiment, a sail into uncharted waters that no other ship of state had ever successfully navigated. There were no maps or charts to guide a republican government claiming to derive its authority and legitimacy from public opinion, that murky source of sovereignty that could be as choppy and unpredictable as waves on the ocean. He had been a member of the crew on this maiden voyage, even taken his turn at the helm, so he knew as well as anyone, better than most, that they had nearly crashed and sunk on several occasions, had argued bitterly among themselves throughout the 1790s about the proper course. Jefferson seemed to think that, once unmoored from British docks and unburdened of European baggage, the ship would sail itself into the proverbial sunset. Adams thought he knew better, and he also would go to his grave believing that a fully empowered federal government on the Federalist model was a fulfillment, rather than a betrayal, of the course they had set at the start. Without a sanctioned central government to steer the still-fragile American republic, the new crew was certain to founder on that huge rock called slavery, which was lurking dead ahead in the middle distance and that even Jefferson acknowledged to be "a breaker."

The more providential Jeffersonian version of the story triumphed in the history books, as Adams knew it would, helped along by one final act of fate that everyone, then and now, regarded as the unmistakable voice of God. On the evening of July 3, 1826, Jefferson fell into a coma. His last discernible words, uttered to the physician and family gathered around the bedside, indicated he was hoping to time his exit in dramatic fashion: "Is it the Fourth?" It was not, but he lingered in a semiconscious condition until shortly after noon on the magic day. That same morning, Adams collapsed in his favorite reading chair. He lapsed into unconsciousness at almost the exact moment Jefferson died. The end came quickly, at about five-thirty that afternoon. He wakened for a brief moment, indicated that nothing more should be done to prolong the inevitable, then, with obvious effort, gave a final salute to his old friend with his last words: "Thomas Jefferson survives," or, by another account, "Thomas Jefferson still lives." Whatever the version, he was wrong for the moment but right for the ages.[71]

NOTES

The notes that follow represent my attempt to adopt a sensible approach to the customary rules of scholarly citation. A full accounting of all the books and articles consulted would produce as many pages of notes as there are of text. This strikes me as cumbersome, more than most readers want, and a clear case of conspicuous erudition. I have cited all primary sources quoted in the text, plus those secondary sources that seem to me seminal or those that had a decided impact on my thinking. The awkward truth is that this book represents a distillation of my reading in the historical literature on the revolutionary era over the past thirty years. A faithful recounting of all the scholarly influences that have shaped my interpretation of the revolutionary generation would entail a massive listing that would still fail to capture the whole truth. In partial compensation for my sins of omission, I have littered the notes below with my assessment of the sources cited, thereby giving them the occasional flavor of a bibliographic essay.

ABBREVIATIONS

Adams	*The Microfilm Edition of the Adams Papers,* 608 reels (Boston, 1954–1959).
AHR	*American Historical Review.*
Boyd	Julian P. Boyd et al., eds., *The Papers of Thomas Jefferson,* 26 vols. to date (Princeton, 1950–).
Cappon	Lester G. Cappon, ed., *The Adams-Jefferson Letters: The Complete Correspondence Between Thomas Jefferson and Abigail and John Adams,* 2 vols. (Chapel Hill, 1959).
Fitzpatrick	John C. Fitzpatrick, ed., *Writings of George Washington,* 39 vols. (Washington, D.C., 1931–1939).

Ford	Paul Leicester Ford, ed., *The Writings of Thomas Jefferson*, 10 vols. (New York, 1892–1899).
JAH	*Journal of American History.*
JER	*Journal of the Early Republic.*
JSH	*Journal of Southern History.*
NEQ	*New England Quarterly.*
Rutland	Robert A. Rutland et al., *The Papers of James Madison*, 22 vols. to date (Charlottesville, 1962–).
Smith	James Morton Smith, ed., *The Republic of Letters: The Correspondence Between Thomas Jefferson and James Madison, 1776–1826*, 3 vols. (New York, 1995).
Spur	John A. Schutz and Douglass Adair, eds., *The Spur of Fame: Dialogues of John Adams and Benjamin Rush, 1805–1813* (San Marino, 1966).
Syrett	Harold Syrett, ed., *The Papers of Alexander Hamilton*, 26 vols. (New York, 1974–1992).
VMHB	*Virginia Magazine of History and Biography.*
WMQ	*William and Mary Quarterly*, 3d ser.
Works	Charles Francis Adams, ed., *The Works of John Adams, Second President of the United States*, 10 vols. (Boston, 1850–1856).
Writings	George Washington, *Writings*, John Rhodehamel, ed., Library of America (New York, 1997).

PREFACE

1. Adams to Nathan Webb, 12 October 1755, *Works*, vol. 1, 23–34; Adams to Abigail Adams, 2 June 1776, Lyman Butterfield, ed., *Adams Family Correspondence*, 3 vols. (Cambridge, 1963), vol. 2, 3; Adams to Benjamin Rush, 21 May 1807, *Spur*, 89.

2. Francis Fukuyama, *The End of History and the Last Man* (New York, 1993).

3. Benjamin Rush to Adams, 20 July 1811, *Spur*, 183.

4. Ira Gruber, *The Howe Brothers and the American Revolution* (Williamsburg, 1972); Kevin Phillips, *The Cousins' War: Religion, Politics, and the Triumph of Anglo-America* (New York, 1999), 291–299.

5. *Writings*, 517.

6. The seminal study of republican ideology as a defiant repudiation of consolidated power is Bernard Bailyn, *Ideological Origins of the American Revolution* (Cambridge, 1967); as applied to the 1780s, the classic work is Gordon Wood, *The Creation of the American Republic* (Chapel Hill, 1969); as applied to the 1790s, the standard source is Lance Banning, *The Jeffersonian Persuasion: Evolution of a Party Ideology* (Ithaca, N.Y., 1978).

7. Adams to Benjamin Rush, 10 July 1812, *Spur*, 231–232.

8. T. H. Breen, "Ideology and Nationalism on the Eve of the American Revolution:

Revisions *Once More* in Need of Revising," *JAH* 84 (June 1997): 13–39; John Murrin, "A Roof Without Walls: The Dilemma of American National Identity," in Richard Beeman, Stephen Botein, Edward Carter, eds., *Beyond Confederation: Origins of the Constitution and American National Identity* (Chapel Hill, 1987), 334–38.

9. Jefferson to William Fleming, 1 July 1776, Boyd, vol. 1, 411–12; U.S. Bureau of Census, *First Census* (Baltimore, 1966), 6–8.

10. Laurel Thatcher Ulrich, *A Midwife's Tale: The Life of Martha Ballard Based on Her Diary, 1785–1812* (New York, 1990); Robert E. Desrochers, Jr., " 'Not Fade Away': The Narrative of Venture Smith, an African American in the Early Republic," *JAH* 84 (June 1997): 40–66. Another approach has been to study the political culture "from below," meaning the way attitudes were shaped at the local level in public ceremonies and rituals. The best analysis of emerging nationalism in this mode is David Waldstreicher, *In the Midst of Perpetual Fêtes: The Making of American Nationalism, 1776–1820* (Chapel Hill, 1997).

11. Mercy Otis Warren, *History of the Rise, Progress, and Termination of the American Revolution*, 3 vols. (Boston, 1805); John Marshall, *The Life of George Washington*, 5 vols. (Philadelphia, 1804–1807).

12. My thinking about the circularity of the debate on the American Revolution was stimulated by the same analysis of the French Revolution by François Furet, *Interpreting the French Revolution*, trans. Elburg Foster (Cambridge, England, 1981).

13. Martin Smelser, "The Federalist Period as an Age of Passion," *American Quarterly* 10 (Winter 1958): 391–419; see also John R. Howe, Jr., "Republican Thought and the Political Violence of the 1790s," *American Quarterly* 19 (Summer 1967): 147–165.

14. Whitehead's assessment is reported as a conversation with Perry Miller in Miller's collection of essays, *Nature's Nation* (Cambridge, 1967), 3–4. For a convenient overview of the ninety-nine men who signed the Declaration of Independence and the Constitution, see Richard D. Brown, "The Founding Fathers of 1776 and 1787: A Collective View," *WMQ* 33 (July 1976): 465–480.

15. Douglass Adair, "Fame and the Founding Fathers," in Trevor Colbourn, ed., *Fame and the Founding Fathers: Essays by Douglass Adair* (New York, 1974), 3–26.

CHAPTER ONE: THE DUEL

1. The most original and recent interpretation of the duel is Joanne Freeman, "Dueling as Politics: Reinterpreting the Burr-Hamilton Duel," *WMQ* 53 (April 1996): 289–318. The fullest narrative of the story is W. J. Rorabaugh, "The Political Duel in the Early Republic," *JER* 15 (Spring 1995): 1–23. All the biographers of Burr and Hamilton obviously cover the duel. The standard collection of documents is Harold C. Syrett and Jean G. Cooke, eds., *Interview at Weehawken* (Middletown, Conn., 1960). The authoritative collection, with an accompanying introductory note of considerable grace and wisdom, is Syrett, vol. 26, 235–349.

2. The standard Burr biography is Milton Lomask, *Aaron Burr*, 2 vols. (New York,

1979–1982). Still helpful because of its original material is James Parton, *The Life and Times of Aaron Burr* (New York, 1864).

3. There are several excellent Hamilton biographies. The standard account is Broadus Mitchell, *Alexander Hamilton*, 2 vols. (New York, 1957–1962). For sheer readability, John C. Miller, *Alexander Hamilton and the Growth of the New Nation* (New York, 1964), is quite good, now joined by Richard Brookhiser, *Alexander Hamilton, American* (New York, 1999). The most incisive and sharply defined portrait is Jacob Ernest Cooke, *Alexander Hamilton: A Biography* (New York, 1979). Old but reliable, and with an excellent account of the duel, is Nathan Schachner, *Alexander Hamilton* (New York, 1946).

4. "Statement on Impending Duel with Aaron Burr," Syrett, vol. 26, 278–281.

5. Parton, *The Life and Times of Aaron Burr,* 349–355, offers a splendid description of the site as it still appeared about fifty years after the duel.

6. On the history of the duel as an institution, the works I found most helpful were: Edward L. Ayers, *Vengeance and Justice: Crime and Punishment in the 19th Century American South* (New York, 1984); V. G. Kiernan, *The Duel in European History: Honor and the Reign of Aristocracy* (Oxford, 1986); Lorenzo Sabine, *Notes on Duels and Dueling . . .* (Boston, 1855); Bertram Wyatt-Brown, *Southern Honor: Ethics and Behavior in the Old South* (New York, 1982).

7. Merrill Lindsay, "Pistols Shed Light on Famed Duel," *Smithsonian,* November 1971, 94–98; see also Virginius Dabney, "The Mystery of the Hamilton-Burr Duel," *New York,* March 29, 1976, 37–41.

8. Syrett, vol. 26, 306–308.

9. David Hosack to William Coleman, 17 August 1804, ibid., 344–347.

10. Joint Statement by William P. Van Ness and Nathaniel Pendleton on the Duel Between Alexander Hamilton and Aaron Burr, 17 July 1804, ibid., 333–336.

11. Benjamin Moore to Coleman, 12 July 1804, ibid., 314–317.

12. Ibid., 322–329.

13. William Coleman, *A Collection of the Facts and Documents, Relative to the Death of Major-General Hamilton* (New York, 1804), which reviews the newspaper coverage and multiple eulogies for Hamilton. I have also looked over James Cheetham's editorial assaults on Burr in the *American Citizen* during July and August of 1804, as well as the pro-Burr editorials in the *Morning Chronicle* at the same time. The story of the wax replica of Burr in ambush comes from Parton, *The Life and Times of Aaron Burr,* 616.

14. See the exchange of letters between Van Ness and Pendleton, then "Joint Statement," Syrett, vol. 26, 329–336.

15. See the several documents and notes in ibid., 335–340.

16. The scholarly consensus accepts the Hamilton version of the duel, primarily because that version dominated the contemporary accounts in the press, and also because it is the only version that fits with Hamilton's purported remarks about the still-loaded pistol. While absolute certainty is not within our grasp, what we

might call "the interval problem" strikes me as an insurmountable obstacle for the Hamiltonian version. For that reason, while the mystery must remain inherently unsolvable in any absolute sense of finality, the interpretation offered here seems most plausible and most compatible with what lawyers would call "the preponderance of the evidence." It also preserves what the Hamilton advocates care about most; namely, Hamilton's stated intention not to fire at Burr. There is a pro-Burr version that argues otherwise. See Samuel Engle Burr, *The Burr-Hamilton Duel and Related Matters* (San Antonio, 1971).

17. Burr to Van Ness, 9 July 1804, Syrett, vol. 26, 295–296. For the tradition of aiming to harm but not kill, see Hamilton Cochrane, *Noted American Duels and Hostile Encounters* (Philadelphia, 1963); Don C. Seitz, *Famous American Duels* (New York, 1919); and Evarts B. Greene, "The Code of Honor in Colonial and Revolutionary Times, with Special Reference to New England," *Publications of the Colonial Society of Massachusetts* 26 (1927): 367–368.

18. Charles D. Cooper to Philip Schuyler, 23 April 1804, Syrett, vol. 26, 243–246; see also Burr to Hamilton, 18 June 1804, ibid., 241–243.

19. Hamilton to Burr, 20 June 1804, ibid., 247–249.

20. Burr to Hamilton, 21, 22 June 1804, ibid., 249–250, 255.

21. Burr to Van Ness, 25 June 1804; "Instructions to Van Ness," 22–23 June 1804; Van Ness to Pendleton, 26 June 1804, ibid., 256–269.

22. Burr to Van Ness, 25 June 1804, ibid., 265.

23. Pendleton to Van Ness, 26 June 1804, ibid., 270–271.

24. Burr to Van Ness, 26 June 1804; Van Ness to Pendleton, 27 June 1804, ibid., 266–267, 272–273. The Randolph quotation is in Syrett and Cooke, eds., *Interview at Weehawken*, 171.

25. Burr's "Instructions to Van Ness," 26 June 1804; Van Ness to Pendleton, 27 June 1804, ibid., 266–267, 272–273.

26. Mary-Jo Kline, ed., *Political Correspondence and Public Papers of Aaron Burr* 2 vols. (Princeton, 1983), vol. 2, 876–883, for the editorial note on Burr and the duel; see also Parton, *The Life and Times of Aaron Burr*, 352–353, for Burr's state of mind on the eve of the duel.

27. Douglass Adair, "What Was Hamilton's 'Favorite Song'?" *WMQ* 12 (April 1955): 298–307, for Trumbull's observation and the song Hamilton probably sang.

28. Editorial notes in Syrett, vol. 26, 292–293; Hamilton to James A. Hamilton, June 1804, ibid., 281–282.

29. Ibid., 279–281.

30. Ibid., 280.

31. Anthony Merry to Lord Harroby, 6 August 1804, Kline, ed., *Burr Papers*, vol. 2, 891–893.

32. Ayers, *Vengeance and Justice*, 8–15, 275; Bertram Wyatt-Brown, "Andrew Jackson's Honor," *JER* 17 (1997): 7–8; Kenneth S. Greenberg, "The Nose, the Lie, and the Duel in the Antebellum South," *AHR* 95 (1990): 57–74.

33. Henry Adams, *History of the United States of America During the Administrations of Thomas Jefferson and James Madison,* 2 vols. (New York, 1986), vol. 1, 429–430.

34. This summary of the political rivalry draws on multiple sources, but the most succinct synthesis is in Syrett, vol. 26, 238–239.

35. Syrett and Cooke, eds., *Interview at Weehawken,* 16–17.

36. Hamilton to Oliver Wolcott, Jr., 16 December 1800, Syrett, vol. 25, 257–258.

37. The most favorable interpretation on Burr's behavior during the presidential drama of 1801 is Lomask, *Aaron Burr,* vol. 2, 268–295, and it does not find Burr innocent so much as conclude that he was not guilty.

38. The best brief character portrait of Burr, simultaneously fair but critical, is Stanley Elkins and Eric McKitrick, *The Age of Federalism: The Early American Republic, 1787–1800* (New York, 1993), 743–746.

39. Adams, *History,* vol. 1, 409–430; see also Henry Adams, ed., *Documents Relating to New England Federalism, 1800–1815* (Boston, 1905), 46–63, 107–330, 338–365.

40. Hamilton to Theodore Sedgwick, 10 July 1804, Syrett, vol. 26, 309; see also the editor's extensive notes in ibid., 310.

41. The best book on the inherent tenuousness of American politics in this era is James Roger Sharp, *American Politics in the Early Republic: The New Nation in Crisis* (New Haven, 1993).

42. The case mentioned here was *People v. Croswell,* argued in February of 1804, in which Hamilton defended the editor of a small country newspaper, appropriately named *The Wasp,* for publishing libelous statements against Adams, Jefferson, and Washington. Hamilton argued that, despite lower court rulings against the principle, truth was a legitimate defense against libel. He lost the case, but the New York legislature enacted a new libel law the following year incorporating Hamilton's language. See the account in Cooke, *Alexander Hamilton,* 359.

43. The seminal essay on the volatile character of politics in the early republic is John R. Howe, Jr., "Republican Thought and the Political Violence of the 1790s," *American Quarterly* 19 (Spring 1967): 148–165. The theme is also a thread in the authoritative history of the political culture, Elkins and McKitrick, *The Age of Federalism,* especially 3–50.

44. On Burr's negligible political prospects, see Lomask, *Aaron Burr,* vol. 1, 302; on Hamilton's, see Cooke, *Alexander Hamilton,* 238. See Adams, ed., *Documents,* 167, for the quotation by John Quincy Adams. The Holmes quotation is from Leonard Levy, ed., *American Constitutional Law: Historical Essays* (New York, 1966), 57.

CHAPTER TWO: THE DINNER

1. See Boyd, vol. 17, 205–207, for Jefferson's version of the dinner. Three scholarly articles capture the interpretive issues at stake: Jacob E. Cooke, "The Compromise of 1790," *WMQ* 27 (1970): 523–545; Kenneth Bowling, "Dinner at Jefferson's: A Note on Jacob E. Cooke's 'The Compromise of 1790,'" *WMQ* 28 (1971):

629–648; Norman K. Risjord, "The Compromise of 1790: New Evidence on the Dinner Table Bargain," *WMQ* 33 (1976): 309–314.

2. *New York Journal*, 27 July 1790, quoted in Boyd, vol. 17, 182.

3. Jefferson to James Monroe, 20 June 1790, Boyd, vol. 16, 536–538. See also Monroe to Jefferson, 3 July 1790, ibid., 596–597.

4. Boyd, vol. 17, 207.

5. On Madison as a seminal political thinker, see Lance Banning, *The Sacred Fire of Liberty: James Madison and the Founding of the Federal Republic* (Ithaca, N.Y., 1995); Drew McCoy, *The Last of the Fathers: James Madison and the Republican Legacy* (Cambridge, 1989); and Marvin Meyers, ed., *The Mind of the Founder: Sources of the Political Thought of James Madison* (Hanover, N.H., 1981).

6. For the most thorough yet succinct account of Madison's career in the 1780s, see the introductory essays for his correspondence with Jefferson during those years in Smith, vol. 1, 204–661.

7. The standard Madison biography is Irving Brant, *James Madison*, 6 vols. (Indianapolis, 1941–1961). See also Ralph Ketcham, *James Madison: A Biography* (New York, 1971), and Jack N. Rakove, *James Madison and the Creation of the American Republic* (Glenview, Ill., 1990). The quotation is from Madison to Jared Sparks, 1 June 1831, Gaillard Hunt, ed., *The Writings of James Madison*, 10 vols. (New York, 1890–1910), vol. 9, 460.

8. The quotation is from McCoy, *The Last of the Fathers*, xiii.

9. Adrienne Koch, *Jefferson and Madison: The Great Collaboration* (New York, 1950). The quote from John Quincy Adams is in Smith, vol. 1, 2.

10. Hamilton to Madison, 12 October 1789, Rutland, vol. 12, 434–435; for Jefferson's views of the Constitution during the Paris years, see Joseph J. Ellis, *American Sphinx: The Character of Thomas Jefferson* (New York, 1997), 97–105.

11. The authoritative work on Jefferson's generational argument is Herbert E. Sloan, *Principle and Interest: Thomas Jefferson and the Problem of Debt* (New York, 1995).

12. The best secondary account of Madison's conversion is Stanley Elkins and Eric McKitrick, *The Age of Federalism: The Early American Republic, 1787–1800* (New York, 1993), 77–92.

13. *Report Relative to a Provision for the Support of Public Credit*, in Syrett, vol. 6, 52–168, which includes a helpful editorial note on the chief features of Hamilton's plan.

14. See Madison's speech in the House on 11 February 1790, in Rutland, vol. 13, 34–39; see also Madison to Jefferson, 24 January 1790, ibid., 3–4. Benjamin Rush to Madison, 18 February 1790, ibid., 45–47.

15. Ibid., 36–37, 47–56, 58–59.

16. Ibid., 60–62, 65–66, 81–82, 163–174, for Madison's major speeches in the House against assumption.

17. Madison to Jefferson, 8 March 1790; Madison to Edmund Randolph, 21 March 1790; Madison to Henry Lee, 13 April 1790, ibid., 95, 110, 147–148.

18. Lee to Madison, 4 March, 3 April 1790, ibid., 87–91, 136–137.

19. Madison to Edmund Pendleton, 2 May 1790; George Nicholas to Madison, 3 May 1790; Edward Carrington to Madison, 7 April 1790, ibid., 184–185, 187, 142.

20. Madison to Jefferson, 17 April 1790, ibid., 151.

21. This personality sketch of Hamilton represents my own interpretive distillation from the multiple biographies. The insecurity theme is a central feature of Jacob Ernest Cooke, *Alexander Hamilton: A Biography* (New York, 1979), v–vi.

22. The hoofprints from several herds of historians and biographers have trampled this ground. Of all the biographers, I found Forrest McDonald, *Alexander Hamilton* (New York, 1979), 117–188, the most provocatively original on these themes and Cooke, *Alexander Hamilton*, 73–84, the most reliably sound. The background to the *Report on the Public Credit* is discussed succinctly and sensibly in the editorial note in Syrett, vol. 6, 51–65.

23. For Hamilton's arguments against "discrimination," see Syrett, vol. 6, 70–78, and the editorial documentation provided in ibid., 58–59.

24. Ibid., 70, 80–82.

25. The quotation about "mending fences" is from Cooke, *Alexander Hamilton*, 94. The interpretation offered here and in the succeeding paragraphs draws on all the standard sources. The two most influential secondary accounts, again as I see it, are Jacob E. Cooke, ed., *The Reports of Alexander Hamilton*, vii–xxiii, and Elkins and McKitrick, *The Age of Federalism*, 93–136. The latter includes a discussion of Hamilton's capacity for "projection," by which the authors mean the tendency to foresee or forecast economic trends. I am suggesting here that the vision Hamilton "projected" was very much a projection of his own distinctive character.

26. Madison to Lee, 13 April 1790, Rutland, vol. 22, 147–148.

27. Hamilton to Lee, 1 December 1789, Syrett, vi, i; Hamilton to William Duer, 4–7 April 1790, ibid., 346–347, for the resignation and editorial note on Duer's unquestionable thievery. The best modern estimate is that he swindled the federal government for personal profits that totaled about $300,000.

28. The best recent study of the economic predicament of Virginia's elite is Bruce A. Ragsdale, *A Planter's Republic: The Search for Economic Independence in Revolutionary Virginia* (Madison, 1994). Older but still useful studies include T. H. Breen, *Tobacco Culture: The Mentality of the Great Tidewater Planters on the Eve of the American Revolution* (Princeton, 1985), and Norman Risjord, *Chesapeake Politics, 1781–1800* (New York, 1978), 84–123. On Jefferson's economic situation and its psychological implications, see Sloan, *Principle and Interest*, 86–124.

29. On Jefferson's condition during the spring, see Jefferson to Thomas Mann Randolph, 9 May 1790, Boyd, vol. 16, 416. On Washington's health, see Jefferson to Randolph, 16 May 1790; Jefferson to William Short, 27 May 1790, ibid., 429, 444. Jefferson's primary focus was his *Report on Weights and Measures*, ibid., 602–675.

30. For Jefferson's Paris years, see Dumas Malone, *Jefferson and His Time*, 6 vols. (Boston, 1948–1981), vol. 2, and Ellis, *American Sphinx*, 64–117. The quotation is from Jefferson to Francis Hopkinson, 13 March 1789, Boyd, vol. 14, 650.

31. Pauline Maier, *American Scripture: Making the Declaration of Independence* (New York, 1997), 154–208.

32. Jefferson to Randolph, 18 April 1790; Jefferson to Lee, 26 April 1790; Jefferson to Randolph, 30 May 1790; Jefferson to George Mason, 13 June 1790, Boyd, vol. 16, 351, 385–386, 449, 493.

33. Kenneth Bowling, *The Creation of Washington, D.C.: The Idea and Location of the American Capital* (Fairfax, Va., 1991), x–xi, 148.

34. Ibid., 129–138, 161–181.

35. Madison to Pendleton, 20 June 1790, Rutland, vol. 13, 252–253; Richard Peters to Jefferson, 20 June 1790, Boyd, vol. 16, 539.

36. Rutland, vol. 12, 369–370, 396, 416–417, for Madison's speeches in the House.

37. Bowling, *The Creation of Washington*, 190–191. Though it appeared too late to shape my interpretation, I much admire C. M. Harris's "Washington's Gamble, L'Enfant's Dream: Politics, Design, and the Founding of the National Capital," *WMQ* 56 (July 1999): 527–564.

38. Ibid., 106–126, 164–166.

39. Madison to Pendleton, 20 June 1790, Rutland, vol. 13, 252–253.

40. Risjord, "The Compromise of 1790," 309; Bowling, *The Creation of Washington*, 179–185; editorial note in Rutland, vol. 13, 243–246.

41. Cooke, "The Compromise of 1790," 523–545, emphasizes the absence of a direct link between the two issues—assumption and residence. His interpretation attributes the bargain to multiple meetings conducted prior to the dinner at Jefferson's. My view is that the latter session sealed the deal by completing the negotiations on Virginia's debt. Without linkage with the residency issue, however, neither Jefferson nor Madison would have concurred.

42. Jefferson to George Gilmer, 27 June, 25 July 1790, Boyd, vol. 16, 269, 575. The standard account of the state and federal debt question is E. James Ferguson, *The Power of the Purse: A History of American Public Finance* (Chapel Hill, 1961). For a few relatively minor revisions, see William G. Anderson, *Price of Liberty: The Public Debt of the American Revolution* (Charlottesville, 1983).

43. Quotations from the *Daily Advertiser* reproduced in Boyd, vol. 17, 452, 460. See also Bowling, *The Creation of Washington*, 201.

44. "Jefferson's Report to Washington on Meeting Held at Georgetown," 14 September 1790, Boyd, vol. 17, 461–462.

45. Thomas Lee Shippen to William Shippen, 15 September 1790, ibid., 464–465, for the Jefferson-Madison tour of the region in September; Jefferson to Washington, 17 September 1790, ibid., 466–467, for the conversation at Mount Vernon. "Memorandum on the Residence Act," 29 August 1790, Rutland, vol. 13, 294–296, for Madison's concurrence on the executive strategy as the preferred solution. Bowling, *The Creation of Washington*, 212–213, for Washington's land holdings within the designated site.

46. Jefferson to Washington, 27 October 1790, Boyd, vol. 17, 643–644; Madison's speech in the House is reprinted in Rutland, vol. 12, 264–266.

47. John Harvie, Jr., to Jefferson, 3 August 1790, Boyd, vol. 17, 296; Carrington to Madison, 24 December 1790, Rutland, vol. 13, 331–332, which includes the language of the Virginia resolution quoted here.

48. *Federal Gazette,* 20 November 1790, quoted in Boyd, vol. 17, 459.

49. "Conjectures About the New Constitution," 17–30 September 1787, Syrett, vol. 6, 59; Hamilton to John Jay, 13 November 1790, Syrett, vol. 7, 149–150.

50. Three scholarly books touch upon these themes in different ways: Richard Buel, Jr., *Securing the Revolution: Ideology in American Politics, 1789–1815* (Ithaca, N.Y., 1972); Roger Sharp, *American Politics in the Early Republic: The New Nation in Crisis* (New Haven, 1993), which is especially good on the contingent character of the constitutional settlement; and Elkins and McKitrick, *The Age of Federalism,* which includes the problematic theme within its panoramic scope.

51. Adams to Francis Vanderkemp, 24 November 1818, *Adams,* reel 122.

52. On the construction of Washington, D.C., in the 1790s, see Bob Arnebeck, *Through a Fiery Trial: Building Washington, 1790–1800* (Lanham, Md., 1991). The seminal study on the distinctive physical conditions the new capital imposed on political life is James Sterling Young, *The Washington Community, 1800–1828* (New York, 1966).

53. Elkins and McKitrick, *The Age of Federalism,* 163–193, for an extended reflection on the national and cultural implications of making the new capital a pastoral place.

CHAPTER THREE: THE SILENCE

1. Linda Grant De Pauw et al., *Documentary History of the First Federal Congress of the United States,* 15 vols. (Baltimore, 1972), vol. 12, 277–87. The debates over the Quaker petitions are mentioned in passing in most secondary accounts of the period. See, for example, Stanley Elkins and Eric McKitrick, *The Age of Federalism: The Early American Republic, 1787–1800* (New York, 1993), 151–152. The fullest and most recent scholarly treatment is by Richard S. Newman, "Prelude to the Gag Rule: Southern Reaction to Antislavery Petitions in the First Federal Congress," *JER* 16 (1996): 571–599. See also Howard Ohline, "Slavery, Economics, and Congressional Politics," *JSH* 46 (1980): 355–360.

2. *First Congress,* vol. 12, 287–288.

3. Ibid., 289–290.

4. *First Congress,* vol. 3, 294. The text of the petitions are most readily available in Alfred Zilversmit, *The First Emancipation: The Abolition of Slavery in the North* (Chicago, 1967), 159–160.

5. More, much more, on this subject shortly. For now, the best surveys of the topic are Donald L. Robinson, *Slavery in the Structure of American Politics* (New York, 1971), 201–247; David Brion Davis, *The Problem of Slavery in the Age of Revolution* (Ithaca, N.Y., 1975), 122–131; Duncan J. MacLeod, *Slavery, Race and the American Revolution* (Cambridge, 1974), 37–39; Paul Finkelman, *Slavery and the Founders:*

Race and Liberty in the Age of Jefferson (London, 1996), 1–33. See also Sylvia R. Frey, *Water from the Rock: Black Resistance in a Revolutionary Age* (Princeton, 1991).

6. *First Congress,* vol. 12, 296.

7. Ibid., 307–308.

8. Ibid., 308–310.

9. Ibid., 297–298, 310–311. There are several versions of the debate recorded in *First Congress,* based on the several newspaper accounts published at the time and the official account in the *Congressional Register.* The accounts seldom disagree, though they vary in length and detail.

10. Ibid., 308.

11. Ibid., 296–297, 307.

12. Ibid., 298–299, 305–306.

13. Ibid., 311.

14. Ibid., 312.

15. *First Congress,* vol. 3, 295–296.

16. Gary B. Nash, *Race and Revolution* (Madison, 1990), 3–24, offers the most robust neoabolitionist interpretation of the revolutionary era. All the standard treatments of the subject emphasize the exuberant expectations generated by the revolutionary ideology: Davis, *The Problem of Slavery in the Age of Revolution,* 48–55; Robinson, *Slavery in the Structure of American Politics,* 98–130; Winthrop Jordan, *White Over Black: American Attitudes Toward the Negro, 1550–1812* (Chapel Hill, 1968), 269–314. On the resonant and quasi-religious power of the Declaration of Independence, see Pauline Maier, *American Scripture: Making the Declaration of Independence* (New York, 1997). See also the collection of essays in Ira Berlin and Ronald Hoffman, eds., *Slavery and Freedom in the Age of the American Revolution* (Charlottesville, 1983).

17. Robinson, *Slavery in the Structure of American Politics,* 124–129; MacLeod, *Slavery, Race and the American Revolution,* 21–29; Quaker Petition to the Continental Congress, 4 October 1783, Record Group 360, National Archives, Washington, D.C. The best collection of documents on this phase of the antislavery movement is Roger Burns, ed., *Am I Not a Man and a Brother: The Antislavery Crusade of Revolutionary America, 1688–1788* (New York, 1977), 397–490. On slavery itself, the authoritative work is Philip Morgan, *Slave Counterpoint: Black Culture in the Eighteenth-Century Chesapeake and Low Country* (Chapel Hill, 1998).

18. Zilversmit, *The First Emancipation,* 109–138.

19. Robert McColley, *Slavery in Jeffersonian Virginia* (Urbana, Ill., 1964), 141–162. For Jefferson's early leadership, see Joseph J. Ellis, *American Sphinx: The Character of Thomas Jefferson* (New York, 1997), 144–146.

20. This paragraph represents my attempt to negotiate the scholarly minefield that confronts anyone trying to explain the anomalous character of slavery within the ideological legacy of the American Revolution. The standard account, still quite impressive for its subtle treatment of the ironies and intellectual disjunctions, is

Davis, *The Problem of Slavery in the Age of Revolution.* The most forceful argument for the radical implications of the revolutionary ideology is Gordon S. Wood, *The Radicalism of the American Revolution* (New York, 1992), which emphasizes the egalitarian legacy that then seeped out slowly to create the democratic society that Alexis de Tocqueville described in the 1830s. If, however, one makes slavery the acid test of the revolutionary ideology, the legacy looks less than radical. The best treatment of that version is William W. Freehling, "The Founding Fathers, Conditional Antislavery, and the Nonradicalism of the American Revolution," in William W. Freehling, ed., *The Reinterpretation of American History: Slavery and the Civil War* (New York, 1994), 76–84.

21. The Madison quotation is from the debates at the Constitutional Convention (28 June 1787) in Max Farrand, ed., *The Records of the Federal Convention of 1787,* 4 vols. (New Haven, 1937), vol. 1, 486–487. The most succinct recent study of the role of slavery at the convention is Finkelman, *Slavery and the Founders,* 1–33. The groundbreaking scholarly analysis is Staughton Lynd, ed., *Class Conflict, Slavery, and the United States Constitution: Ten Essays* (Indianapolis, 1967). The most comprehensive assessment within the larger context of "original intent" is Jack N. Rakove, *Original Meanings: Politics and Ideas in the Making of the Constitution* (New York, 1996), 58, 70–74, 90–93.

22. *Records,* vol. 2 221–223, 364–365, 396–403.

23. *Records,* vol. 1, 605; vol. 2, 306.

24. Finkelman, *Slavery and the Founders,* 34–57, for the most recent scholarly assessment of the Northwest Ordinance, which emphasizes its inherent ambiguity. A more optimistic interpretation is suggested in William W. Freehling, "The Founding Fathers and Slavery," *AHR* 77 (1972): 81–93. See also Peter Onuf, "From Constitution to Higher Law: The Reinterpretation of the Northwest Ordinance," *Ohio History* 94 (1985): 5–33.

25. Finkelman, *Slavery and the Founders,* 19–31; Rakove, *Original Meanings,* 85–89.

26. Jonathan Elliot, ed., *The Debates in the Several State Conventions on the Adoption of the Federal Constitution,* 5 vols. (Philadelphia, 1896), vol. 2, 41, 149, 484.

27. Elliot, ed., *Debates,* vol. 4, 286.

28. McColley, *Slavery and Jeffersonian Virginia,* 120, 163–190. For Madison's remark on the three-fifths clause, see Clinton Rossiter, ed., *The Federalist Papers* (New York, 1961), 338–339.

29. Elliot, ed., *Debates,* vol. 3, 273, 452–453, 598–599. An excellent overview of the larger set of issues raised by the ambiguity of the Constitution on slavery is William Wiecek, *The Sources of Antislavery Constitutionalism in America, 1760–1840* (Ithaca, N.Y., 1977).

30. *First Congress,* vol. 12, 649–662.

31. This is a large claim, but it is rooted in the evidence (coming up in the next few pages) and in keeping with the best scholarly overview of the subject by Larry Tise, *Proslavery: A History of the Defense of Slavery in America, 1701–1840* (Athens, Ga., 1987).

32. *First Congress,* vol. 12, 719–721, 725–735.

33. Ibid., 750–761.

34. Tise, *Proslavery,* 97–123, which claims that even the "positive good" argument was part of the Deep South's position in the revolutionary era. I cannot go quite that far, even though the Deep South did argue that Africans actually preferred slavery to impoverished freedom or to life in Africa. What is missing in the revolutionary era, however, is the claim that the conditions of life for slaves in the South were preferable to the conditions for factory workers in the North, which would have been a historic impossibility, since factories had yet to appear. The late-eighteenth-century proslavery position, I believe, was more defensive. See, for example, Eric R. Papenfuse, *The Evils of Necessity: Robert Goodloe Harper and the Moral Dilemma of Slavery* (Philadelphia, 1997), and John P. Kaminski, ed., *A Necessary Evil? Slavery and the Debate Over the Constitution* (Madison, 1994).

35. The most elegant argument for the creation of a distinctive racial ideology in this period is Barbara Jeanne Fields, "Slavery, Race and Ideology in the United States of America," *New Left Review* 181 (1990): 95–118. The magisterial argument for the long-standing existence of racial attitudes and convictions is Jordan, *White Over Black.* What I am attempting to argue here is that a coherent or explicit racial ideology had been unnecessary before this period, because slavery institutionalized the presumption of white Anglo-Saxon superiority and rendered an explicit or systematic racial ideology superfluous. Just as the most virulent racial legislation in American history appeared after slavery was ended in the late nineteenth century, the most potent racial arguments surfaced when slavery was threatened in the late eighteenth century. But the underlying values on which all the formal arguments and laws were based had been present for centuries. For a discussion of the racial implications of the proposed seal for the United States, see Robinson, *Slavery in the Structure of American Politics,* 135.

36. The phrase about "revolutionary time" is from Davis, *The Problem of Slavery in the Age of Revolution,* 306. On the one hand, Davis's book remains the most sophisticated and comprehensive assessment of the extended historical moment when the fate of slavery seemed to hang in the balance after the Revolution. On the other hand, because it considers the fifty-year period as a single piece, the patterns within the period are blurred into the larger whole and the inevitability of the eventual failure shadows the entire survey. The strongest case for the viability of a national antislavery program is Nash, *Race and Revolution,* which emphasizes the historic opportunity without putting a specific date on the closing of that opportunity, but which ignores altogether the powerful forces confronting any antislavery initiative and then makes the rather bizarre claim that the chief responsibility, even culpability, for the failure rests with the North. The argument here, which strikes me as incontrovertible, is that the key was Virginia.

37. The Fairfax and Tucker plans are conveniently reprinted in Nash, *Race and Revolution,* 146–165. The best analysis of the components contained in all

gradual emancipation plans coming out of Virginia is Jordan, *White Over Black,* 555–567.

38. Robinson, *Slavery in the Structure of American Politics,* 6–8, offers the most specific economic estimates and the clearest negative judgment, concluding that "slavery could not have been eliminated by political processes during the founding period." Nash, *Race and Revolution,* 5–6, 20, offers no economic evidence that emancipation was feasible, but it assumes the failure to take decisive action was moral and political, emphasizing the lack of leadership in the North, thereby implying the costs were not prohibitive. Freehling, "The Founding Fathers, Conditional Antislavery, and the Nonradicalism of the American Revolution," 76–84, takes a more circumspect middle course, providing no systematic economic argument but suggesting that the combination of political, economic, and racial factors converged to limit the options and virtually assure that slavery would persist. For Jefferson's backward evolution from the vanguard to the rear guard of the antislavery movement, see Ellis, *American Sphinx,* 146–152.

39. The Tucker plan, for example, would have freed only female slaves at twenty-eight years of age, then their children when they reached the same age. (The gradual emancipation plans adopted in New York and New Jersey had analogous provisions, designed to stagger the effect of liberation as well as the costs.) Tucker emphasized the time delay as a central feature of his plan, which was cost-free to the present generation. He did not provide specific estimates of the compensation levels, and my own estimate of the size of the sinking fund, about $50 million, is no more than an educated guess. Nevertheless, my estimate is designed to expose the realistic economic parameters implicit in the most practical of the available plans. Perhaps there should have been a sliding compensation scale that encouraged earlier emancipations by rewarding slave owners who acted before the legal deadline.

40. Freehling, "The Founding Fathers, Conditional Antislavery, and the Nonradicalism of the American Revolution," 83, makes the same point even more assertively: "no such color-blind, ethnically-blind, gender-blind social order had ever existed, not on these shores, not anywhere else."

41. P. J. Staudenraus, *The African Colonization Movement, 1816–1865* (New York, 1961), is the standard history. See also George M. Fredrickson, *The Black Image in the White Mind: The Debate on Afro-American Character and Destiny, 1817–1914* (New York, 1971). Of all the prominent statesmen at the time, Madison gave the African option the most thought. For an elegant summary of this thinking, see Drew McCoy, *The Last of the Fathers: James Madison and the Republican Legacy* (Cambridge, 1989), 279–283.

42. The great Franklin biography remains Carl Van Doren, *Benjamin Franklin* (New York, 1938). The best recent biography is Esmond Wright, *Franklin of Philadelphia* (Cambridge, 1986). For Franklin's contribution as a scientist, see I. Bernard Cohen, *Science and the Founding Fathers* (New York, 1995), 135–195. The classic effort to undermine Franklin's historical reputation is D. H. Lawrence, *Studies in*

Classic American Literature (New York, 1924), 15–27. On the changing images of Franklin, see Nian-Sheng Huang, *Benjamin Franklin in American Thought and Culture* (Philadelphia, 1994). A perceptive appraisal of Franklin's character emerges in Robert Middlekauf, *Benjamin Franklin and His Enemies* (Berkeley, 1996). And these scholarly sources are but the tip of the proverbial iceberg. For Jefferson's ranking of Franklin as next to Washington, with all others "on the second line," see Jefferson to William Carmichael, 12 August 1788, Boyd, vol. 13, 502.

43. For Franklin's early career in Pennsylvania politics, see William Hanna, *Benjamin Franklin and Pennsylvania Politics* (Stanford, 1964). For his English phase, see Verner W. Crane, *Benjamin Franklin's Letters to the Press, 1758–1775* (Chapel Hill, 1950). For his Parisian phase, see Claude-Ann Lopez, *Mon Cher Papa: Franklin and the Ladies of Paris* (New Haven, 1990).

44. *Records,* vol. 3, 361, for Franklin's antislavery petition at the Constitutional Convention. Tench Coxe was the member of the Pennsylvania Abolition Society who urged him to withdraw the petition on the grounds that "it would be a very improper season & place to hazard the Application" (quoted in Davis, *The Problem of Slavery in the Age of Revolution,* 321).

45. Albert H. Smyth, ed., *The Writings of Benjamin Franklin,* 10 vols. (New York, 1907), vol. 10, 87–91.

46. *First Congress,* vol. 12, 809–810, 812–822, 825–827.

47. Of all the prominent statesmen who chose to regard silence as the highest form of leadership at this moment, Washington is the most intriguing, in part because he was the largest slave owner (over three hundred slaves lived on his several plantations), and in part because he, perhaps alone, possessed the stature to have altered the political context if he had chosen to do so. The Washington quotation is from Washington to John Mercer, 9 September 1786, John C. Fitzpatrick, ed., *The Writings of George Washington,* 39 vols. (Washington, D.C., 1931–1944), vol. 29, 5. See also Fritz Hirschfeld, *George Washington and Slavery: A Documentary Portrayal* (St. Louis, 1997). For a conversation with the editors of the modern edition of the Washington papers on this topic, see Sarah Booth Conroy, *Washington Post,* February 16, 1998. Of course, Washington was the supreme example in the founding generation of what John Adams called "the gift of silence." In hindsight, this was one occasion when one could only have wished that the gift had failed him.

48. Madison to Edmund Randolph, 21 March 1790; Madison to Benjamin Rush, 20 March 1790, Rutland, vol. 13, 109–110.

49. Madison to Rush, 20 March 1790; Thomas Pleasants, Jr., to Madison, 10 July 1790; Madison to Robert Pleasants, 30 October 1791, Rutland, vol. 13, 109, 271, vol. 14, 117. See also McColley, *Slavery in Jeffersonian Virginia,* 182.

50. Madison to Rush, 20 March 1790, Rutland, vol. 13, 109. The shrewdest assessment of Madison's inherently equivocal thinking about slavery is McCoy, *The Last of the Fathers,* 217–322.

51. Madison to Randolph, 21 March 1790, Rutland, vol. 13, 110.

52. *First Congress,* vol. 12, 832–844. John Pemberton to James Pemberton, 16 March 1790, quoted in Nash, *Race and Revolution,* 41.

53. *First Congress,* vol. 3, 338–339, for the debate and vote on the committee report.

54. Ibid., 340–341.

55. Ibid., 341, for the final version of the resolution. Madison's comment is from *First Congress,* vol. 12, 842. The Washington quotation is from Washington to David Stuart, 28 March 1790, Fitzpatrick, vol. 31, 28–30.

56. In the petition of 1792, see *Annals of Congress,* 2d Congress, 2d Session, 728–731. For the Webster comment, see Daniel Webster to John Bolton, 17 May 1833, Charles Wiltse, ed., *The Papers of Daniel Webster,* 7 vols. (Hanover, N.H., 1974–1986), vol. 3, 252–253.

57. *First Congress,* vol. 3, 375.

CHAPTER FOUR: THE FAREWELL

1. On the Washington mythology, three books provide excellent surveys: Marcus Cunliffe, *George Washington, Man and Monument* (Boston, 1958); Paul Longmore, *The Invention of George Washington* (Berkeley, 1988); Barry Schwartz, *The Making of an American Symbol* (New York, 1987).

2. Longmore, *The Invention,* 24; Schwartz, *The Making of an American Symbol,* 127; Richard Brookhiser, *Founding Father: Rediscovering George Washington* (New York, 1996), 22–23.

3. Albert H. Smyth, ed., *The Writings of Benjamin Franklin,* 10 vols. (New York, 1907), vol. 10, 111–112.

4. Jefferson to Washington, 23 May 1792, Boyd, vol. 22, 123; Schwartz, *The Making of an American Symbol,* 38–39; Gary Wills, *Cincinnatus: George Washington and the Enlightenment* (New York, 1984).

5. Victor H. Paltsits, ed., *Washington's Farewell Address* (New York, 1935), 2–3.

6. Matthew Spalding and Patrick J. Garrity, *A Sacred Union of Citizens: George Washington's Farewell Address and the American Character* (Lanham, Md., 1996) is the most recent and comprehensive scholarly study. On the historiography, see Burton J. Kaufman, *Washington's Farewell Address: The View from the Twentieth Century* (Chicago, 1969). The account in Stanley Elkins and Eric McKitrick, *The Age of Federalism: The Early American Republic, 1787–1800* (New York, 1993), 489–528, provides the best incisive summary of the larger implications of Washington's retirement within the political culture of the 1790s.

7. Spalding and Garrity, *A Sacred Union,* 45–48; Paltsits, ed., *Washington's Farewell Address,* 308–309.

8. Syrett, vol. 20, 169–173, for an excellent editorial note on Hamilton's role; Paltsits, ed., *Washington's Farewell Address,* 30–31; Smith, vol. 2, 940, for the Ames quotation; Madison to Monroe, 14 May 1796, Smith, vol. 2, 941. James Thomas Flexner, *George Washington: Anguish and Farewell, 1793–1799* (Boston, 1972), 292–307.

9. John Adams to Abigail Adams, 14 January 1797, quoted in Smith, vol. 2, 895. For Jefferson's version of the Ciceronian posture, see Joseph J. Ellis, *American Sphinx: The Character of Thomas Jefferson* (New York, 1997), 139–141.

10. Schwartz, *The Making of an American Symbol,* 18–19, for an excellent physical description of Washington, which also includes the quotation from Rush. Brookhiser, *Founding Father,* 114–115, is also excellent on Washington's physical presence. Mantle Fielding, *Gilbert Stuart's Portraits of Washington* (Philadelphia, 1933), 77–80, offers the best contemporary description of Washington's physical features as rendered by an artist whose eye was trained to notice such things. Washington to Robert Lewis, 26 June 1796, Fitzpatrick, vol. 35, 99, provides Washington's own testimony on aging.

11. Adams to Benjamin Rush, 22 April 1812, Alexander Biddle, ed., *Old Family Letters* (Philadelphia, 1892), 161–173, 375–381, for Adams on Washington and "the gift of taciturnity."

12. The Jefferson quotation is from his "Anas" in Ford, vol. 1, 168. In the same vein, see Jefferson to Madison, 9 June 1793, Smith, vol. 2, 780–782. For the manifestations of physical decline, see Flexner, *George Washington,* 156–157.

13. *Aurora,* 17 October 1796.

14. Ibid., 6 March 1796; Schwartz, *The Making of an American Symbol,* 68, 99; John Keane, *Tom Paine: A Political Life* (Boston, 1995), 430–452.

15. Washington to David Humphreys, 12 June 1796, Fitzpatrick, vol. 35, 91–92.

16. The newspaper quotation is quoted in Douglas S. Freeman, *George Washington: A Biography,* 7 vols. (New York, 1948–1957), vol. 7, 321. On Washington's royal style, see especially Schwartz, *The Making of an American Symbol,* 48–61.

17. The most insightful contemporary commentator on Washington's unique and highly paradoxical status was John Adams, who recognized the utter necessity of a singular leader to focus the national government, and who simultaneously recognized the dangers inherent in making Washington superhuman. The most explicit discussion of this dilemma occurs in the letters Adams wrote to Benjamin Rush soon after his own retirement. See *Spur,* 185–186.

18. The best synthesis of the different scholarly interpretations of the Farewell Address is Arthur A. Markowitz, "Washington's Farewell and the Historians," *Pennsylvania Magazine of History and Biography,* 94 (1970): 173–191. See especially, Felix Gilbert, *To the Farewell Address: Ideas of Early American Foreign Policy* (Princeton, 1961).

19. The most incisive account of Washington's dramatic sense of departure is Wills, *Cincinnatus,* 3–16.

20. For his speech to the army, then his address to the Congress upon resigning, see *Writings,* 542–545, 547–550. For the remark by George III, see Wills, *Cincinnatus,* 13.

21. The two outstanding scholarly books on the subject are Don Higginbotham, *George Washington and the American Military Tradition* (Athens, Ga., 1985), and

Charles Royster, *A Revolutionary People at War: The Continental Army and American Character* (Chapel Hill, 1979).

22. Washington to John Barrister, 21 April 1778, Fitzpatrick, vol. 6, 107–108.

23. The decision to execute André was Washington's most unpopular decision during the war and generated a spirited correspondence. See *Writings*, 387–390.

24. Washington to Henry Laurens, 14 November 1778, Fitzpatrick, vol. 13, 254–257. The significance of this observation was emphasized by Edmund S. Morgan in his biographical essay on Washington in *The Meaning of Independence* (New York, 1976), 47–48.

25. *Writings*, 516–517.

26. Ibid., 517.

27. Isaiah Berlin, *The Hedgehog and the Fox: An Essay on Tolstoy's View of History* (London, 1954).

28. Washington to Humphreys, 3 March 1794, Fitzpatrick, vol. 32, 398–399.

29. *Writings*, 840; Washington to Charles Carroll, 1 May 1796, Fitzpatrick, vol. 37, 29–31.

30. Lawrence Kaplan, *Entangling Alliances with None: American Foreign Policy in the Age of Jefferson* (Kent, Ohio, 1987), emphasizes the consensus that existed among American political leaders; Elkins and McKitrick, *The Age of Federalism*, 375–450, take the party divisions as more serious expressions of deep division. I tend to think they are closer to the truth.

31. Three scholarly accounts are seminal here: Samuel Flagg Bemis, *Jay's Treaty: A Study in Commerce and Diplomacy* (New Haven, 1962); Jerald A. Combs, *The Jay Treaty: Political Background of the Founding Fathers* (Berkeley, 1970); Elkins and McKitrick, *The Age of Federalism*, 375–450.

32. Smith, vol. 2, 882–883; Adams to William Cunningham, 15 October 1808, *Correspondence Between the Honorable John Adams . . . and William Cunningham, Esq.* (Boston, 1823), 34; Washington to Edmund Randolph, 31 July 1795, Fitzpatrick, vol. 34, 266.

33. Madison to Jefferson, 4 April 1796, Smith, vol. 2, 929–930; Jefferson to Edward Rutledge, 30 November 1795, Ford, vol. 7, 39–40.

34. Smith, vol. 2, 887–888; Jefferson to Monroe, 21 March 1796, Ford, vol. 7, 67–68.

35. Jefferson to Madison, 27 March 1796; Madison to Jefferson, 9 May 1796, Smith, vol. 2, 928, 937; Jefferson to Monroe, 12 June 1796, Ford, vol. 7, 80. Jefferson's political assessment of the reasons for passage of Jay's Treaty were shrewd, but Washington's influence, while crucial, was aided immeasurably by a shift among voters primarily concerned with access to lands in the West. The English promise to withdraw from forts, in effect to implement commitments made in the Treaty of Paris (1783), was itself important in producing the shift. But equally important was the news of Pinckney's Treaty, in which Spain granted access to the Mississippi River and thereby enhanced the prospects for settlements and commerce in the vast American interior.

36. For a fuller version of this side of Jefferson's mentality, see Ellis, *American Sphinx,* especially 151–152.

37. This is the conspiratorial perspective Jefferson embraced in his "Anas," the collection of anecdotes and gossip he gathered for eventual publication during his retirement years. For the anecdotes themselves, see Ford, vol. 1, 168–178. The best analysis of the "Anas" is Joanne Freeman, "Slander, Poison, Whispers and Fame: Jefferson 'Anas' and Political Gossip in the Early Republic," *JER* 15 (1995): 25–58. The most revealing statement by Jefferson, which includes the "They all live in cities" remark, was "Notes on Professor Ebeling's Letter of July 30, 1785," Ford, vol. 7, 44–49.

38. On the Whiskey Rebellion, see Thomas P. Slaughter, *The Whiskey Rebellion* (New York, 1986). On Washington's response to the insurrection, see Richard H. Kohn, "The Washington Administration's Decision to Crush the Whiskey Rebellion," *JAH* 59 (1972): 567–574.

39. Jefferson to Mann Page, 30 August 1795, Ford, vol. 7, 24–25. See also Jefferson to Monroe, 26 May 1795, Ford, vol. 7, 16–17; Jefferson to Madison, 30 October 1794, Smith, vol. 2, 858. The standard assessment of Jefferson's conspiratorial perspective is Lance Banning, *The Jeffersonian Persuasion: Evolution of a Party Ideology* (Ithaca, N.Y., 1978).

40. Jefferson to Phillip Mazzei, 24 April 1796, Ford, vol. 7, 72–78. The letter was eventually published in a New York newspaper, *The Minerva,* on March 14, 1797. After its publication, all correspondence between Mount Vernon and Monticello ceased.

41. The quotation is from Jefferson to Tench Coxe, 1 June 1795, Ford, vol. 7, 22.

42. Jefferson to Coxe, 1 May 1794; Jefferson to William Short, 3 January 1793, Ford, vol. 6, 507–508, 153–156.

43. Jefferson to Monroe, 16 July 1796, Ford, vol. 7, 89.

44. Washington to Jefferson, 6 July 1794, *Writings,* 951–954. For the pro-Jefferson version of this episode, see Dumas Malone, *Jefferson and His Times,* 6 vols. (Boston, 1948–1981), vol. 3, 307–311.

45. The best analysis of Monroe's behavior as minister to France is Elkins and McKitrick, *The Age of Federalism,* 497–504. The correspondence in which Washington tried to fathom Monroe's statements includes: Washington to Hamilton, 26 June 1796, Syrett, vol. 20, 239; Washington to Secretary of State, 25 July and 27 July, 1796; Washington to Monroe, 26 August 1796, Fitzpatrick, vol. 35, 155, 157, 187–190. See also the note on Monroe's support for French seizures of American shipping in Fitzpatrick, vol. 35, 155, 157, 187–190. See also the note on Monroe's support for French seizures of American shipping in Syrett, vol. 20, 227.

46. The most succinct summary of Randolph's fiasco in the modern scholarly literature is Elkins and McKitrick, *The Age of Federalism,* 424–431. See also two old but helpful accounts: W. C. Ford, "Edmund Randolph on the British Treaty, 1795," *AHR* 12 (1907): 587–599; Moncure D. Conway, *Omitted Chapters in the History Disclosed in the Life and Papers of Edmund Randolph* (New York, 1988).

47. The correspondence on the episode includes: Randolph to Washington, 20, 29, 31 July 1795; Washington to Randolph, 22 July, 3 August 1795, Fitzpatrick, vol. 34, 244–255; see also Washington to Hamilton, 29 July 1795, Syrett, vol. 18, 525. Randolph's reputation is defended in a somewhat excessive fashion in Irving Brant, "Edmund Randolph. Not Guilty!" *WMQ* 7 (1950): 179–198.

48. For a convenient summary of the debate over the authorship question, see Spalding and Garrity, *A Sacred Union,* 55–58.

49. Paltsits, ed., *Washington's Farewell Address,* 160–163, 212–217, 227.

50. Ibid., 14–15, 241–243. The story is nicely summarized in Spalding and Garrity, *A Sacred Union,* 46–49.

51. Paltsits, ed., *Washington's Farewell Address,* 242.

52. Ibid., 246–247; the "first draft" Washington sent to Hamilton is reproduced in ibid., 164–173.

53. Ibid., 249–250.

54. Ibid., 250–253, 257. See also Syrett, vol. 20, 265–268, 292–293.

55. Washington to Hamilton, 25 August 1796, Syrett, vol. 20, 307–309. The "incorporating draft" that Washington did not like as well is reproduced in ibid., 294–303. On the editorial process and the changes Washington made, see Spalding and Garrity, *A Sacred Union,* 53–54.

56. *Writings,* 968.

57. Ibid., 974–975.

58. Paltsits, ed., *Washington's Farewell Address,* 260.

59. Ibid., 172.

60. Ibid., 252–253.

61. Ibid., 258–259.

62. Ibid., 245–257; *Writings,* 972.

63. For Washington's Eighth Annual Address, see *Writings,* 978–985. The Hamilton draft is in Syrett, vol. 20, 382–388.

64. Flexner, *George Washington,* 324–327, and Elkins and McKitrick, *The Age of Federalism,* 495–496, call attention to the strongly nationalistic message Washington delivered. While some historians dismiss the message as Hamilton's handiwork, and therefore as evidence that Washington capitulated to the Hamiltonian wing of the Federalist party in his last executive statement, it seems to me this interpretation misses the larger point, which is that Washington required no instruction from Hamilton on these issues, and retained his own reasons for regarding the enhanced powers of the federal government as indispensable instruments, the chief reason being that his own departure created a vacuum that would need to be filled by federal institutions. Even Jefferson, who ascended to the presidency in 1801 fully intending to dismantle rather than buttress those institutions and policies, discovered in his first term that Washington's projection, though the great man was now in the grave, still haunted the political landscape. Even with the Jefferson triumph in the early years of the nineteenth century and the parallel defeat

of the Federalist party as a national force, the core of Washington's vision remained alive, because without it the American nation itself would have ceased to exist. A reincarnated Washington, I am suggesting, would have gone with Lincoln and the Union in 1861.

65. Paltsits, ed., *Washington's Farewell Address,* 252–253.

66. Though inadequate, the only book-length treatment of the subject is Fritz Hirschfeld, *George Washington and Slavery: A Documentary Portrayal* (St. Louis, 1997). Still valuable for its discussion of Washington's posture as a slave owner is Flexner, *George Washington,* 432–448. The most thorough assessment in the recent works is Robert E. Dalzell, Jr., and Lee Baldwin Dalzell, *George Washington's Mount Vernon: At Home in Revolutionary America* (New York, 1998), 112, 211–219.

67. *Writings,* 956–957.

68. Ibid., 957–960.

69. Paltsits, ed., *Washington's Farewell Address,* 261–262; William Duane, *A Letter to George Washington . . . Containing Strictures of His Address* (Philadelphia, 1786), 11–12; *Aurora,* 17 October 1796; Washington to Benjamin Walker, 12 January 1797, Fitzpatrick, vol. 35, 363–365.

70. Washington to Citizens of Alexandria, 23 March 1797, Fitzpatrick, vol. 35, 423.

71. Washington's opinion concerning the state of Virginia's politics is best expressed in Washington to Patrick Henry, 9 October 1795, ibid., 335. His views of the Republican party in the state after his retirement are illustrated in Washington to Henry Knox, 2 March 1797, *Writings,* 986–987, and Washington to Lafayette, 25 December 1798, Fitzpatrick, vol. 37, 66. Jefferson's immediate opinion of Washington was equally critical: "The President is fortunate to get off just as the bubble is bursting, leaving others to hold the bag. . . . He will have his usual good fortune of reaping credit from the good arts of others, and leaving to them that of his errors." See Jefferson to Madison, 8 January 1797, Smith, vol. 2, 955, and Malone, *Jefferson and His Times,* vol. 3, 307–311, who tries to paper over the rift. For Washington's role in the construction of the nation's capital, and his dedication to national rather than Virginia priorities, see C. M. Harris, "Washington's Gamble, L'Enfant's Dream: Politics, Design, and the Founding of the National Capital," *WMQ* 56 (July 1999): 527–564.

72. Flexner, *George Washington,* 456–462.

CHAPTER FIVE: THE COLLABORATORS

1. Merrill Peterson, *Adams and Jefferson: A Revolutionary Dialogue* (Oxford, 1978), views the collaboration from Jefferson's perspective. I have offered two accounts of the Adams-Jefferson partnership: *Passionate Sage: The Character and Legacy of John Adams* (New York, 1993), 113–142; and *American Sphinx: The Character of Thomas Jefferson* (New York, 1997), 235–251.

2. Abigail Adams to Jefferson, 6 June 1785, Cappon, vol. 1, 28.

3. This sketch of Adams's career draws on the standard biographies: Gilbert Chinard, *Honest John Adams* (Boston, 1933); Page Smith, *John Adams*, 2 vols. (New York, 1962); Peter Shaw, *The Character of John Adams* (Chapel Hill, 1976). The most satisfying one-volume life, covering his entire public career with respect for the history in which it was imbedded, is John Ferling, *John Adams: A Life* (Knoxville, Tenn., 1992). Two succinct and shrewd appraisals of the Adams temperament are Bernard Bailyn, *Faces of Revolution: Personalities and Themes in the Struggle for American Independence* (New York, 1990), 3–21; and Edmund S. Morgan, "John Adams and the Puritan Tradition," *NEQ* 34 (1961): 518–529. The freshest and fullest study of Adams as a political thinker is C. Bradley Thompson, *John Adams and the Spirit of Liberty* (Lawrence, Kans., 1998).

4. Adams to Abigail Adams, 19 December 1793, Charles Francis Adams, ed., *Letters of John Adams, Addressed to His Wife*, 2 vols. (Boston, 1841), vol. 2, 133. There is no satisfactory book on the Adams vice presidency. Ferling, *John Adams*, 185–217, offers the fullest coverage among the biographies. See also Linda Dudek Guerrero, *John Adams's Vice-Presidency 1789–97: The Neglected Man in the Forgotten Office* (New York, 1982).

5. Adams to Abigail Adams, 19 December 1793, 12 March 1794, *Adams*, reel 377; Adams to Thomas Brand-Hollis, 19 February 1792, *Adams*, reel 375.

6. See the exchanges between Adams and Abigail, most especially during the period from 1794 to 1796, *Adams*, reels 378–381. Adams to Benjamin Rush, 4 April 1790, Alexander Biddle, ed., *Old Family Letters* (Philadelphia, 1892), 168–170.

7. Adams to Ebenezer Stokes, 20 March 1790, *Adams*, reel 115.

8. James H. Hutson, "John Adams's Title Campaign," *NEQ* 41 (1968): 30–39; Jefferson to Madison, 29 July 1789, Boyd, vol. 15, 315–316.

9. Adams to William Tudor, 28 June 1789; Adams to Rush, 5 July 1789, *Adams*, reel 115.

10. For an analysis of Adams's political thought as reflected in *Discourses on Davila*, see Ellis, *Passionate Sage*, 143–173, and Thompson, *John Adams*, 149–173. For a convenient synthesis of the press coverage of Adams as a closet monarchist, see Dumas Malone, *Jefferson and His Times*, 6 vols. (Boston, 1948–1981), vol. 3, 283–285.

11. *Discourses on Davila* first appeared as a series of thirty-one articles in the *Gazette of the United States*, starting in April of 1790. Jefferson to Washington, 8 May 1791, Ford, vol. 5, 328–330; see also Jefferson in his "Anas," Ford, vol. 1, 166–167; Jefferson to Adams, 30 August 1791; Adams to Jefferson, 39 July 1791, Cappon, vol. 1, 245–250.

12. Jefferson to Adams, 30 August 1791, Cappon, vol. 1, 250. For Jefferson's latter-day recollection of the episode, in which he emphasizes his abiding sense of Adams as a traitor to the republican tradition, see Jefferson to William Short, 3 January 1825, Ford, vol. 10, 328–335. Jefferson simply told Adams a different version of the story than he told everyone else.

13. Adams to Abigail Adams, 3 February 1793, *Adams,* reel 376.

14. For a convenient summary of Adams's most colorful fulminations against the French Revolution, see Ellis, *Passionate Sage,* 91–98. For his assessment of Jefferson's motives for supporting the French Revolution, see Adams to Abigail Adams, 3 February, 26 December 1793, *Adams,* reel 376.

15. Adams to Abigail Adams, 6 January 1794, *Adams,* reel 377.

16. Adams to John Quincy Adams, 3 January 1794, ibid.

17. The seminal study of the Jefferson-Madison collaboration is Adrienne Koch, *Jefferson and Madison: The Great Collaboration* (New York, 1950). Madison to Jefferson, 5 October 1794, Smith, vol. 2, 857.

18. Jefferson to Madison, 5 October 1794, 27 April 1795, Smith, vol. 2, 857, 897–898; Jefferson to Adams, 25 April 1794, Cappon, vol. 1, 254; Jefferson to Washington, 14 May 1794, Ford, vol. 6, 509–510. And these are merely illustrative of the much larger exchange in this vein.

19. See Malone, *Jefferson and His Times,* vol. 3, 276–283, for an incisive discussion of the Burr visit and the political context in Virginia at this time. See Ellis, *American Sphinx,* 121–133, for Jefferson's capacity to seclude himself at Monticello while silently and surreptitiously launching a campaign for the presidency.

20. Madison to Monroe, 26 February 1796, Smith, vol. 2, 940–941; Jefferson to Archibald Stuart, 4 January 1797, Ford, vol. 7, 103.

21. Three modern biographies of Abigail Adams are especially useful: Charles W. Akers, *Abigail Adams: An American Woman* (Boston, 1980); Lynne Withey, *Dearest Friend: A Life of Abigail Adams* (New York, 1981); Phyllis Lee Levin, *Abigail Adams: A Biography* (New York, 1987). Though not a full life, the best character study of Abigail is Edith B. Gelles, *Portia: The World of Abigail Adams* (Bloomington, IL, 1992). For the quotations, see Adams to Abigail Adams, 5 December, 16 December 1794, *Adams,* reel 378; Abigail Adams to Adams, 5 January 1795, *Adams,* reel 379.

22. Adams to Abigail Adams, 2 December, 1793, 12 March 1794; Abigail Adams, 6 December 1794, *Adams,* reel 378.

23. Abigail Adams to Adams, 4 January 1795; Adams to John Quincy Adams, 25 August 1795, *Adams,* reel 379.

24. Adams to Abigail Adams, 2, 6 December 1794, *Adams,* reel 378; Abigail Adams to Adams, 10 April 1796, *Adams,* reel 381.

25. Adams to Abigail Adams, 10 February 1796, *Adams,* reel 381.

26. Adams to Abigail Adams, 14 February 1796, ibid.

27. Abigail Adams to Adams, 21 January, 20 February 1796; Adams to Abigail Adams, 15, 19 March 1796, ibid.

28. Adams to Abigail Adams, 7 January 1796, ibid.; Abigail Adams to Adams, 31 December 1796, 1 January 1797, *Adams,* reel 382.

29. Adams to Abigail Adams, 8 April, 8, 12 December 1796, *Adams,* reels 381, 382.

30. Jefferson to Madison, 1 January 1797, Smith, vol. 2, 953; Jefferson to Stuart,

4 January 1797, Ford, vol. 7, 102–103; Abigail Adams to Adams, 31 December 1796, *Adams,* reel 382.

31. Jefferson to Madison, 22 January 1797, Smith, vol. 2, 959–960; Abigail Adams to Adams, 15 January 1797, *Adams,* reel 382.

32. Fisher Ames to Rufus King, 24 September 1800, Charles R. King, ed., *The Life and Correspondence of Rufus King,* 6 vols. (New York, 1895), vol. 3, 304; Adams to Elbridge Gerry, 20 February 1797, *Adams,* reel 117.

33. Madison to Jefferson, 22 January 1797, Smith, vol. 2, 961.

34. Adams to Abigail Adams, 15 March 1797, *Adams,* reel 382.

35. Jefferson to Edward Rutledge, 27 December 1796, Ford, vol. 7, 93–95; Jefferson to Thomas Mann Randolph, 28 November 1796, quoted in Malone, *Jefferson and His Times,* vol. 3, 290–291; Jefferson to Madison, 16 January 1797, Smith, vol. 2, 958–959.

36. Jefferson to Madison, 8 January 1797, Smith, vol. 2, 955; Merrill D. Peterson, *Visitors to Monticello* (Charlottesville, 1989), 31.

37. Jefferson to Adams, 28 December 1796, Smith, vol. 2, 954–955.

38. Madison to Jefferson, 15 January 1797, ibid., 956–958.

39. Jefferson to Madison, 30 January 1797, ibid., 962–963.

40. Ford, vol. 1, 272–273; Smith, vol. 2, 966–997.

41. Adams to Abigail Adams, 9, 17, 27 March 1797, *Adams,* reel 383.

42. This is my own interpretive synthesis based on the standard accounts of the Adams presidency: Stephen G. Kurtz, *The Presidency of John Adams: The Collapse of Federalism, 1795–1800* (Philadelphia, 1957); Manning Dauer, *The Adams Federalists* (Baltimore, 1953); Ralph A. Brown, *The Presidency of John Adams* (Lawrence, KS, 1975). The authoritative account of this entangled moment in American politics is Stanley Elkins and Eric McKitrick, *The Age of Federalism: The Early American Republic, 1787–1800* (New York, 1993), 513–528.

43. Jefferson to Rutledge, 24 June 1797, Ford, vol. 7, 154–155; Jefferson to John Wise, 12 February 1798; Jefferson to Martha Jefferson Randolph, 17 May 1798, Smith, vol. 2, 996, 1063.

44. Adams to John Quincy Adams, 3 November 1797, *Adams,* reel 117.

45. Abigail Adams to Cotton Tufts, 8 June 1798, *Adams,* reel 392; Smith, *John Adams,* vol. 2, 933.

46. Adams to John Quincy Adams, 2 June 1797, *Adams,* reel 119.

47. Abigail Adams to Mary Cranch, 20 March 1798, Stewart Mitchell, ed., *New Letters of Abigail Adams, 1788–1801* (Boston, 1947), 146–147.

48. Smith, *John Adams,* vol. 2, 937.

49. Ibid., 958; Abigail Adams to William Smith, 20, 30 March 1798, *Adams,* reel 392; Smith, vol. 2, 1010.

50. The standard work on the Alien and Sedition Acts is James Morton Smith, *Freedom's Letters: The Alien and Sedition Laws and American Civil Liberties* (Ithaca,

N.Y., 1956). Among Adams's biographers, Smith, *John Adams,* vol. 2, 975–978, tends to defend Adams by playing down the severity of the threat to civil liberties; Ferling, *John Adams,* 365–368, sees this episode as a major blunder by Adams. The discussion in Elkins and McKitrick, *The Age of Federalism,* 590–593, 694–695, is elegantly balanced and warns against imposing our modern notion of civil liberties or freedom of the press on an age that was still groping toward a more expansive version of First Amendment protections. This latter warning, which strikes me as historically, if not politically, correct, clearly needs to be underlined. As a monumental example of how to make all the presentistic mistakes, see Richard Rosenfeld's blunderbuss of a book, *American Aurora: A Democratic-Republican Returns* (New York, 1997).

51. Abigail Adams to Mercy Otis Warren, 25 April 1798, quoted in Ferling, *John Adams,* 365; Abigail Adams to Cranch, 26 April 1798, Mitchell, ed., *New Letters,* 165; Smith, vol. 2, 1003–1005.

52. Richard Welch, *Theodore Segwick, Federalist: A Political Portrait* (Middletown, Conn., 1965), 185–186; Syrett, vol. 22, 494–495; Abigail Adams to Adams, 3 March 1799, *Adams,* reel 393.

53. Adams to Abigail Adams, 31 December 1798, 1 January 1799; Abigail Adams to Adams, 27 February 1799, *Adams,* reels 392, 393.

54. Abigail Adams to Elizabeth Peabody, 7 April 1799, *Adams,* reel 393.

55. Adams to James McHenry, 22 October 1798, *Adams,* reel 119. The standard work on the threat posed by the New Army is Richard W. Kohn, *Eagle and Sword: The Beginnings of the Military Establishment in America* (New York, 1975). See also Syrett, vol. 22, 452–454.

56. Abigail Adams to William Smith, 7 July 1798, *Adams,* reel 392.

57. Jefferson to Madison, 2, 21, 22 March 1798, Smith, vol. 2, 1024, 1029.

58. Madison to Jefferson, 18 February 1798, ibid., 1021.

59. Jefferson to Madison, 6 April 1798; Madison to Jefferson, 15 April 1798, 13, 20 May 1798, ibid., 1002, 1036–1038, 1048–1049, 1051.

60. Jefferson to Madison, 24 May 1798, 3 January, 19, 26 February 1799, ibid., 1053, 1056, 1085, 1086.

61. For Callender's career, see Michael Durey, *With the Hammer of Truth: James Thomas Callender and America's Early National Heroes* (Charlottesville, 1990). Jefferson to Monroe, 26 May 1801, 15 July 1802, Ford, vol. 8, 57–58, 164–168. The best scholarly study of the Republican effort to smear Adams is C. O. Lerche, Jr., "Jefferson and the Election of 1800: A Case Study in the Political Smear," *WMQ* 8 (1948): 467–491.

62. Jefferson to Monroe, 5 April 1798, Ford, vol. 7, 233; Madison to Jefferson, 18 February 1798; Theodore Sedgwick to Rufus King, 9 April 1798, Smith, vol. 2, 997, 1021.

63. Jefferson's draft of the Kentucky Resolutions is reprinted in Smith, vol. 2,

1080–1084. The introductory essay in ibid., 1063–1075, provides the fairest and fullest coverage of the context. The previous account, more charitable toward Jefferson, is Adrienne Koch and Harry Ammon, "The Virginia and Kentucky Resolutions: An Episode in Jefferson's and Madison's Defense of Civil Liberties," *WMQ* 5 (1945): 170–189.

64. Smith, vol. 2, 1108–1112; see also the editorial notes in Rutland, vol. 17, 199–206, 303–307.

65. Jefferson to Madison, 23 August 1799, Smith, vol. 2, 1118–1119; Jefferson to Wilson Cary Nicholas, 5 September 1799, Ford, vol. 7, 389–392. For an elegant appraisal of the Madisonian influence on Jefferson, and the huge constitutional gap the two colleagues managed to ignore, see Drew R. McCoy, *The Last of the Fathers: James Madison and the Republican Legacy* (Cambridge, 1989). See also Leonard Levy, *The Emergence of a Free Press* (New York, 1985), 315–325.

66. Madison to Jefferson, 4 April 1800, Smith, vol. 2, 1131–1132. For the enforcement of the Sedition Act, see Smith, *Freedom's Letters,* 176–187.

67. Smith, *Freedom's Letters,* 270–274; Elkins and McKitrick, *The Age of Federalism,* 694–713; Ellis, *American Sphinx,* 217–219. The scientific evidence establishing Jefferson's paternity of at least one of Sally's children, Eston Hemings, was published in *Nature,* November 1998, 27–28. See also the explanatory note by Eric S. Lander and Joseph J. Ellis, "DNA Analysis: Founding Father," *Nature,* November 1998, 13–14.

68. Jefferson to John Breckenridge, 29 January 1800, Ford, vol. 7, 417–418; Jefferson to Madison, 4 March 1800, Smith, vol. 2, 1128–1130. For an overview of the election from the Jeffersonian perspective, see Daniel Sisson, *The American Revolution of 1800* (New York, 1974).

69. Ferling, *John Adams,* 403–404; Abigail Adams to Cranch, 5 May 1800, Mitchell, ed., *New Letters,* 251, 265.

70. Syrett, vol. 25, 178–202, for the text of Hamilton's pamphlet as well as the correspondence by Adams and other Federalists in response to it.

71. Jefferson to Levi Lincoln, 25 October 1802, Ford, vol. 8, 175–176; see the concluding thoughts of Elkins and McKitrick, *The Age of Federalism,* 750–754.

72. The first Adams quotation is from Zoltán Haraszti, *John Adams and the Prophets of Progress* (Cambridge, 1953), 57; Adams to Thomas Boylston Adams, 24, 26 January 1801, *Adams,* reel 400; Ferling, *John Adams,* 405–413, provides a nice summary of Adams's sense of resignation.

73. Adams to Gerry, 30 December 1800, *Adams,* reel 399. This is a much-condensed version of the historic vote in the House to choose between Jefferson and Burr. The standard account is now Elkins and McKitrick, *The Age of Federalism,* 743–750.

74. Jefferson to Madison, 19 December 1800, Smith, vol. 2, 1154, for Jefferson's expectations concerning civility. I have told the story of these last days of the Adams presidency more fully in *Passionate Sage,* 19–25.

CHAPTER SIX: THE FRIENDSHIP

1. Adams to Samuel Dexter, 23 March 1801; Adams to Benjamin Stoddert, 31 March 1801, *Works,* vol. 10, 580–582.

2. Abigail Adams to Thomas Boylston Adams, 12 July 1801, *Adams,* reel 400; Adams to Francis Vanderkemp, 25 January 1806, *Adams,* reel 118.

3. Adams to William Cranch, 23 May 1801, *Adams,* reel 118; Adams to Benjamin Waterhouse, 29 October 1805, Worthington C. Ford., ed., *Statesman and Friend: The Correspondence of John Adams and Benjamin Waterhouse, 1784–1822* (Boston, 1927), 31.

4. Abigail Adams to Jefferson, 20 May 1804, Cappon, vol. 1, 268–269.

5. Jefferson to Abigail Adams, 14 June 1804, ibid., 270–271.

6. Abigail Adams to Jefferson, 1 July 1804, ibid., 271–274.

7. Jefferson to Abigail Adams, 22 July, 11 September 1804, ibid., 274–276, 279–280.

8. Abigail Adams to Jefferson, 25 October 1804, ibid., 280–282.

9. Jefferson to Francis Hopkinson, 13 March 1789, Boyd, vol. 14, 650.

10. Adams postscript, 19 November 1804, Cappon, vol. 1, 282.

11. Adams to Benjamin Rush, 18 April 1808, *Spur,* 107.

12. Adams to Rush, 30 September 1805, Alexander Biddle, ed., *Old Family Letters* (Philadelphia, 1892), 86; Lyman H. Butterfield, ed., *The Diary and Autobiography of John Adams,* 4 vols. (Cambridge, 1961), vol. 3, 335–336; Adams to Rush, 21 June 1811, *Spur,* 182.

13. I have covered these early years of the Adams retirement in greater detail in *Passionate Sage: The Character and Legacy of John Adams* (New York, 1993), 57–83. Mercy Otis Warren to Adams, 7, 15 August 1807, Charles Francis Adams, ed., *Correspondence Between John Adams and Mercy Otis Warren,* reprinted in *Collections of the Massachusetts Historical Society,* vol. 4 (1878), 422–423, 449; Adams to William Cunningham, 22 February, 31 July 1809, *Correspondence Between the Honorable John Adams . . . and William Cunningham, Esq.* (Boston, 1823), 93, 151; Adams to Nicholas Boylston, 3 November 1819, *Adams,* reel 124.

14. Adams to Rush, 23 July 1806, *Spur,* 61.

15. Rush to Adams, 23 March 1805; Adams to Rush, 29 November 1812, ibid., 25, 254–255.

16. Adams to Rush, 22 December 1806, ibid., 72–73.

17. Adams to Rush, 17 August 1812, Biddle, ed., *Old Family Letters,* 420.

18. Adams to Rush, 12 June, 17 August 1812, *Spur,* 225, 242.

19. Adams to Rush, 20 June 1808, 14 November 1812, ibid., 110, 252.

20. Adams to Rush, 30 September 1805, 14 March 1809, 21 June 1811, 11 November 1807, 8 January, 14 May 1812, *Spur,* 39–42, 97–99, 181, 204, 216–217.

21. Ellis, *Passionate Sage,* 143–173; Adams to Rush, 27 September 1809, *Spur,* 155; John Ferling and Lewis E. Braverman, "John Adams's Health Reconsidered," *WMQ* 55 (1998): 83–104.

22. Adams to Cunningham, 16 January 1804, *Correspondence Between the Honorable John Adams . . . and William Cunningham, Esq.,* 7–9; Adams to Rush, 18 April 1808, *Spur,* 107–108.

23. Adams to Rush, September 1807, *Spur,* 93.

24. Adams to Rush, 10 October 1808, ibid., 122–123.

25. Adams to Rush, 23 March 1809, ibid., 139.

26. Rush to Adams, 16 October 1809, ibid., 156–157.

27. Adams to Rush, 25 October 1809, ibid., 158–159.

28. Rush to Jefferson, 2 January 1811, quoted in *Spur,* 157–158.

29. Jefferson to Rush, 5 December 1811, Ford, vol. 9, 300. See also Lyman H. Butterfield, "The Dream of Benjamin Rush: The Reconciliation of John Adams and Thomas Jefferson," *Yale Review* 40 (1950–1951): 297–319.

30. Adams to Rush, 25 December 1811, *Spur,* 200–202.

31. Adams to Jefferson, 1 January 1812, Cappon, vol. 2, 290; Adams to Rush, 10 February 1812, *Adams,* reel 118; Rush to Adams, 17 February 1812, *Spur,* 211; the remark about "a brother sailor" is in Donald Stewart and George Clark, "Misanthrope or Humanitarian? John Adams in Retirement," *NEQ* 28 (1955): 232.

32. The quotation is from Adams to Jefferson, 15 July 1813, Cappon, vol. 2, 357. I have explored the Adams-Jefferson correspondence in two previous books: from the Adams perspective in *Passionate Sage,* 113–142; from the Jefferson perspective in *American Sphinx: The Character of Thomas Jefferson* (New York, 1997), 281–300. My account here represents an attempt to combine the perspectives of both men and to assess the correspondence as a self-conscious capstone to the work of the revolutionary generation.

33. Jefferson to Adams, 12 October 1823; Adams to Jefferson, 10 November 1823, Cappon, vol. 2, 600–602. A typical letter took from a week to ten days to go from Quincy to Monticello, or vice versa, and both men were amazed at the relative speed of delivery, seeing it as a measure of technological progress and the arrival of a "new age" quite different from that of their time.

34. Jefferson to Adams, 21 January 1812; Adams to Jefferson, 3 February 1812, ibid., 291–292, 295.

35. Jefferson to Adams, 5 July 1814; Adams to Jefferson, 16 July 1814, ibid., 430–431, 435.

36. Jefferson to Adams, 11 June 1812; Adams to Jefferson, 11 June 1813; Jefferson to Adams, 12 September 1820, ibid., 305–307, 328, 566–567. The Adams quotation on Samuel Johnson comes from his correspondence with Catherine Rush, 23 February 1815, *Adams,* reel 118.

37. Adams to Jefferson, 1 May 1812; Jefferson to Adams, 27 May 1813, Cappon, vol. 2, 301, 324.

38. Adams to Jefferson, 10 June 1813; Jefferson to Adams, 15 June 1813, ibid., 326–327, 331–332.

39. Jefferson to Adams, 15 June 1813, ibid., 331–332.

40. Adams to Jefferson, 14, 25, 28, 30 June 1813, ibid., 329–330, 333–335, 338–340, 346–348.
41. Adams to Jefferson, 15 July 1813, ibid., 358.
42. Jefferson to Adams, 27 June 1813, ibid., 335–336.
43. Jefferson to Adams, 27 June 1813, ibid., 336–338.
44. Jefferson to Adams, 27 June 1813, ibid., 337.
45. Adams to Jefferson, 9 July 1813, ibid., 350–352.
46. Adams to Jefferson, 9, 13 July, 14 August, 19 December 1813, ibid., 351–352, 355, 365, 409.
47. Jefferson to Adams, 28 October 1813, ibid., 387–392.
48. Jefferson to Adams, 24 January 1814, ibid., 421–425.
49. Adams to Jefferson, 15 November 1813, 16 July 1814, ibid., 397–402, 438.
50. Adams to Jefferson, 2, 15 September, 15 November 1813, ibid. 371–372, 376, 398.
51. *Works,* vol. 6, 461–462.
52. Jefferson to Adams, 11 January 1816, Cappon, vol. 2, 458–461.
53. Adams to Jefferson, 2 February 1816, ibid., 461–462.
54. Adams to Jefferson, 16 December 1816, ibid., 500–501.
55. Adams to Jefferson, 16 December 1816, ibid., 501–503.
56. Adams to Jefferson, 2 February 1816, ibid., 462.
57. Adams to Reverend Coleman, 13 January 1817, *Adams,* reel 124; Jefferson to George Logan, 11 May 1805, Ford, vol. 9, 141.
58. Jefferson to Adams, 10 December 1819, 20 January 1821, Cappon, vol. 2, 448–450, 569–570. Jefferson's extreme reaction to the Missouri crisis is a major problem for his more admiring biographers. See Dumas Malone, *Jefferson and His Times,* 6 vols. (Boston, 1948–1981), vol. 6, 328–344. More balanced and critical assessments include Robert Shalhope, "Thomas Jefferson's Republicanism and Antebellum Southern Thought," *JSH* 72 (1976): 529–556, and Donald S. Fehrenbacher, "The Missouri Controversy and the Sources of Southern Separatism," *Southern Review* 14 (1978): 653–667. My own appraisal is in *American Sphinx,* 314–334.
59. Adams to Jefferson, 23 November 1819, Cappon, vol. 2, 547–548; Adams to William Tudor, 20 November 1819; Adams to Louisa Catherine Adams, 29 January 1820, *Adams,* reel 124.
60. Jefferson to John Holmes, 22 April 1820, Ford, vol. 10, 157–158; Adams to Jefferson, 3 February 1821, Cappon, vol. 2, 571–572. If one were to take the generational argument literally, the Adams family provides a perfect example of the unwritten rules. John Adams sustained his commitment to silence and avoidance, but his son John Quincy Adams became a leader in the antislavery movement. Moreover, John Quincy's leadership was rooted in his personal knowledge of the sectional compromise consented to by his father and his strong sense that the South, especially Virginia, had not kept its end of the bargain.
61. Adams to Jefferson, 22 June 1819; Jefferson to Adams, 9 July 1819; Adams to Jefferson, 21 July 1819, Cappon, vol. 2, 542–546; Adams to Vanderkemp, 21 August 1819,

Adams, reel 124. For the best and most recent scholarly study of the Mecklenburg matter, see Pauline Maier, *American Scripture: Making the Declaration of Independence* (New York, 1997), 172–177.

62. Butterfield, ed., *The Diary and Autobiography,* vol. 3, 335–352.

63. For the deathbed scene with Abigail, see Paul C. Nagel, *Descent from Glory: Four Generations of the John Adams Family* (New York, 1983), 129–130; Jefferson to Adams, 1 June 1822, Cappon, vol. 2, 578–579.

64. Jefferson to Adams, 12 October 1823; Adams to Jefferson, 25 February 1825, Cappon, vol. 2, 599–601, 610.

65. Jefferson to Adams, 11 April 1823; Adams to Jefferson, 25 February 1825, ibid., 591–594, 610; Adams to Vanderkemp, 27 December 1816, *Works,* vol. 10, 235.

66. Adams to Jefferson, 10 February 1823; Jefferson to Adams, 25 February 1823, Cappon, vol. 2, 587–589.

67. Bennett Nolan, ed., *Lafayette in America: Day by Day* (Baltimore, 1934), 247–257; Jefferson to Madison, 18 October 1825, Smith, vol. 2, 1942, for the Browere incident; Jefferson to Adams, 25 March 1826, Cappon, vol. 2, 613–614.

68. Jefferson to Roger C. Weightman, 24 June 1826, Ford, vol. 10, 390–392. The handwritten draft, with its multiple deletions and revisions, is reproduced in Ellis, *Passionate Sage,* 207.

69. Douglass Adair, "Rumbold's Dying Speech, 1685, and Jefferson's Last Words on Democracy, 1826," in Trevor Colbourn, ed., *Fame and the Founding Fathers: Essays by Douglass Adair* (New York, 1974), 192–202.

70. Adams to John Whitney, 7 June 1826, *Works,* vol. 10, 416–417; Lyman H. Butterfield, "The Jubilee of Independence, July 4, 1826," *VMHB* 61 (1953): 119–140.

71. Sarah N. Randolph, *The Domestic Life of Thomas Jefferson* (Charlottesville, 1978), 422–432, for Jefferson's last hours and words; see also Ellis, *American Sphinx,* 280–281. For the deathbed scene at Quincy, see Eliza Quincy, *Memoirs of the Life of Eliza S. M. Quincy* (Boston, 1861); see also Ellis, *Passionate Sage,* 209–210.

INDEX

abolitionist movement, *see* slavery debate

Adams, Abigail, 3, 17, 163, 164, 206

    Adams's correspondence with, 123–4, 166, 170, 171, 174–5, 176–7, 178, 181, 184, 185, 192, 193

    as Adams's presidential adviser, 188, 190

    Adams's relationship with, 174, 185

    Alien and Sedition Acts, 190, 191

    bipartisan effort regarding Adams presidency, 179, 183

    death of, 243

    federal government's transition to permanent location, 205

    on Gerry, 188

    on Hamilton, 194

    Jefferson and, 177, 178, 207–10, 211, 230

    peace delegations to France, 180, 183, 189, 192–3, 194

    presidential election of 1796, 175, 176–7

    presidential election of 1800, 203, 208–10

Adams, Henry, 40, 44, 195

Adams, John, 3, 14, 17, 59, 67, 79, 101, 109, 123

    Abigail Adams and, *see under* Adams, Abigail

    Alien and Sedition Acts, 190–1, 193, 201

    American Revolution, account of, 215–18, 242–3, 247–8

    background, 164

    candor of, 18

    death of, 225, 248

    Declaration of Independence, composition of, 212–13, 216, 242

    dreams, reports on, 214–15

    "enlightened perversity" style, 195

    erratic habits, 214, 218

    executive leadership, approach to, 188, 190, 194–5

    Federalists, alienation from, 193

    Franklin and, 165, 217, 218

    on frustration of governing, 8

    Great Britain, attitude toward, 239

    Hamilton and, 22, 37, 41, 193–4, 203, 206–7, 214, 218

    historical explanation, realistic approach to, 215–20

    historical vindication, desire for, 213–14, 224

    inauguration of, 184

    Independence Day comments (1826), 247–8

    Jay's Treaty, 137, 138, 175

    Jefferson-Madison campaign against, 195–201, 228–30

    judicial appointments, 208

    Madison's attitude toward, 196–7

    memoir projects, 213–14

    "monarchist" label, 167–9

    nepotism charge against, 189

Adams, John *(cont'd)*
New Army, 193–4, 202
peace delegations to France, 180, 185–6,
188–90, 191–5, 197, 202
political foes, attitude toward, 179–80
presidency of, 185–201, 204–5
presidential election of 1796, 163, 175–8
presidential election of 1800, 202–3, 205
presidential form of address, 167–8
on retirement by politicians, 123–4
retirement from public life, 206
revolutionary career, 164–5
Rush's correspondence with, 214–22
slavery debate, 112–13, 240–1
vice presidency of, 166–7
Washington and, 124, 125, 175, 217
see also Adams–Jefferson correspondence;
Adams–Jefferson relationship
Adams, John Quincy, 47, 54, 156, 169, 170,
171, 187, 194, 195, 223
diplomatic appointment, 189
slavery debate, 278*n* 60
Adams, Samuel, 163, 165, 180
Adams, Thomas Boylston, 194
Adams–Jefferson correspondence, 169, 170
Adams's motives, 223–4
on aging and death, 226, 243–4
as argument between competing versions
of the revolutionary legacy, 227–42
beginning of retirement correspondence,
220–3
delivery of letters, 277*n* 33
elegiac tone, 224, 242–5
on French Revolution, 237–9
friendship recovered through, 224–5, 230,
244
as historical record, 223, 244
Jefferson's apology, 238
on presidential election of 1796, 178
on slavery, 239–42
on social equality and the role of elites,
231, 233–7
verbal prowess, 225–7
Adams–Jefferson relationship, 17
Adams's criticisms of Jefferson, 171, 187,
212
Adams's jealousy of Jefferson's
revolutionary reputation, 212–13

Adams's satirical account of, 220
Adams's sense of betrayal, 207
bipartisan effort regarding Adams
presidency, 178–85
bonding during revolutionary period,
163–4, 180
breakdown of, 169–71, 188
Jefferson–Madison collaboration,
comparison with, 171–2
Jefferson's defamation of Adams, 198, 211,
228
Jefferson's failed attempt at reconciliation,
207–10
odd-couple status, 163
reconciliation under Rush's influence, 218,
220–2
silence following Jefferson's election, 205,
211
see also Adams–Jefferson correspondence
Addison, Joseph, 139
African Americans, *see* blacks
Alien and Sedition Acts, 190–1, 193, 199–200,
201, 229, 273*n* 50
American Colonization Society, 107
American Daily Advertiser, 121
American nationhood, origins of, 10
American Philosophical Society, 170
American Revolution, 134
Adams's nonmythologized account of,
215–18, 242–3, 247–8
alternate possible outcomes, 5
factionalism of revolutionaries, 15
improbability of, 5–6
as improvisational affair, 5, 216
inevitability of, 3–4, 5
Jefferson's vision of, 246–7
most decisive moment, 242–3
participants' historical perspective,
4–5
slavery debate and, 89
Washington's realist approach to
command, 131–3, 135
Ames, Fisher, 59, 72, 116, 118, 123, 180
André, Maj. John, 132
Antifederalists, 9, 59
aristocracy, 231, 233–7
Arnold, Benedict, 27, 38, 126, 132
Articles of Confederation, 7, 8, 52, 138

assumption of state debts by the federal
government, 48
consolidation issue, 58, 59, 63–4
Hamilton's answer to objections, 62
Hamilton's proposal, 57
Jefferson's views on, 51, 68–9
long-term effects, 80
Madison's views on, 57–60, 62, 64
philosophical foundations, 62–5
recalculation of Virginia's debt, 73
secession issue and, 77, 80
Virginians' objections, 58–9, 65, 76–7
see also Compromise of 1790
Augustus, Caesar, 16
Aurora (newspaper), 126, 146, 160, 190, 198

Bache, Benjamin Franklin, 126, 146, 160, 191,
198
Baldwin, Abraham, 85–6
Ballard, Martha, 12
Bayard, James, 26
Beckley, John, 173
Benezet, Anthony, 110
Berlin, Isaiah, 134
Bill of Rights, 53
blacks
Washington's attitude toward, 158
see also slavery debate
Boone, Daniel, 120
Braddock, Gen. Edward, 120
Browere, John Henri, 245
Burke, Aedanus, 84
Burr, Aaron, 17, 18–19, 53, 175
physical appearance, 21, 22
political career, 40–1, 43–4
presidential election of 1796, 173, 176, 178
presidential election of 1800, 41, 42, 43,
203, 205
as threat to American nation, 44, 45–6
western adventure, 38–9
see also Burr–Hamilton duel
Burr, Theodosia, 36
Burr-Hamilton duel, 18–19, 20–1, 60
anti-dueling crusade following, 39
Burr's challenge to Hamilton, 35–6
Burr's disgrace, 27, 38–9
Burr's intentions, 30–1

Burr's surprise and regret at outcome,
25–6, 30–1
contradictory accounts, 27, 30, 31
core meaning, 40, 45–7
eyewitness' statement about, 27–9
feud immediately preceding the duel, 31–8
firing of weapons, 25, 26, 27–31, 253*n*16
Hamilton's alleged suicidal intentions, 37
Hamilton's derogatory comments about
Burr, 32, 41–3, 44, 45
Hamilton's final hours, 26
Hamilton's thoughts about, 22–3, 25, 26,
37–8
Hamilton's wound, 25
legendary status, 39–40
location of, 23
long-standing conflict between Burr and
Hamilton, 40–6
motives of participants, 38
public's perception of, 26–7
rules of, 23, 24
scholarly consensus on, 253*n*16
serious or mortal injury, unlikelihood of,
24
weapons for, 24
Butler, Pierce, 92

Caesar, Julius, 6
Calhoun, John C., 94, 241
Callender, James, 198, 201, 208–9
Canada, 132
Carroll, Charles, 246
Catiline, 42–3
Cato (Addison), 139
census of 1790, 102–4
centralized political power, Americans'
suspicion of, 7–8, 9
Church, John, 24
Cicero, 6, 42, 123
Cincinnatus, 123
Civil War, 12, 16, 101, 241
Clay, Henry, 156
Clinton, George, 40
Cobbett, William, 190, 217
Coles, Edward, 221
Compromise of 1790
congressional approval, 50

Compromise of 1790 *(cont'd)*
  dinner-table bargain, 48–50, 51, 73
  direct link between two issues, 257*n* 41
  Jefferson-Madison collaboration and,
    80
  Jefferson's views on, 50–1, 73–4
  preliminary negotiations, 72–3
  slavery debate and, 116
  survival of American nation and, 50–2,
    78
Confederation Congress, 93
Congress, U.S., *see* House of Representatives;
  Senate
consolidation
  assumption issue and, 58, 59, 63–4
  slavery debate and, 108
Constitution, 13
  criticisms of, 9
  ratification of, 52–3
  slavery debate and, 82, 83, 84, 85–6, 87,
    91–6, 112, 116–18
  Washington's retirement and, 122
Constitutional Convention, 52, 121, 130, 132,
    165, 212, 213
  compromises to produce consensus,
    9–10
  extralegal nature, 8
  minutes of secret deliberations, 137
  "miraculous" quality, 8–9
  slavery debate, 85–6, 91–4, 110–11
Continental Army, 11, 121, 130–1, 165
Continental Congress, 67, 89, 101, 165
Cooper, Charles, 32
Courier of New Hampshire, 121
Coxe, Tench, 72

Declaration of Independence, 11, 67, 68, 122,
    127–8, 139, 143, 163, 165, 247
  composition of, 212–13, 216, 242
  slavery debate and, 86, 88–9
*Defence of the Constitution of the United States
  of America* (Adams), 165, 218, 234
Destutt de Tracy, Antoine, 238
Discourses on Davila (Adams), 168, 169, 170,
  218
Douglas, Stephen, 241
Duer, William, 65, 256*n* 27

early republic, *see* revolutionary era and the
  early republic
economic philosophy, 60–5
Edwards, Jonathan, 21, 109
Embargo Act of 1807, 212
England, *see* Great Britain
Eppes, Maria Jefferson, 207

Fairfax, Fernando, 105, 106
Fauchet, Joseph, 147
Federalist Papers, The, 17, 52, 54, 55, 61, 164
Federalists, 149, 162
  Adams's alienation from, 193
  downfall of, 202–4
  ideological warfare, 186–7
  interpretation of revolutionary era and the
    early republic, 14
  Jefferson-Madison campaign against,
    195–201, 228–30
  Jefferson's conspiracy theory regarding,
    139–41, 147
  political elitism and, 237
  presidential election of 1796, 173
  secession conspiracy, 44
fiscal policy, *see* assumption of state debts by
  the federal government; funding of the
  domestic debt
"Founding Fathers" myth, 12
France, 165, 219
  invasion of Canada during American
    Revolution, proposed, 132
  Monroe's assurances to, 146
  peace delegations to, 180, 183, 184, 185–6,
    188–90, 191–5, 197, 202, 229
  "quasi-war" with United States, 156, 185,
    192, 202, 205
  XYZ Affair, 189–90, 196
  see also French *headings*
Franklin, Benjamin, 13, 17, 53, 101, 163, 164
  Adams and, 165, 217, 218
  memorial service for, 119
  slavery debate, 83, 109, 110–13
  stature of, 108–10
  timing, sense of, 109
  Washington and, 120–1
French and Indian War, 120, 134
French Revolution, 142–3, 170, 175, 202, 219

Adams-Jefferson argument about, 237–9

funding of the domestic debt, 55–7, 61–2, 64

Gallatin, Albert, 191

"General Wolfe's Song," 36

George III of Great Britain, 68, 130, 163, 175

Gerry, Elbridge, 5, 86–7, 180

  peace delegations to France, 188–9, 197

Gettysburg Address, 10, 122

Great Britain (England), 156, 219

  Adams's attitude toward, 239

  Jay's Treaty agreement, 136–7

  Jefferson's condemnation of, 143

Hamilton, Alexander, 13, 14, 17, 52, 132, 155, 163, 164, 187, 198

  Adams and, 22, 37, 41, 193–4, 203, 206–7, 214, 218

  Alien and Sedition Acts, 191

  assumption issue, 57, 62–5, 77;

    Compromise of 1790, 48–50, 72, 73

  background, 22

  death and funeral, 26

  economic philosophy, 60–5

  funding of the domestic debt, 55–6, 61–2, 64

  Jay's Treaty, 137, 150

  Jefferson and, 37, 41

  Jefferson's conspiracy theory and, 140, 141

  libel case, 45, 254n 42

  Madison and, 54

  New Army, 21, 193–4

  personal qualities, 22, 60

  physical appearance, 21

  political downfall, 203

  presidential election of 1796, 177–8

  presidential election of 1800, 41, 42

  secession conspiracy of New England Federalists, 44

  slavery debate, 113

  treasonable activities, 199

  trusting nature, 64–5

  Washington's Farewell Address, 123, 148, 149, 150–4, 157

  see also Burr-Hamilton duel

Hamilton, Elizabeth, 26

Hamilton, Philip, 24

Hannibal, 131

Harrison, Benjamin, 5

Hartford Convention of 1815, 44

Hemings, Sally, 201–2, 209

Henry, Patrick, 52–3, 76, 163

historical explanation, 13–14

  Adams-Jefferson argument, 227–42

  Adams's realistic approach, 215–20

History of the American Revolution (Warren), 13, 213

Holmes, Oliver Wendell, 46

Hosack, David, 21, 23, 25, 26, 28, 29, 31

House of Representatives

  assumption issue, 50, 57

  Franklin's memorial service, 119

  funding of the domestic debt, 56

  Jay's Treaty, 138

  Missouri Compromise, 240

  presidential election of 1800, 42, 43

  residency issue, 50, 69–71, 72

  slavery debate, 81–8, 96–101, 112–13, 116–18

  treaty-making powers, 138

Hume, David, 61

"ideology," 238–9

imperialism, 12

Indians, *see* Native Americans

isolationism, 129

Jackson, Andrew, 156

Jackson, James, 81, 82, 84–5, 97–100, 111, 116

Jay, John, 52, 77, 136, 137, 152–3

Jay's Treaty, 136–9, 141, 143, 144, 145–6, 149, 150, 156, 167, 175, 186, 267n 35

Jefferson, Thomas, 3, 4, 11, 14, 16, 17, 57, 58, 60, 70, 71, 101, 123, 127, 128, 155, 165

  Abigail Adams and, 177, 178, 207–10, 211, 230

  Alien and Sedition Acts, 199–200

  American Revolution, vision of, 246–7

  assumption issue, 51, 68–9; Compromise of 1790, 48–51, 72, 73–4

  conspiracy theory regarding Federalist takeover of government, 139–41, 147

Jefferson, Thomas, *(cont'd)*
  death of, 225, 248
  debt problem, 170–1
  Declaration of Independence,
    composition of, 212–13, 216, 242
  detachment from American developments
    while in Paris, 65–7
  dichotomous world view, 231
  dishonorable behavior, accusations of,
    208–11
  economic philosophy, 65
  European affairs, misunderstanding of, 219
  Federalists' attitude toward, 149
  First Inaugural Address, 128
  foreign policy, 142–3, 202
  Franklin and, 109, 110
  global revolution, belief in, 141–3
  Great Britain, condemnation of, 143
  Hamilton and, 37, 41
  Hemings affair, 201–2, 209
  Independence Day letter (1826), 245–7
  Jay's Treaty, 138, 139, 143, 145–6
  party leadership role, 183
  peace delegations to France, 184
  personal and political ideals, 68
  on political parties, 186, 210, 230–1
  politics, distaste for, 67–8
  presidency after Washington, perspective
    on, 181–2
  presidency of, 212
  presidential election of 1796, 163, 173–4,
    177, 178, 181
  presidential election of 1800, 41, 42, 43,
    203, 205, 208–11
  presidential form of address, 168
  press criticism of, 190
  reclusive period in mid-1790s, 172–3
  residency issue, 74–6; Compromise of
    1790, 48–51, 72, 73–4
  reticent nature, 67
  retirement in 1793, 171, 218–19
  romanticized versions of history,
    beneficiary of, 212–13, 219–20
  secession issue, 200–1
  self-deception, capacity for, 197–8, 210–11,
    219–20
  slavery debate, 90, 95, 99, 100, 105, 106,
    113, 158

  "sovereignty of each generation" idea, 54–5
  treasonable action, defense of, 145–6
  treasonable activities, 198–9
  on treaty-making powers, 138
  vice presidency of, 184
  vision for American nation, 139–42
  on Washington's physical decline, 125
  Washington's relationship with, 138–9,
    140–1, 143–5, 269*n* 71
  Whiskey Rebellion, 140–1, 145
  see also Adams-Jefferson correspondence;
    Adams-Jefferson relationship;
    Jefferson-Madison collaboration
Jefferson-Madison collaboration, 164, 188
  Adams-Jefferson relationship, comparison
    with, 171–2
  bipartisan effort regarding Adams
    presidency and, 182–3
  character of, 54, 171–2
  Compromise of 1790 and, 80
  constitutional questions and, 66, 200–1
  correspondence, 172–3
  Kentucky and Virginia Resolutions,
    199–201
  partisan campaign against Adams
    presidency, 195–201, 228–30
  presidential election of 1796, 173–4, 178
  Republican triumph over Federalists,
    202–4
  Virginian perspective, 172
Johnson, Samuel, 226

Kentucky and Virginia Resolutions, 199–201

Lafayette, Marquis de, 89, 245
Laurance, John, 86
Laurens, Henry, 132
Lectures on Rhetoric and Oratory (Adams), 223
Lee, Henry, 58, 64, 68, 76
Lee, Robert E., 131
Lewis and Clark expedition, 71
libel law, 45, 254*n* 42
Liberia, 107
Life of George Washington, The (Marshall), 14
Lincoln, Abraham, 10, 16, 156, 241
Louisiana Purchase, 74, 212, 241

Madison, James, 8, 17, 66, 68, 155, 163, 164
  Adams, attitude toward, 196–7
  Alien and Sedition Acts, 200
  assumption issue, 57–60, 62, 64;
    Compromise of 1790, 48, 49–50, 72, 73
  constitutional government, efforts on
    behalf of, 52–3
  economic philosophy, 65
  Federalist orientation prior to 1790, 54–5
  Federalists' attitude toward, 149
  Franklin's memorial service, 119
  funding of the domestic debt, 55–7, 61
  Hamilton and, 54
  Jay's Treaty, 137, 138
  peace delegations to France, 180, 183, 184
  personal qualities, 53
  political skills, 53–4, 113
  Republican conversion, 55
  residency issue, 70–1, 72, 74, 75–6;
    Compromise of 1790, 48, 49–50, 72, 73
  Sectional Compromise, 94
  slavery debate, 82–3, 87, 91, 94, 95, 113–18,
    119, 158
  on treaty-making powers, 137–8
  Washington's Farewell Address, 123, 148–9
  see also Jefferson-Madison collaboration
Marshall, John, 14, 53, 155, 191
  Supreme Court appointment, 208
Martin, Luther, 92, 94–5
Mason, George, 68, 95, 96
Massachusetts Constitution, 165
Mather, Cotton, 109
Mazzei, Phillip, 141, 145
Mecklenburg Declaration, 242
Mifflin, Warner, 97–8
Missouri Compromise, 239–40, 241
monarchical principle, 168–9, 204
Monroe, James, 50, 51, 123, 174, 198
  extreme Republican mentality, 146
Monroe Doctrine, 136
Moore, Benjamin, 26
Morris, Gouverneur, 26, 92

Napoleon I of France, 131, 135, 185, 202, 237,
  238
national capital, permanent residence for, *see*
  residency issue

national university, proposal for, 153–4
Native Americans, 12, 100, 133, 226
  Washington's policy toward, 158–9
natural rights, 10
navy, 185, 193, 227
Necker, Jacques, 61
neutrality policy, 134–6
New Army, 21, 193–4, 199, 202
New York Manumission Society, 113
Northwest Ordinance of 1787, 93–4
Notes on the State of Virginia (Jefferson), 90,
  99, 100, 105, 158
nullification issue, 93, 199–200

Page, John, 87
Paine, Tom, 3, 5, 126, 139, 169, 207
Peale, Charles Willson, 18
Pemberton, John, 116
Pendleton, Nathaniel, 21, 23, 24, 26, 27–9, 31,
  34, 35
Pennsylvania Abolition Society, 83, 110
Pennsylvania Avenue, 75
People v. Croswell, 254n 42
Pickering, Timothy, 44, 192
Pinckney, Charles Cotesworth, 92, 95
Pinckney, Thomas, 177–8
Pinckney's Treaty, 267n 35
political parties, 15, 162, 186–7, 204, 210,
  230–1
  see also Federalists; Republicans
Porcupine's Gazette, 190, 192, 193
Postlethwayt, Malachai, 61
Potomac Magazine, 71
Potomac mythology, 70–2
presidential election of 1796
  Adams's candidacy, 175–7
  electoral vote, 177–8, 181
  Jefferson's candidacy, 173–4, 181
  Jefferson's congratulatory letter to Adams,
    178
  prospective candidates, 163
  qualifications for presidency, 162
  uncertainty about, 162, 177
presidential election of 1800, 41, 42, 43,
  202–3, 205
  Jefferson's "dishonorable" behavior, 208–11
presidential form of address, 167–8

press, the, 187
Priestley, Joseph, 228
Proclamation of Neutrality (1793), 135
property rights, 91
Prospect Before Us, The (Callender), 198

Quakers, 81, 97, 110, 117

Randolph, Edmund, 60, 66, 96, 146–7
Randolph, John, 35
Randolph, Thomas Jefferson, 245
recovery of public debt, *see* assumption of
state debts by the federal government;
funding of the domestic debt
Report on the Public Credit (Hamilton), 54,
55, 60–1, 62, 63
republican paradigm, 6
Republicans, 162
Alien and Sedition Acts and, 190–1
ideological warfare, 186–7
interpretation of revolutionary era and the
early republic, 13–14
Jefferson's leadership role, 183
partisan campaign against Adams
presidency, 195–201, 228–30
political elitism and, 237
presidential election of 1796, 173
rise to political domination, 202–4
Washington, rejection of, 160–1
residency issue
congressional debate, 69–71, 72
diffusion's victory over consolidation,
79–80
as executive concern following
congressional passage, 74–6
federal government's transition to
permanent location, 205
Philadelphia's status as likely permanent
capital, 74, 76
Potomac site, case for, 70–2
Virginia-writ-large myth and, 78–9
Washington's site selection, 75
see also Compromise of 1790
revolutionary era and the early republic
American nationhood, origins of, 10
assets of the new nation, 10–11
common themes regarding revolutionary
generation, 17–18
constitutional settlement, importance of,
8–10
dissolution of American nation, potential
for, 8
historical perspective for understanding,
6–8
ideological debate over, 13–15, 145–6
institutionalization of ongoing national
debate, 15–16
liabilities of the new nation, 11
as most crucial period in American
history, 11–12
nonviolent conflict within revolutionary
generation, 39–40
paradox of, 7–8
political cacophony of, 16
political leaders' central role, 12–13
see also American Revolution
Reynolds, Maria, 198
Rights of Man, The (Paine), 139, 169
Roman Republic, 6
Roosevelt, Franklin Delano, 122
Rumbold, Col. Richard, 246–7
Rush, Benjamin, 4–5, 114, 124, 167, 168, 180,
183, 188, 213, 237
Adams-Jefferson reconciliation, 218, 220–2
Adams's correspondence with, 214–22
funding of the domestic debt, 56
Rutledge, John, 92–3

Schuyler, Philip, 40
Scott, Thomas, 84, 86
Scott, William, 112–13
seal for the United States, 101
secession
assumption issue and, 77, 80
Federalist conspiracy, 44
Jefferson's advocacy of, 200–1
slavery debate and, 93, 97, 105, 115
Sectional Compromise, 94, 95, 98, 111
Sedgwick, Theodore, 191–2
Senate, 69, 137
oratory in, 174
president pro tem position, 166–7
slavery debate, 113

Shays's Rebellion, 141
Short, William, 36–7, 66
Sidi Mehemet Ibrahim, 111–12
slavery debate, 8, 11, 12, 17–18, 248
    abolition in northern states, 89–90
    abolitionist position, 91–2
    in Adams-Jefferson correspondence,
        239–42
    J. Q. Adams's leadership of abolitionist
        movement, 278n 60
    American Revolution and, 89
    Compromise of 1790 and, 116
    congressional debate, 83–8, 96–101,
        112–13; rejection of right to end slavery,
        115–18
    consolidation issue, 108
    constitutionality issue, 82, 83, 84, 85–6, 87,
        91–6, 112, 116–18
    Declaration of Independence and, 86,
        88–9
    demographic dimension, 102–4
    expansion of slavery into the West, 87, 90,
        91, 92, 93–4
    Franklin's involvement in abolitionist
        movement, 83, 109, 110–13
    gradual emancipation plans, 103, 103–8,
        262n 39
    historical perspective on, 88
    "inevitable extinction" viewpoint, 89,
        90–1, 94, 103–4
    insurrections, fears about, 87
    intractability of slavery problem, 91, 98,
        105
    Islam's enslavement of Christians and,
        111–12
    Jefferson's views, 90, 99, 106
    Madison's views, 113–15
    national leadership's attitude toward, 113
    "original intentions" issue, 88–97
    owner compensation plans, 86–7, 89, 92,
        106–7, 262nn 38, 39
    petitions for abolition presented to
        Congress, 81–3, 118
    proslavery argument, 85, 92–3, 97–102,
        261n 34
    racial dimension, 99–101, 102–3, 261n 35
    relocation of freed slaves, 100, 106, 107–8
    secession issue, 93, 97, 105, 115

    Sectional Compromise, 94, 95, 98, 111
    silence about slavery, 84, 87, 93, 102, 115,
        157–8, 239, 241–2
    in state legislatures, 84, 94–6
    total emancipation, southern concerns
        about, 82
    viability of a national emancipation policy
        in 1790, 105–8, 118–19, 262n 36
    Virginia's paradoxical position, 95–6, 103
    Washington's Farewell Address and, 157–8
Smith, Abigail Adams, 37
Smith, Adam, 61
Smith, John, 71
Smith, Venture, 12
Smith, William Loughton, 81–2, 85, 97,
        100–1, 112, 116, 118
social equality and the role of elites, 231,
        233–7
"Statement on the Impending Duel"
        (Hamilton), 37–8
Stuart, Gilbert, 18
Supreme Court, 116, 208

Talleyrand, Charles, 189, 194, 196, 197
Taylor, John, 236
"Thesis on Discretion" (Hamilton), 37
Thoughts on Government (Adams), 165
Tolstoy, Leo, 216
treaty-making powers, 137–8
Treaty of Mortefontaine (1800), 205
Treaty of Paris (1783), 136
Trumbull, John, 18, 36
Tucker, St. George, 105, 106, 262n 39
Tudor, William, 240
Twenty-second Amendment, 122

Van Ness, William, 21, 23, 24, 25, 27–9, 33,
        34, 35
vice presidency, 166–7
Virgil, 123
Virginia-writ-large myth, 78–9, 161
Voltaire, 109, 139

War and Peace (Tolstoy), 216
War of 1812, 135, 227

Warren, Mercy Otis, 13, 180, 213–14

Washington, D.C., 75–6, 79, 161
see also residency issue

Washington, George, 11, 14, 17, 43, 51, 53, 60, 70, 71, 89, 163, 164, 165, 184, 197
Adams and, 124, 125, 175, 217
"Address to the Cherokee Nation," 158–9
American Revolution military command, 130–3, 135
blacks, attitude toward, 158
childlessness of, 169
Circular Letter of 1783, 133–4
courage under fire, 120
decision-making process, 150
enlarged federal power, program for, 156–7, 269*n* 64
final message to Congress, 156–7, 269*n* 64
final years at Mount Vernon, 160–1
Franklin and, 120–1
illness of 1790, 66, 124–5
Jay's Treaty, 136–9, 144, 149
Jefferson's relationship with, 138–9, 140–1, 143–5, 269*n* 71
last will and testament, 158
monarchical tendencies, 127, 139
mythology surrounding, 120–1
Native American policy, 158–9
neutrality policy, 134–6
physical appearance, 124
realist outlook in political and military matters, 131–3
Republican opposition, 160–1
residency issue, 69, 75–6
slavery debate, 113, 118, 263*n* 47
surrendering power, flair for, 129–30
vice presidency, views on, 167
vision for American nation, 7, 133–4
Whiskey Rebellion, 140–1, 145
see also Washington's Farewell Address; Washington's retirement

Washington's Farewell Address, 123
authentic meaning, means for understanding, 129
composition of, 148–53
foreign policy message, 128–9, 131–6, 148, 150
historical commentary on, 129
as justification for strong executive leadership, 155
misnaming of, 122
national unity message, 128, 130–1, 148–9, 154–6
national university proposal, omission of, 153–4
as prophecy accompanied by advice, 155
publication of, 121
reactions to, 159–60
slavery, silence about, 157–8
target audience, 157
transcendental status, 122
Washington's intentions, 128, 147–8

Washington's retirement
age and health reasons, 124–5
as confirmation of republican government, 127–8
consitutional significance, 122
departure from office, 160
"disposable president" principle and, 125
first indications of, 123
press attacks and, 125–7
tradition of retirement and, 123–4
voluntary nature, 149–50
see also Washington's Farewell Address

Webster, Daniel, 118

Whiskey Rebellion, 140–1, 145, 147, 167, 186

Whitehead, Alfred North, 16

Wilson, James, 94

Wythe, George, 67

XYZ Affair, 189–90, 196

From the author of the Pulitzer Prize-winning best-seller *Founding Brothers* and the National Book Award-winning best-seller *American Sphinx*—a landmark biography that brings to life in all his complexity the most important and perhaps least understood figure in American history.

GEORGE WASHINGTON

BY JOSEPH J. ELLIS

Available October 2004 in hardcover from Knopf
$26.95 (Canada: $37.95) • 1-4000-4031-0

PLEASE VISIT www.aaknopf.com

Available in Vintage paperback:

American Sphinx • 0-679-76441-0
Founding Brothers • 0-375-70524-4